Christian Warfare
in Rhodesia-Zimbabwe

Christian Warfare
in Rhodesia-Zimbabwe

The Salvation Army and African Liberation, 1891–1991

NORMAN H. MURDOCH

Foreword by
N. M. BHEBE

◥PICKWICK *Publications* · Eugene, Oregon

CHRISTIAN WARFARE IN RHODESIA-ZIMBABWE
The Salvation Army and African Liberation 1891–1991

Copyright © 2015 Norman H. Murdoch. All rights reserved. Except for brief quotations in critical publications or reviews, no part of this book may be reproduced in any manner without prior written permission from the publisher. Write: Permissions. Wipf and Stock Publishers, 199 W. 8th Ave., Suite 3, Eugene, OR 97401.

Pickwick Publications
An Imprint of Wipf and Stock Publishers
199 W. 8th Ave., Suite 3
Eugene, OR 97401

www.wipfandstock.com

ISBN 13: 978-1-62564-681-1

Cataloguing-in-Publication Data

Murdoch, Norman H.

   Christian warfare in Rhodesia-Zimbabwe : the Salvation Army and African liberation 1891–1991 / Norman H. Murdoch, edited by Harold Hill, with a foreword by N. M. Bhebe

   xxxii + 218 p. ; 23 cm. Includes bibliographical references.

   ISBN 13: 978-1-62564-681-1

   1. Salvation Army—History. 2. Salvation Army—History—20th century. 3. Salvation Army—Rhodesia/Zimbabwe. 4. Zimbabwe—Church history. 5. Africa—Church history. I. Hill, Harold. II. Bhebe, N. M. III. Title.

BX9715 M87 2015

Manufactured in the U.S.A.   01/19/2015

To
Corps Sergeant Major Jonah Blessing Matsvetu,
the Salvationists of Zimbabwe,
and the Missionaries in "the Bush."

Corps Sergeant Major Jonah Blessing Matsvetu, with Mrs Matsvetu, on the occasion of his receiving the Salvation Army Certificate in Recognition of Exceptional Service. According to Salvation Army Regulations, "the Certificate in Recognition of Exceptional Service is awarded by the territorial commander after full consideration by an appropriate council, to Salvationists (officers and soldiers) and friends whose work in and for The Salvation Army is outstanding in length or quality, unusual in nature and of particular benefit to the Territory."

Contents

Illustrations | ix
Editorial Note | xi
Foreword | xiii
Preface | xv
Acknowledgments (2014) | xxi
Norman Murdoch as Colleague, Historian and Teacher | xxiii
Norman Murdoch, Historian of The Salvation Army | xxvii

Chapter 1
Christian and Cultural Warfare in Rhodesia/Zimbabwe, 1890–1990 | 1

Chapter 2
The Salvation Army Invades Mashonaland, 1891–95 | 8

Chapter 3
The First *Chimurenga* (1896–97) and the death of Captain Cass | 21

Chapter 4
Rhodes and Booth: "Wholesale Salvation," 1901–8 | 36

Chapter 5
Father and Son in 1908: "My dear General"—"My dear Chief" | 53

Chapter 6
The Salvation Army and the Rhodesian State, 1908–65 | 89

Chapter 7
Colonial, Conciliar, and Communist Forces Collide, 1950s and 1960s | 109

Chapter 8
Paying the Piper, Calling the Tune: A Salvation Army Power Shift, 1970–78 | 118

Chapter 9
Conciliar Movements and The Salvation Army, 1970–78 | 131

Chapter 10
The Program to Combat Racism and the Salvation Army Reaction, 1969–78 | 140

Chapter 11
The 1978 Deaths at Usher Institute | 149

Chapter 12
Salvation Army Reaction to the Usher Killings, 1978–83 | 158

Chapter 13
African Salvationists React to the Salvation Army's Withdrawal from the World Council of Churches, 1981 | 173

Chapter 14
Conclusions | 183

Epilogue | 199
Bibliography | 203
Index | 209

Illustrations

Captain Edward Cass (22)

Survivors of the party who took refuge at the Alice Mine and of the relief forces sent to escort them to safety. Mrs Cass third from left in front row. Major John Pascoe seated atop the wagon (26)

Cass Memorial beside road in Mazowe Valley (27)

Nehanda Nyakasikana (c.1840–98) as a prisoner after the Chimurenga (29)

Cecil John Rhodes portrayed on stamp to mark 50th anniversary of Pioneer Column (37)

William and Bramwell Booth motoring, circa 1907 (54)

Leander Starr Jameson. Cartoon by 'Spy' from Vanity Fair, 9 April 1896 (61)

Abe Bailey. Cartoon by 'Spy' from Vanity Fair, 9 September 1908 (61)

Local Salvationists holding an open-air meeting in a village, 1930s (93)

Salvation Army congress meeting near Howard Institute in the late 1930s (94)

Homecraft class and women Cadets at Howard Institute, late 1930s (98)

School prefects at Howard Institute, late 1930s (98)

Open-air lesson at a village school, 1930s (99)

Ian Douglas Smith as a Federation of Rhodesia and Nyasaland MP, in the late 1950s (113)

Robert Mugabe and Josiah Tongogara in Rhodesian Government propaganda leaflet produced in the late 1970s (123)

Joshua Mqabuko Nkomo (124)

Rev. Philip Potter, General Secretary of the World Council of Churches (146)

General Eva Burrows visits the grave of Sharon Swindells and Lieut. Diane Thompson in 1987 (156)

Commissioner Paul Kaiser presenting classroom maps to Howard Secondary School, 1977, with Lieut. Linda Schearing and Headmaster Lemuel C. Tsikirayi (159)

Group of retired Salvation Army officers at Mazowe with Commissioner Richard Atwell and Mrs Doris Atwell. In the centre of the group is Major Leonard Kirby O.F. and top right, Major Ben Gwindi, both then aged over ninety (160)

General Arnold Brown (165)

Editorial Note

This book has been a long time in the making. Norman Murdoch began archival and field research towards it at the beginning of the 1990s, and it was largely finished within ten years. Unfortunately busyness with other tasks and then illness in retirement meant that he was unable to complete his work on it and others have had the opportunity of seeing it into print.

This is an absorbing but perhaps not an easy read, nor a comfortable one for Salvationists. Norman Murdoch combines his love for the Salvation Army (he is the child of officers) with his love for justice and truth, and truth-tellers have a mixed reception. The historian has elements of the prophet in his experience and his task, and merely romanticized or triumphalist histories do not always bring the greatest glory to God or most needful insight to the people. Professor Bhebe's candid and appreciative Foreword presents in stark summary some of the less palatable realities explored in the text. This book is not intended as a comprehensive history of the Salvation Army in Zimbabwe but it does tease out one strand in its history. Realism about the present should be predicated on honesty about the past. Faithful are the wounds of a friend.

As this book was the last project to be worked on by Norman Murdoch before his illness, his friends thought the opportunity should be taken to pay tribute to him and to his work. Representative contributors are Dr. Andrew Villalon on Norman as a university colleague, and Dr. John Coutts on his contribution to the Salvation Army's understanding of its own history. Andrew Villalon Ph.D. (Yale) is Senior Lecturer in the Department of History, University of Texas, Austin, and formerly taught at the University of Cincinnati. John Coutts M.A. (Oxon.) B.D. (London) Ph.D. (Edin.) of Stirling, Scotland, is a scholar, linguist and former Salvation Army officer who has served as a missionary in Nigeria. I am grateful to them and to others mentioned for their contributions, to Dr Robin Parry of Wipf and Stock for his guidance and patience, and to Norman and Grace for their friendship and the privilege of assisting in bringing this project to completion.

Harold Hill
Wellington, New Zealand

Foreword

The Salvation Army is a respected institution in Zimbabwe today. Although it is not one of the major Christian bodies, its Zimbabwean membership is the largest of any Salvation Army "territory" internationally and its history deserves attention. Professor Murdoch's *Christian Warfare in Rhodesia-Zimbabwe* is a scrupulously researched and multi-layered text that is essential reading for anyone interested in the modern history of Christianity in Africa. It is a seminal examination of the Salvation Army's problematic encounters with Africans from the formative days of the colonial interlude to the first decade of black majority rule.

Through a systematic interrogation of multiple oral and written sources, Professor Murdoch's narrative reveals some hitherto little known details about the Salvation Army's ambivalent relations with Africans. Foremost, its basic aim between 1891 and 1908 was to promote mass emigration of England's urban unemployed to settle on land seized from Africans. The Army's later focus on Africans was initially a pragmatic response to Rhodes' imperial preference for funding the 'civilising' of Africans through educational services, medical facilities and churches.

Christian Warfare in Rhodesia-Zimbabwe also reveals the Army's exclusive recognition of white victims of the country's nationalist struggles as martyrs. The Army's pantheon of martyrs included three individuals; Captain Edward T. Cass was killed by Africans during the First Chimurenga in 1896 and two white teachers were killed by 'unknown' assailants at Usher Institute in June 1978, at the height of the Second Chimurenga. Many Africans also died because of their association with the Salvation Army, especially during the Second Chimurenga, but they were not recognized.

Professor Murdoch also explores the political and religious intricacies behind the Salvation Army's ill-advised withdrawal of its membership from the World Council of Churches (WCC) in 1981. This move was triggered by the aforementioned killings of two white teachers at Usher Institute in June

1978 and the WCC's availing of grants to Zimbabwe's liberation movements for the procurement of educational material and food for Zimbabwean refugees resident in neighboring countries. Opposition to the WCC's support of the liberation movements was stirred by the Cold War anxieties of the Army's membership in the West. Again, though the Army condemned the purported violence of the African liberation fighters it never condemned the state sanctioned excesses of Ian Smith's right-wing regime.

In a nuanced way, Professor Murdoch's narrative also shows that Africans and many international Salvationists supported struggles for majority rule and opposed their organization's withdrawal from the WCC. That the Army's then international leadership disregarded these sentiments, coupled with their apparent indifference to the concerns of the oppressed Africans, shows that they were on the wrong side of history. That the Salvation Army has changed with the times and attempts to serve Africa more even-handedly today is to its credit.

Finally, *Christian Warfare in Rhodesia-Zimbabwe* is a rigorously researched and accessible text. It is both an excellent intervention and complement to Zimbabwe's burgeoning histories on the interface between Church and politics.

N. M. Bhebe
Professor of History and Vice Chancellor,
Midlands State University, Zimbabwe.
Author of *The ZAPU and ZANU Guerrilla Warfare and The Evangelical Lutheran Church in Zimbabwe.*

Preface

In 1991 and 1998 I visited Zimbabwe in the course of research towards an international history of The Salvation Army. I realized that the history of a global enterprise like The Salvation Army must include Salvationists in the two-thirds world where a majority of the Army's soldiers (members) live.[1] The day before my wife Grace and I left Zimbabwe to return home Major Godfrey Mufanechiya asked if we were aware of a 1981 Salvation Army soldiers' protest march in Harare, Zimbabwe's recently renamed capital. I had not seen reports of the march in Salvation Army journals or in the Western press. Mufanechiya agreed that the Army had not published accounts of the march, but he suggested that it ought to have been recorded in Army histories.

At the office of the Zimbabwean daily, the *Herald*, Grace and I found press coverage of the soldiers' protest march. A front page headline shouted the soldiers' case against Salvation Army leaders in London, the Army's international headquarters. The reporter revealed that there was a rift between Zimbabwean Salvationists and Army leaders. At its heart it was a dispute over who would rule the Army in Zimbabwe. Would it be the leader in London, or in the United States, or newly liberated African Salvationists who had toppled minority white political rule in a decade-long war that had ended in 1979?

Subsequent archival research led to another discovery. The Salvation Army's leaders in the United States had encouraged a rift between the Army and the World Council of Churches (WCC). In the 1970s the WCC, through a Program to Combat Racism, had campaigned to end apartheid and to support African wars of liberation from colonial rule, including the white minority-rule of Rhodesia, now black-ruled Zimbabwe. Many Americans

---

1. Since the early 1980s, the term, "two-thirds world," has been used—mostly by evangelical Christians—to indicate the less-developed countries of the world, as in "third world" but signifying proportionality rather than precedence. The term is used in this sense in this book.

opposed all Marxist-financed wars of liberation in the wake of America's defeat in the Vietnam War in 1973. Now, after the defeat of Prime Minister Ian Smith's Rhodesian Front in Rhodesia in 1979 by the African Patriotic Front forces of Robert Mugabe and Joshua Nkomo, the American leaders asked their International Headquarters in London to dissolve the Army's thirty-three-year membership of the WCC which had backed "communist" financed struggles.

In the Zimbabwe National Archives and at Salvation Army archives in London I found an ancient tale, full of colonial mythology, which lay behind the Soldiers' 1981 protest march. There had been a "martyrdom" of a British Salvationist missionary during an 1896–97 African rising (the Shona term is Chimurenga), just six years after Cecil John Rhodes' British South Africa Company (BSAC) imposed colonial rule on the Shona and Ndebele tribes. The Africans fought to reclaim land Rhodes had taken from them and renamed Rhodesia.

The 1896 killing of Captain Edward T. Cass near a farm the BSAC had given to the Salvation Army in 1893 was well-known to African Salvationists in 1978 when two Salvationist women missionary teachers were killed at the peak of the independence war in Matabeleland, during the second rising or Chimurenga. Newspaper and Police reports blamed Patriotic Front "terrorists" for the killings but many Africans believed that the culprits were African soldiers recruited into the Selous Scouts, an élite unit of the Rhodesian army.

The 1981 African Salvationist march, the year after the creation of a new African-led state of Zimbabwe, brought long-buried issues to the surface. Claims that in 1896 Shona tribesmen had martyred Captain Cass during the first Chimurenga, and claims that Africans had killed Lieutenant Sharon Swindells and Ms. Diane Thompson during the second Chimurenga both needed investigation. Interviews and research at the Zimbabwe National Archives in Harare and at Salvation Army Archives in London and Alexandria, Virginia, convinced me that the Army's account of these events needed to be probed to connect political and religious history in Rhodesia-Zimbabwe in 1891 and 1981. I also concluded that a colonial mythology had been imprinted on the Salvation Army in its colonial empire, nurtured by Britain's imperial state.

Rhodesian history began at Fort Salisbury (now Harare) in 1890 with the blessing of Britain's government and its agent, Cecil Rhodes' British South Africa Company.[2] With its arrival in Salisbury in 1891 the Salvation

2. For early Zimbabwe history, see: D. N. Beach, *The Shona and Zimbabwe, 900–1850: An Outline of Shona History* (Masvingo: Mambo, 1980); *A Zimbabwean Past: Shona Dynastic Histories and Oral Traditions* (Gweru: Mambo, 1994); *War and Politics in*

Army became part of that heritage for the next ninety years through its marriage to white colonial rule. As a Christian Imperium the Army found a role in African subjugation in the name of Western Christian Civilization. When Africans rebelled against colonial rule in 1896 the Salvation Army stood with white settlers. Between 1890 and 1980 only a few Christian missions and settlers supported African rights. In the 1970s Rhodesia's state-run media, the Western press, and Salvation Army journals blamed African "guerrillas" or "terrorists" for the deaths of missionaries of several denominations. They also blamed the World Council of Churches, of which the Salvation Army was a founding member in 1948, for its humanitarian grants to African liberation movements. While there were churches that supported African independence forces, including Robert Mugabe's and Joshua Nkomo's Patriotic Front in Rhodesia, the Salvation Army did not.

The incident that made me look again at the 1896 and 1978 events was the Salvation Army soldiers' protest march on Wednesday August 26, 1981. The Army's international leader in London, Canadian Arnold Brown, had decided to suspend the Army's World Council of Churches' affiliation because of humanitarian aid given to Patriotic Front refugees in Zambia and Mozambique until the war ended with the signing of the Lancaster House Agreement in 1979. That agreement brought African rule to the new nation of Zimbabwe in 1980. General Brown's decision came in a Cold War context that included the American withdrawal from Vietnam in 1973. Now, as American Salvation Army leaders saw it, a pivotal African country was falling under anti-Christian Marxist control.

To defend themselves from a public airing of dirty laundry officials of organizations hide stories of conflict, hoping not to stir publicity that might lead to negative public reactions. If a philanthropic agency depends on public funds for survival the situation is critical.³ This problem faced Salvation Army leaders in 1896–97 and again in 1978–81. When the dispute became public the Army's Commander in the US appeared on "60 Minutes" on CBS

Zimbabwe, 1840–1900 (Gweru: Mambo, 1986); Michael Bourdillon, *The Shona Peoples: An Ethnography of the Contemporary Shona, with special reference to their religion*, 3rd ed. (Gweru: Mambo, 1987); Frank McLynn, *Hearts of Darkness: The European Exploration of Africa* (New York: Caroll & Graf, 1992); and Elizabeth Schmidt, *Peasants, Traders and Wives: Shona Women in the History of Zimbabwe, 1870–1939* (Harare: Baobab, 1992).

3. Henry Gariepy, *Mobilized for God: The History of The Salvation Army, Vol. 8, 1977–1894* (Atlanta GA: The Salvation Army, 2000) 323–34, claimed that the Army in the U.S. had for three years, 1992–94, "received $726 million in private contributions, more than any other non-profit agency," including $199 million from federal, state and local governments and over $1.3 billion in total support.

to defend the Americans' push for the Salvation Army's withdrawal from the World Council of Churches.

The Salvation Army-World Council of Churches dispute remained in the public eye until 1983, but there was little investigation of this international Christian conflict. Since historians analyze what lies behind "facts" and "myths" I will try to record faithfully this story and analyze the passions that lay behind it. At its best, history destroys myth. The Greek word *historia* means to learn through research, to investigate. Investigation is uncomfortable for the investigated. Many fear that evidence of friction will damage the glue of loyalty that binds an organization together or will harm its external reputation and income, so they offer the world an image of single-minded teamwork. I will deal with distortions of fact while trying to avoid damage to those who were well meaning. I will not pluck people out of the era in which they made their decisions, nor will I judge them by standards of a later time. Historians do not assert what persons *should* have done. The word *should* is not in our vocabulary. My aim is to understand why people did what they did when and how they did it.

Among public agencies the Salvation Army has been known for managerial integrity and spiritual sensitivity, a standing that permits it to seek public and private funds for its social and religious work. I will not shake confidence in people for whom I have high regard, but I will point to rifts in the ranks that led to the Army's 1978–81 break with the World Council of Churches. This decision revealed fault lines in its leaders and a parochial mentality held by American leaders, many of whom had spent their careers entirely in America. Tensions between leaders in London and New York, and with Zimbabwe Salvationists, led Africans to side with the World Council and to oppose Anglo-American leaders. In the overall leadership there were divergent views that isolated some Anglo-Americans from colleagues in Asia, South America, Europe, Australia and New Zealand, many of whom had served as missionaries in Africa.

Why has the Salvation Army not told this African story of international conflict? Like many organizations the Army is not enthusiastic about historians' attempts to reveal "warts and all." Official histories aim to protect the Army's reputation. Western authors have written nearly all of its histories, leaving Asian, African, and Latin American voices largely unheard. My aim is to let Africans speak of events as they saw them to the extent that a Western author can achieve that end. For this reason I have conducted oral interviews as well as depended on written archived records.

I pieced this puzzle together out of information I gathered on trips to Zimbabwe and correspondence with Africans, missionaries and leaders. I have also gone to Salvation Army centers in Chile (1993), India (1994),

Britain, Canada, Australia, New Zealand, France, Switzerland and the US, but Zimbabwe epitomizes Army history in the two-thirds world and its conflicted colonial ties to the West. In the 1950s Europe's colonies sought liberation from imperial rule and from oversight by Western organizations including churches. The word "Liberation" describes colonial emancipation from Western hegemony. Africans and Asians did not reject every Western contribution to their civilizations. Medicine, education and religion have had salutary effects. They did reject Western paternalism and imperial rule.

These are my reasons for writing this book. History studies the past, of both fools and heroes. It must be its own reward. It is not intended to guide decision-making, although some may learn from it. Historians explain human conditions as they find them in documents and people from whom they are able to pry loose ideas. And of course the *"why"* of the past follows from the how, what, when and where. Factual accuracy, as best it can be found, leads the historian to uncover *why* individuals and groups acted as they did. To this end historians, as time and resources permit, immerse themselves in cultures in which events occurred and people lived. Here the cultures are African and Western, the Salvation Army and World Council of Churches, with their political, religious, economic, and social nuances. In all I set out to find what happened in Rhodesia/Zimbabwe between 1891 and 1991, during the pre- and post-independence era in Rhodesia-Zimbabwe.

ACKNOWLEDGEMENTS

I owe many debts to those who led me into new fields of intellectual-social-cultural and global history. To do history where participants are still alive was new to me. I did oral interviews and corresponded with persons who posed hard questions. Jonah Blessing Matsvetu, whom I met in Harare in 1991, and interviewed by mail, and then in person 1998, wrote a narrative of his leadership of the 1981 Salvation Army Soldiers' March. John Ncube, a teacher at Usher Institute in 1978, gave me an eyewitness account of the killing of two of his British colleagues and the wounding of two others. I will name others who aided my work in the text or in footnotes. They all have my deep gratitude.

Some Salvation Army leaders with whom I corresponded were Arnold Brown, Harry Williams, Denis Hunter, Paul du Plessis, Eva Burrows, and Earl Robinson. Army missionaries Ruth Chinchen, John and Heather Coutts, Leonard F. Kirby, Stephen Pallant, Jim Watt, Geoffrey T. Perry, Lyndon Taylor, and Pat and Harold Hill, helped me understand the expatriate experience in Africa and tensions between missionaries in the field and administrators at headquarters in Salisbury/Harare, London, and New York. In the text I list American leaders with whom I corresponded. The best source for their views in the 1970s–80s is letters in my possession and at the Army's Alexandria, Virginia Archives. I regret that neither of the two missionaries injured at Usher in 1978 responded to my requests for their reactions.

For interviews with World Council of Churches leaders I travelled to its Archives and headquarters in Geneva, Switzerland in 1999 and met staff members to discuss their interactions with the Salvation Army. General Secretary Konrad Raiser, Baldwin Sjollema, Dwayne Epps, and Bob Scott were most helpful. Former WCC leaders who were involved in WCC–Salvation Army negotiations in London did not respond to inquiries.

In 1991 the Pew Charitable Trust gave me a grant for research in London, Geneva, and Harare through the Centre on Philanthropy at Indiana University. In 1998 the University of Cincinnati Research Council provided a grant for a second research trip to Zimbabwe. The University College Humanities Department provided research grants for my work in Harare, Geneva, London, and Alexandria. I profited from reactions to my research from University of Cincinnati colleagues: Professors Janine C. Hartman, L. J. Andrew Villalon and Mark A. Lause, who have supported my work for over thirty years. The Association of Third World Studies published my essay on part of this study in its 1996 Conference Proceedings, and as "'Darkest Africa': Martyrdom and Resistance to Colonialism in Rhodesia," *Journal of Third World Studies* (Spr. 2005).

The University of Zimbabwe gave me a Research Associate title for my work in Zimbabwe's National Archives and invited me to lead a graduate seminar of the Religious Studies Department. I am in debt to Professors D. N. Beach; Ngwabi Bhebe; Terence Ranger; and C. J. M. Zvobgo, who read and critiqued versions of this work.

For hospitality in Zimbabwe I thank expatriates and Zimbabweans: Alan and Brenda Coles, André Cox, April Foster, Judith Johansen, Clement A. Jumbe and the Mazowe Secondary School faculty, Paul and Jajuan Kellner, Gideon and Lister Moyo, Audrey Ridout and the Officer Training School faculty, Tadeous Shipe, Jim and Bette Watt. Special friends, Sydney and Gladys Mabhiza, and the Lambon-Jacobs family introduced us to Zimbabwe's culture and landscape, and enriched our bookish experience with joy.

Norman H. Murdoch Ph.D.
Professor Emeritus of History
University of Cincinnati

Acknowledgments (2014)

This work is a labor of love, love for history, for The Salvation Army, and for the people who care about the academic integrity of its record. My husband used to say that history is invented because facts must be interpreted. Therefore, the integrity and commitment of those who are doing the interpretation is essential. We are fortunate to have such people as dear friends. As a result of Alzheimer's disease, Norman could not finish this manuscript. Fortunately he had completed a first draft of the narrative, which represented significant research. A dinner-table conversation about the work led to the contribution of Major Dr. Harold Hill. Harold took on the work of editing, finding a publisher, and preparing for publication. This represents hours of time and effort that he took on only because he believed in the importance of seeing the work completed. He also solicited the assistance of kind mutual friends, Dr. John Coutts and his wife Heather, as readers. Without Harold's unceasing efforts and the work of the readers, this manuscript would not be available.

I also want to express my appreciation for the help of Norman's University of Cincinnati friends and colleagues, Dr. Janine Hartman and Dr. Mark Lause. They were so helpful in the publication process and their support for the effort was invaluable.

Grateful thanks are due also to Professor Ngwabi Bhebe for his foreword, to Drs. Andrew Villalon and John Coutts for their tributes, to Commissioners John Swinfen and Stuart Mungate, Professors Gordon Moyles and Norman Etherington, and Dr. Isabel Mukonyora for their commendations, and to Major Don Hutson for preparing the illustrations for printing. Thank you one and all for making this book possible and helping Norman's work come to fruition.

Grace Murdoch, Ed.D.
Professor Emeritus of Psychology
University of Cincinnati

Norman Murdoch as Colleague, Historian and Teacher

Andrew Villalon

How does one write a personal tribute to an individual who, without any exaggeration, saved one's academic career, with whom one locked arms in an on-going struggle to make the university where they both taught a more equitable, reasonable, and honest place, who was one's closest friend for the better part of two decades, with whom one discussed anything and everything, a person who always had one's back, even in the dark days of a wearing and costly libel suit? How does one write such a thing without sounding either hackneyed or embarrassingly over-the-top? That is precisely the problem I face when writing about Norman Murdoch. But I'll give it my best shot.

    Norman and I met for the first time in the mid-1980s during an academic field trip to the Yucatan conducted by the University of Cincinnati's Geography Department. Although not a member of that department, my wife is a Latin American historian and was asked to help lead the tour. I was part of a package deal. Norman and his wife, Grace, numbered among the tour's adult contingent, what were dubbed "the big spenders" whose somewhat higher fee helped underwrite student participation. During a long conversation sitting by a pool at Chitzen Itza, I told Norman of my chequered career in academe and he told me about a job that was opening up in the section of the university where he taught. At the time, although my wife had a good position in the UC History Department, I was cobbling together employment as an adjunct, university parlance for part time faculty who were in those days woefully underpaid at the University of Cincinnati. And there was no indication that things would get better anytime soon.

    An incident that occurred during that trip impressed Norman, not so much with my intellect, but rather with my willingness to pitch in during a crisis. Late in the afternoon on what was scheduled to be our last day in Yucatan, we were on our way back to Cancun from an inland Maya site called

Coba. Suddenly, our tour bus went belly up along a fairly lonely road cutting through the jungle. After a while, when no traffic went by in either direction, I volunteered to run the ten or so miles back to the site to try to get some help. We had seen another bus there which might be available to rent on an emergency basis. Meanwhile, the tour head, a member of the Geography Department, would try to flag down a car if by chance one came our way. Fortunately, I didn't have to make good on my attempt. I had only run several miles when a car came up behind me; riding in the backseat was the head who had flagged it down and gotten the ride back to the Coba. I then jogged back leisurely to the bus, finishing, however, with a flourish. Ever thereafter, Norman and I would joke about this, as he would often introduce me to others as the person he had met "chasing after a bus in the jungle."

For nearly three years, through the many vicissitudes of the academic search process, Norman never ceased working to get me a fulltime position. His efforts were finally rewarded and for the next dozen years or so we taught together in the University College, an on-campus open access unit of the university. During those years, we became fairly inseparable comrades. On most days, Norman was the first person I would talk with when I arrived in the morning and last whom I saw when leaving for the day. Except for a two year period when the university was renovating our building, we had offices side by side. During that renovation, we were roommates sharing a cubicle in the building to which they moved us. Since both of us were what the university would categorize as "radicals" (i.e., we would not suffer the stupidities of university life in silence), the wall to our cubicle where we posted our latest thoughts on the subject became fairly widely-known in the college as "freedom wall."

Just as he had worked hard to get me hired, Norman did everything he could to help me get tenure, heading committees, writing letters, and doing all of the other time consuming things that are part of the process. It was that intervention that saved my academic career. I remain thoroughly convinced that without his unwavering friendship and support, I would not be in academe today. Let me hasten to add, mine is not the only career on which Norman has a profound effect. There are a number of other people who taught in University College, particularly historians, but some non-historians as well, who owe him a considerable debt of gratitude, including one who following a long battle on both of our parts to hire and then tenure him ultimately became the most prolific historian at the University of Cincinnati.

During the years that Norman and I were together at the University of Cincinnati, he demonstrated an amazing work ethic. In addition to teaching the 4–4–4 schedule that characterized University College, he performed a significant amount of college and university service, much of it for the American Association of University Professors which functioned at UC as both a professional association and a faculty union. Among other things, Norman served two consecutive terms as the organization's president. Throughout those years, he bent every effort to increase the faculty role in university governance and to protect faculty and staff against arbitrary and unfair treatment by the university.

Some of these efforts were high profile, involving significant conflicts with higher administration as well as leading the faculty through a strike. On the other hand, Norman never eschewed "the little things." Serving as a member of the University Grievance Committee, he represented many of our colleagues who were taking individual grievances against the university. In fact, given his equitable temperament and sympathy for the underdog, he was not infrequently assigned to cases involving people who were notorious for being difficult to deal with.

Despite the teaching load and extensive service, Norman also made time to conduct meaningful research into his chosen subject, the history of religion; in particular, the origins and development of the Salvation Army as both a religious and a charitable entity. He explained to me that his having chosen that topic at least in part reflected his having been raised in a family where both his father and mother were deeply involved with the organization. We occasionally talked about his childhood when he had "beaten the bass drum" for the Army and I kidded him about being a latter-day Sky Masterson in reverse. But while much of the history of the Salvation Army has been written by insiders and tends toward the panegyric, Norman brought his historical insight and honesty to the endeavor. While treating the Army fairly, he did not hesitate to be critical where criticism was merited. This did not always make him popular with the powers-that-be, but it did make his historical work on the Salvation Army some of the best available.

Finally, let me say that no one has ever been a better friend as anyone who has ever been Norman's friend will tell you. He always makes allowances for our failings while inspiring us to be better people and scholars.

I would like to mention one instance in particular where that friendship was enormously important to me. When you are a radical voice on an academic faculty, sometimes unfortunate things happen. In the mid-1990s, the historians in University College led the charge to bring about the downfall of a particularly obnoxious Dean. As part of this effort, I wrote (with help from several of my colleagues) a report showing that that individual (who will here remain nameless) had submitted at the time of his employment a curriculum vitae claiming publications that existed only in his imagination. Although the university lacked the courage to fire him outright for what is after all one of the major academic transgressions, it did transfer him out of our college and gave him a year to look for another job. After that year, he was gone.

Five years later, he resurfaced as a university president at a small college in Kentucky. (At least occasionally, the wages of sin are a college presidency!) At about the same time, in answer to continuing criticism of my report within my own college, I placed it on the web along with the supporting evidence for all my colleagues at UC to read. As it turned out, they read it in Kentucky as well. Someone from a Louisville newspaper came to Cincinnati, interviewed us, and wrote a front page story on the issue. This led to a libel suit filed against the newspaper and me, one which dragged on for two agonizing years. Although we eventually won and the individual in question was fired by his college for seemingly unrelated reasons, the whole thing cost my wife and me a very pretty penny in lawyer fees, not to mention psychic angst. Given American libel law and the fact that the individual in question pulled up stakes and left Kentucky jurisdiction, neither I nor the newspaper ever received any compensation for what is known among lawyers as "a slap suit."

I struggled through this extraordinary experience with the case never far from my thoughts and with virtually no help from the University of Cincinnati or the AAUP. Although originally encouraged by our president to write the report (he too was not happy with the Dean), when the suit materialized the university ran for cover. By contrast, Norman Murdoch was always right at my side. He helped me find a lawyer and prepare the case. He defended me from my detractors in the college. Most importantly, he was there when I simply (or desperately) needed to talk to someone.

Not long after this ordeal ended, a university reorganization dissolved the college where we had taught and transferred the faculty either to other sectors of the university or pensioned them off. For a year, I continued to work at UC in the Department of Romance Languages while Norman was more or less compelled by the administration to retire, despite the fact that not a few members of the Arts and Sciences History Department wanted him to join them. After that year, my wife and I left for Austin, Texas where we still teach at the university. Meanwhile, Norman had retired to Oregon.

When all is said and done, I tend to judge people, at least in part, according to what might be characterized as a military metaphor: if tomorrow I found it necessary to "go over the top" and charge across a field at the enemy, could I count on this or that person to go with me? For most people, even friends, the answer would have to be no. On the other hand, in the case of Norman Murdoch, I have no doubt whatsoever that during that charge, were I to look to my side, he would be there. Live long and prosper my friend.

Norman Murdoch, Historian of The Salvation Army

John Coutts

On an autumn morning in 1981 I switched on the radio and tuned in to the BBC World Service. Normally I gave it only half an ear, for a long day in the classroom lay ahead: but this occasion was different. Top of the 8 a.m. news programme was the announcement that General Arnold Brown had withdrawn the entire international Salvation Army from the World Council of Churches in protest against the latter's support for the Fund to combat Racism in Southern Africa.

Church news is often non-news, at least in the United Kingdom, but on this occasion the Army had hit unwanted headlines. To me it seemed obvious that General Brown's decision would be deeply divisive. For some—inside The Salvation Army and elsewhere —it would be seen as a principled stand against Communist-inspired terrorism. To others, it would look like backing for a racist regime.

Years before, way back in 1965, Mr Ian Smith, leader of a white minority government, had made a unilateral declaration of the independence of Rhodesia. I was a missionary teacher at the time, Principal of The Salvation Army Secondary School at Akai in Nigeria, and had the none-too-easy task to announce this unwelcome news in school assembly. For a whole generation—and more—the wrongs and rights of minority rule in Southern Africa were to loom large in the consciousness of the Western world, and disturb the conscience of the Christian churches.

As African resistance in Rhodesia grew, the World Council of Churches had set up the controversial Fund to Combat Racism, providing financial assistance to liberation movements which were regarded as terrorist groups by those who opposed them. The international Salvation Army had been an uneasy member of the WCC since its foundation in 1948, but had made no contribution to the Fund. Violent resistance grew and led to the tragic death of two young teachers at the Army's Usher Institute in what was then

Rhodesia. For General Brown, enough was enough. It was time for the Salvation Army to part company from the WCC.

The conflicts, hopes, suspicions and misunderstandings that surrounded his controversial decision set the scene for Norman Murdoch's heartfelt and scholarly book.

Times change, and attitudes shift. Communism is no longer a serious threat. Apartheid has come to an end in South Africa and Zimbabwe is no longer subject to white minority rule. But the relevance of Norman's work remains, for it shows, without cynicism, how prejudices and presuppositions color the plans that Christians make and the ways in which they carry them out.

But it does more; for Norman's work as a historian—of which this book is the latest and probably the last example—also is a landmark on The Salvation Army's long march to self-understanding, a process which Norman did much to assist.

Enthusiasts—political and religious—are naturally eager to promote their new-found and exciting cause, and have little time to discuss its shortcomings in public. Not surprisingly, analysis is often left to the second generation. For The Salvation Army, that process was to be delayed.

Not long after its foundation in nineteenth-century London, the Army adopted an autocratic form of government, with General William Booth in sole command. Autocracies cannot function without censorship, and full-time officers were required not to publish without the General's permission. Small wonder then, that Salvation Army biographies have read more like hagiographies, and attempts at objective analysis—from inside the movement—were not made available to the public.

In this, of course The Salvation Army was far from unique. 'Investigative' newspapers rarely investigate their own proprietors, and University Principals, seeking to impress potential donors, may not welcome candid accounts of infighting in the ranks of the academic faculty. Even in democracies, the hard-pressed administrator would often prefer that dissenters would prudently refrain from rocking the boat.

But religious bodies profess to rely on Divine Providence, and every follower of Jesus must suppose that works of faith, hope and charity—however inadequate—are blessed and sustained by their Lord. How then should they deal with bad news of moral failure, which might cause simple souls to stumble and reflect badly on the Almighty himself? Good news may become the only news, and the desire to 'avoid scandal' may lead to prevarication and cover-up. And some disasters, like quarrels in the family, can be too painful to discuss.

For many Salvationists of my parents' generation the crisis of 1929 was such an occasion. That was a year of revolution in which the second General, Bramwell Booth, was deposed by the High Council—a group of senior officers. The Army became a self-perpetuating oligarchy—a system which remains, with modification, at the present time. For me, as a young man, this high tragedy was a matter of great interest—yet my officer-parents, who had lived through it, were reluctant to discuss it at all. My father, General Frederick Coutts, details the course of the First High Council in Volume 6 of *The History of the Salvation Army*. The facts are laid out, detailed documentation is provided—but no analysis is attempted. That's as far as he, and I believe many of that generation, felt able go to. But let no one feel smug or superior: for we too are hemmed in—more than we realize—by the attitudes of the world we live in.[4]

But the times they were a-changing: an early attempt at critical biography, which General Coutts encouraged, was *Soldier Saint* by Bernard Watson. This account of the stormy and colorful life of George Scott Railton, the Salvation Army's first Commissioner, appeared with official approval in 1971. So far, so progressive.

But Watson was writing about the receding past. My own book *The Salvationists* [1977] fell foul of censorship when I attempted to analyze—guess what!—The Salvation Army's relationship with the World Council of Churches and yes—the situation in Southern Africa! Some potatoes were simply too hot to handle. But my book also attracted the interest and attention of Norman Murdoch, then a Professor of History at the University of Cincinnati.

Norman Murdoch has devoted much of his professional life to the study of The Salvation Army because he understands the faith and idealism that drives much of the Army's work. He has been a critical but never a cynical observer—an independent scholar and a candid friend.

The titles of his published essays bear witness to his wide range of interests: these include "Salvation Army invasions of Montreal, 1884-5,"[5] "Salvation Army disturbances in Liverpool, England, 1879-1887,"[6] "Wesleyan Influence on William and Catherine Booth,"[7] "Female Ministry in

---

4. The story has been told in detail by John Larsson in *1929: A Crisis that Shaped The Salvation Army's Future* (London: Salvation Books, 2009).

5. "Marching as to War: Salvation Army Invasion of Montreal, 1884-5." *Fides et Historia* 35.1 (2003) 59-90.

6. "Salvation Army Disturbances in Liverpool, 1879-1887." *Journal of Social History* 25 (1992) 575-83.

7. "Wesleyan Influence on William & Catherine Booth." *Wesleyan Theological Journal* 20 (1985) 97-103.

the Thought and Work of Catherine Booth,"[8] "Anglo-American Salvation Army Farm Colonies, 1890–1910,"[9] "The Salvation Army & Church of England, 1882–3,"[10] and "The Salvation Army: A Model Late 19th Century Anglo American Youth Organization."[11] He also served as Edition Editor of a special number of *Christian History* celebrating William and Catherine Booth.[12] Relevant to the present work is "Darkest Africa: Martyrdom and Resistance to Colonialism in Rhodesia."[13]

Norman also explored the past history of the city in which he spent much of his professional life, writing *A Centennial History—The Salvation Army in Cincinnati 1885–1985*.[14] Detailed research, including personal interviews, enabled him to tell a story full of human interest, to analyze the Army's response to social and spiritual need throughout the course of a turbulent century, and to commemorate honourable lives that would otherwise be forgotten.

He also gave detailed consideration to the roots of the Salvation Army in English Methodism, its far-from-easy birth as the East London Christian Mission, and its sudden sensational growth and expansion world-wide. He broke new ground with the publication in 1994 of *Origins of The Salvation Army*.[15] Norman was not convinced that 'The Founder'—William Booth—was its sole creator under God, or that its early history was a triumphant march to glory. On the contrary, Booth's revivalist mission "never won the heathen masses of the cities to its Wesleyan gospel," and the famous 'Darkest England Scheme' for social reform was in part the brain-child of Frank Smith, who later turned to politics and ended his career as a Member of the U.K. Parliament and as a government junior minister.[16]

---

8. "Female Ministry in the Thought & Work of Catherine Booth." *Church History* 53 (1984) 363–78.

9. "Anglo-American Salvation Army Farm Colonies, 1890–1910." *Communal Societies* 3 (1983) 111–21.

10. *Historical Magazine of the Protestant Episcopal Church* 55 (Mar. 1986) 31–55.

11. In *La Jeunesse Et Ses Mouvements*, ed. by Joel Colton (Paris: Editions du CNRS, 1992).

12. *Christian History* (May 1990). Author of: "The General," 5–8; "The Army Mother," 5–9; "The Booths' Children," 26; "In Darkest England," 33–35; "Sources of Booth's Reforming Ideas," 36, and edited articles by six historians.

13. "'Darkest Africa': Martyrdom and Resistance to Colonialism in Rhodesia." *Journal of Third World Studies* (Spr. 2005).

14. Cincinnati: The Salvation Army, 1985.

15. *Origins of The Salvation Army* (Knoxville: University of Tennessee Press, 1994).

16. See also his *Frank Smith: Salvationist Socialist (1854–1940)* (Alexandria VA: The Salvation Army, 2003).

For Norman Murdoch, historian, it was clear that the Lord moved 'in mysterious ways,' and that dedicated human beings—fallible and fascinating—were often the instruments of His purposes. Two of these were Susie Swift and David Lamb, whose lives were retold in *Soldiers of the Cross*, a book whose subtitle, *Pioneers of Social Change*, shows where its author's interests lie.[17] The former went from being a Salvation Army officer to a Roman Catholic nun—equally dedicated in both vocations—while the latter played a major and long-lasting part in the Army's development as it grew into an international and multiracial Christian society.

Norman's attention had already turned to Southern Africa. How did the Army's plans for Christian evangelism and social reform play out in the world of the expanding British Empire? What happened when two giants—William Booth and Cecil Rhodes—met and compared notes? To what extent were Salvation Army policies colored by the social and racial presuppositions of the age? What was the truth behind the tragic events at the Usher Institute? The result of his labor is *Christian Warfare in Rhodesia Zimbabwe*—a work which studies a specific slice of human history, but may help us to understand what happened at other times and in other places.

Norman's work shows that an army 'raised up by God' is nonetheless kept going—and at times misdirected—by fallible human beings. Writing of the church in his own day, St. Paul summed up the paradox precisely: "We have this treasure in earthenware pots." But, the apostle continues, this serves "to show that the transcendent power belongs to God and not to us."[18] Let this text serve as a citation for the work of Norman Murdoch, good and faithful historian.

---

17. *Soldiers of the Cross, Susie Swift and David Lamb* (Alexandria VA: Crest, 2006).

18. 2 Corinthians 4:7.

Chapter 1

Christian and Cultural Warfare in Rhodesia/Zimbabwe, 1890–1990

> The Protestant missionaries who took their Bibles to Africa in the nineteenth century . . . represent in the most acute form the prescriptions of a faith and the spirit of an age. They came from every white nation whose social and moral values had been sculpted by the descendants of the Christian Reformation in the sixteenth century. They came, significantly, in proportions approximating to purely national instincts for expansion and appetites for colonialism. Of these missionaries, it was the men and women representing the British societies who bore most of the burdens in the nineteenth century, who took most of the spoils, who were supported most extensively by their kinsmen at home. Much of Africa as we know it today, to a degree which cannot yet be assessed, is their legacy.—Geoffrey Moorhouse[1]

Between 1890 and 1990 three forces collided in Rhodesia/Zimbabwe: colonialism (1890–1979), church councils (conciliarism),[2] and two liberation wars or Chimurenga (1896–97 and 1970s) which ended with a treaty in 1979. Rhodesia was the name British invaders gave a land-locked area of

---

1. Moorhouse, *The Missionaries*, 18.
2. The word "conciliarism" is used here as a convenient short-hand term for the phenomenon of national and international councils of churches in the twentieth century, rather than in its narrower sense of a fourteenth- to sixteenth-century movement within the Catholic Church, or of a particular theory of church government.

southern Africa just north of the British-Afrikaner colony of South Africa.[3] British and American Christian missions contested or joined forces to proclaim the gospel and obtain a share of the land Cecil Rhodes took by force from Africans for his British South Africa Company (BSAC) in the name of Queen Victoria in 1890. By accepting land and financial grants from the BSAC, Christian missions, including the London-based Salvation Army, were entwined in political and cultural intrigues to further their religious and humanitarian causes, often to their credit, but often to their shame.

The main subject of this history is The Salvation Army, a British mission whose "pioneer column," mimicking the name Rhodes gave his military invasion force in 1890, arrived at Fort Salisbury in Mashonaland in 1891 from South Africa. In this period Christian missions were subsumed in an imperial state that both aided and stunted their work. From 1891 to 1980, the colonial period, the Salvation Army interacted with the state in the same manner as other missions. It sought land and subsidies from the government for its churches, clinics, and schools. It generally shared cordial relations with other missions, Roman Catholic and Protestant, and with white settlers. As the colonial era drew to a close in Africa in the 1950s to 1980, the Army tried to maintain apolitical neutrality during an independence war that fused in some minds, especially Americans', with an international "Cold War" conflict with international communism.

The United Kingdom, United States, United Nations, African frontline states, and Eastern European and Asian communist-bloc nations all had a political interest in Rhodesia/Zimbabwe. Christian conciliar movements, the World Council of Churches (WCC) and the Christian Council of Rhodesia (CCR), played roles that some Salvation Army leaders saw as overtly political as well as humanitarian. As a result, in the late 1970s the Army dissolved its conciliar relations with the national church coalition (RCC), and then with the World Council (WCC) in the 1980s.

For some twenty-five years beginning in the 1960s there was some disagreement between pro- and anti-conciliar movement factions of Salvation Army leaders in London, New York, and other nations. American leaders asked leaders in the rest of the Army's then eighty-six-nation ranks to withdraw the Army from the World Council of Churches, headquartered in Geneva, Switzerland. Their reason was the WCC's tendency not to acknowledge a "Cold War" between the West and Communist bloc nations. I propose to examine the three forces—colonialism, conciliarism, and the

3. Names for this area of Southern Africa changed after the arrival of the British South African Company (BSAC) in 1890 from Mashonaland, Manicaland, and Matabeleland to "Rhodesia," which became "Zimbabwe" in 1980. I will use the name appropriate for the period that I am discussing.

Cold War (communism vs. the West) in the context of the effect they had on Salvationists in Rhodesia in the 1890s and then again in the 1970s–80s when Shona and Matabele (Ndebele speaking) tribes initiated two *Chimurenga* (risings). In the second of these, the Patriotic Front (PF), an alliance of the Zimbabwe African People's Union (ZAPU) of Joshua Nkomu and the Zimbabwe African National Union (ZANU) led by Robert Mugabe, gained support from Eastern European and Asian communist nations in their struggle against minority white rule in the 1960s and 1970s. Churches, both in Rhodesia and beyond, had to choose sides.

Rhodesia was a British colony from 1890 to 1980. Until 1923 Britain ruled through the British South Africa Company. After 1923 Britain ruled through a white settler regime until 1965, when Ian Smith's Rhodesian Front Party made a Unilateral Declaration of Independence (UDI) from Britain. Britain did not accede to this change and worked, without success, to alter minority white rule. From 1890 Africans did not accept British rule, but challenges were muted by armed force.

In the first *Chimurenga*, a Shona warrior killed the Salvation Army's first "martyr" and member of its pioneer party, Captain Edward T. Cass. The killing took place in the Mazoe Valley north of Fort Salisbury in 1896.[4] In a second *Chimurenga*, Ndebele guerrillas killed two British Salvationist women teachers at the Army's Usher secondary school near Figtree, east of Bulawayo, in 1978. In his 2009 history of the Salvation Army, Henry Gariepy describes the latter event under the heading "Modern-Day Martyrs."[5] These deaths form historical bookends to the Army's relations with white settlers and African inhabitants of the British colonial state.

To place inverted commas around "martyr" and "martyrdom," with reference to either Edward Cass in the first *Chimurenga* or Sharon Swindells and Diane Thompson in the second is not to discount either the value of their missionary endeavors or the tragedy of their deaths.[6] Rather, it acknowledges that they died primarily because they were caught up in social, political, and national circumstances wider than simply the defense of their faith per se. At the same time, many African Salvationists died for the same reasons, regarded as "sell-outs" because of their involvement with the Salvation Army, and in some cases specifically because they would not deny their faith. As Major Misheck Nyandoro records, "On occasion, Salvationists

---

4. Post-majority rule, the spelling of many African place-names has been altered to better approximate their correct pronunciation. Hence "Mazoe" is now "Mazowe." Spelling and place-names current in the times being discussed will be used in this book.

5. Gariepy, *Christianity in Action*, 230.

6. The names of Sharon Swindells and Diane Thompson are enrolled in the Chapel of the Saints and Martyrs of our Time, in Canterbury Cathedral, Kent, England.

were visited by night, ordered to put on their Salvation Army uniform, and then inhumanely beaten or hacked to death."[7] Over four and a half thousand Salvationists were reported to have been killed in the long conflict.[8]

After the Patriotic Front forces of Robert Mugabe and Joshua Nkomo obliged the Rhodesian government to accept a negotiated settlement in 1979, Africans set up their state of Zimbabwe in 1980. As a protest against the Salvation Army's colonial rule from London, in 1981 an estimated 200 African Salvationists marched through the streets of Harare (the new name of the capital, formerly Salisbury), to ask Salvation Army leaders in London to cancel their decision to withdraw the Army from the World Council of Churches. During the conflict the WCC had helped to seal a bond between Christian churches and the new African state by offering humanitarian aid through a Program to Combat Racism. The Salvation Army, mainly its American leaders, saw aid to the Marxist-led movement as aid to atheistic communists. African Salvationists saw the aid as humanitarian-political sympathy for their liberation struggle.

In 1904 Rhodesia's Christian missions had begun a conciliar movement by joining in a Missionary Conference to deal with the government on matters of education and health. This produced comity agreements that determined how missions would divide Rhodesia's districts and land among the Christian denominations. They also encouraged Bible translating that reduced African languages to writing. Africans organized a separate Southern Rhodesia Bantu Christian Conference in 1928. During the Second *Chimurenga* (1964–79) a bi-racial Christian Council of Rhodesia (CCR) with ties to the World Council of Churches tried to stem rising tensions over majority rule and minority rights. The Salvation Army was a reluctant member of the RCC. In 1979 the RCC became the Zimbabwe Council of Churches (ZCC) and joined with the Roman Catholic Church in order to speak with one voice to Prime Minister Ian Smith's government. The ZCC opened ties to the All Africa and British Councils of Churches.

From the late 1960s to 1983 the Salvation Army increasingly disliked what it termed "liberal" tendencies in conciliar organizations. Tensions between the Army and the WCC, RCC, and ZCC strained relations among the Army's international leaders. After the killings at its Usher Institute (girls' school at Figtree near Bulawayo), US Salvation Army leaders reacted

---

7. Nyandoro, *A Flame of Sacred Love*, 122.

8. Gariepy, *Mobilized for God*, 20, notes that an estimated 4,600 Salvationists, mostly African, also died during the Second *Chimurenga*. However, this figure may have been based on a simple comparison of Salvation Army Soldiers' numbers before and after the *Chimurenga* and does not indicate how many had died, or show responsibility for those deaths.

with outrage to a WCC humanitarian grant to support the Patriotic Front nationalists and urged the Army's leader in London to sever WCC ties. In 1978 General Arnold Brown, a Canadian, suspended the Army's membership and made the split final in 1981. The African Salvationists' reaction to withdrawal was a protest march on the Army's headquarters in Harare to denounce General Brown for leaving an organization that supported their liberation with humanitarian aid. They also opposed the sale of land at Pearson Farm that Cecil Rhodes had given the Army as a patrimony for its African church.

A third force, international communism, supported majority African rule and an end to Western colonialism. Eastern European and Asian Marxist states had armed and trained Zimbabwe African National Liberation Army (ZANLA) Shona guerrillas led by Robert Mugabe, and Joshua Nkomo's Zimbabwe People's Revolutionary Army (ZIPRA) Ndebele forces. African nationalists, including Christians, accepted this support for their struggle. After all, colonial powers did not offer them financial or military aid, although they had assisted the Soviets in World War II. Salvation Army leaders, especially in the U.S., were adamantly anti-communist, all the more so in the wake of the US defeat in Vietnam.

A debate had begun in the 1950s between African Christians and Western missions that had evangelized, taught, and healed them. Ties between white-led missions and colonial governments, dating from 1890, were hard to break and protagonists on neither the Christian right nor the Marxist left would yield to divided loyalties. State treason was religious heresy in much the way it was when Europe's medieval state and church had bonded together. Neither white Rhodesians nor African liberationists would relinquish Euro-Christian or Marxist-nationalist creeds. African Christians who welcomed communist aid for their nationalist cause did so for reasons similar to the Americans' acceptance of French aid in their 1776–81 revolution.

Prime Minister Ian Smith's Rhodesia Front maintained minority rule up to the day the United Kingdom and United States joined to force Smith to negotiate with African nationalists in 1976 at Geneva. Smith portrayed himself as Christian and staunchly anti-communist. He was upset that churches did not see his regime as a savior of Western Christian civilization. To be Christian was, in his mind, to be white, European, and anti-Marxist. His vague notions of Christian and Marxist ideologies were born in a post–World War II world of dying imperialism. He liked to say that Rhodesians were "more British than the British" in their fight for the empire.[9] But Professor Anthony J. Chennells argues that there were "many more Christians

---

9. Smith, *The Great Betrayal*, 9.

in the nationalist [African] leadership than there were in [Smith's] cabinet." And that "there is little evidence . . . that white Rhodesians ever perceived themselves as being engaged in some civilizing mission, let alone as agents of Christianity—white missionaries were in fact regarded as dangerous subversives and black Christians appear in many novels as political subversives."[10] Furthermore, Smith was no democrat. "One man one vote" had no part in his political philosophy.

The ideological heritage of Africans, since most had been educated in mission schools, was largely Christian. Which Rhodesian leader—Robert Mugabe, Joshua Nkomo, Methodist Bishop Abel Muzorewa, or Ian Smith—would win the prize as the most Christian? Can there be any doubt that Africans who favored majority rule honored a Western heritage that they had learned in mission-run schools? They were grateful to the Protestant conciliar movement and the Roman Catholic Church for supporting their freedom fight, but they also had a debt to communist benefactors whose military aid helped release them from a white racist regime. Africans were debtors, in St. Paul's words, to "Greek and barbarian," to churches and communists. Many Africans recognized that Christianity, conveyed to them in mission schools, churches, and hospitals, had formed their values, including that of freedom.

After independence in 1980 missionaries learned to work with their schools' African alumni. White Zimbabweans came to terms with church-state and conciliar alliances. But the post-independence period was hard for churches like the Salvation Army which had opposed the independence movement's leaders and had been slow to install African leaders for their churches before 1980. But historically the Army had thrived on adaptability. Fortunately for its mission, its international leaders in London, and its principal source of funds in the US, gradually learned to accept the grace and wisdom of African officers and soldiers.

In the 1890s, the BSAC intrusion meant altered place names, demeaning of native culture, including language and religion, theft of land and minerals, all blessed by Queen Victoria's charter issued to the Company. Britain vested power in Rhodes' BSAC whose interest in Rhodesia was purely financial. He expressed no interest in the natives' welfare. Professor T. O. Ranger observes that "Rhodes' biographers have disputed as to whether he regarded Africans as children or as animals, [and] did not really pay much regard to Africans at all. As a result he felt no need to evolve any continuous native

---

10. Chennells, "White Rhodesian Nationalism—The Mistaken Years," 124.

policy."[11] Instead Rhodes turned to white settler farmers and miners to rule for him, while he devoted himself to aggrandizing wealth.

With that mercenary goal the BSAC made alliances with white settlers and agencies that would further its end, including Christian missions. Colonizers claimed that their intrusion into African polity and culture was done to give Rhodesia European free enterprise and Christian faith. The mix of those two cultural accoutrements they labelled "Western civilization." The new culture also included proper dress, English language and tea preparation, and Western medicine, drama, music, religious sectarianism, and dance. European settlers dubbed everything African as "heathen" or "pagan" and referred to anything Western, including a capitalist economic system that had commenced only a century earlier, as civilized and Christian.

After the Salvation Army arrived in Mashonaland in 1890, it interacted with the BSAC and white settler governments. In this relationship the Army proved to be impressively imperial, with a pragmatism that mimicked that of Cecil Rhodes. In adjusting to colonial regimes the Army secured its position in relation to those who held state authority.

The Army was not courageous. It took few stands that would antagonize the colonial state. Roman Catholics, Methodists, and even Anglicans were more prone to chastise the state for denying Africans the franchise and for taking African land. The Army was a resilient survivor in the midst of better-heeled missions with better-educated leaders. A few Salvationists showed courage that allowed the Army to claim "martyrs," a claim that it granted only to Europeans. Africans whose courage deserved the appellation "martyr" did not receive it from the Army, either because their views did not coincide with those of the Army's leaders or simply because they were African. What criteria did Army historians and journalists apply to those whom they found to be deserving of an investiture of sainthood? That is the story we begin in 1891 with the initial Salvation Army interaction with Rhodes' BSAC.

---

11. Ranger, *Revolt in Southern Rhodesia, 1896–97*, 51–53.

Chapter 2

The Salvation Army Invades Mashonaland, 1891–95

> To black and white the Gospel preach,
> To save poor sinners, and to teach
> Salvation is within their reach,
> Mashonaland! Mashonaland!¹

The story of Rhodesia and Zimbabwe is a tale of land and its possession as much as it is of land and its people. John White, a Methodist missionary in Rhodesia at the time the Salvation Army arrived in 1891, foresaw a danger in the British taking land from Africans. He said that "If the African became landless he would either sink down to a serf-like condition on some European's farm, or else he would drift into mines or the towns and become rapidly in danger of losing his moral character, and along with it some of his best qualities as the member of a great race."[2] Europeans came to Africa to claim the land and the wealth it contained. King Leopold of Belgium said that all around him he saw stirrings of a new age of colonialism.[3] This was the era in which the future South African politician and diamond magnate Cecil Rhodes would say, "I would annex the planets if I could."[4]

On May 5, 1891, the Rhodesia-bound Salvation Army pioneer column began a rugged 952-mile, six-month trek from the center of Cecil Rhodes'

---

1. *The War Cry* (South Africa), 28 March 1891, 1, and 1 August 1891, 1, 24.
2. Mazobere, "Christian Theology of Mission," 148.
3. Hochshild, *King Leopold's Ghost*, 41.
4. Millin, *Rhodes*, 138.

gold and diamond enterprise at Kimberley, South Africa. They travelled in a wagon they named the "Enterprise," pulled by eighteen bullocks. Their goal was to join other Christian missionaries at the Fort Salisbury stockade in central Mashonaland, a land-bound territory north of South Africa. They arrived on November 18. Commissioner Thomas Estill, the Army's Southern Africa commander, made it clear that he had not sent the Salvationists to convert Africans to Christianity. Instead, his charge to the pioneer party was to teach South African white men, who had gone to Mashonaland as gold miners, to seek the "Pearl of Greatest Price." The commander of the pioneer party, Major John Pascoe, his wife and two daughters, and Captains David Crook, Edward Cass, Bob Scott, Edgar Mahon, and Theodore Searle, comprised the Army's invasion force. But in spite of Estill's command to save whites, the Army's South African magazine, the *War Cry*, printed a broader message in the form of an evangelical hymn at the head of this chapter, to be sung to the tune: "Maryland, My Maryland."

This ambiguity in the mission's purpose, whether to save white miners or black Shona tribesmen, signaled the Salvation Army's mixed motives in its missionary campaign. Other missions shared in the confusion. Some of the misunderstanding of goals can be understood by the fact that the Salvation Army's General, William Booth, an evangelist by profession, had just published his social reform opus, *Darkest England, and the Way Out*, in 1890.

Booth's plan for the social regeneration of England's impoverished masses included a major role for the Salvation Army in Britain's colonies, including those in Southern Africa. Booth would eliminate unemployment in English cities by sending London's unemployed to farms in England for training. After they were trained to farm, he would move them "back to the land" in "Little Englands" in the British colonies—Canada, Australia, New Zealand, South Africa, and hopefully, Rhodesia. Booth soon asked Cecil Rhodes' British South Africa Company (BSAC) for land in Mashonaland. On to this allegedly "manless land" Booth proposed to move thousands of unemployed "landless men" from England. But Mashonaland was *not* "manless." The land the Army and other missions acquired by purchase or as gifts from Rhodes British South Africa Company belonged to African farmers who had lived on the land for several centuries.

Southern Africa's unemployed and landless Dutch-speaking Afrikaners and British whites did not want to compete with Booth's poor from London's East End slums for either work or land. Rhodes, after creating false hope in Booth when the two men met in South Africa and in England, ultimately did not support Booth's "Darkest England" venture. Still, as late as 1908, six years after Rhodes' death, Booth still believed that the BSAC might invest in his Rhodesia emigration scheme.

Put bluntly, Booth's principal aim in Mashonaland in 1891 was not to convert Africans to his Wesleyan form of Christianity, but rather to promote mass emigration of England's urban unemployed to African farms under the Salvation Army's supervision. By this means he would achieve his economic and soul-salvation goals for destitute English whites. But within a decade Booth's Rhodesia mission failed. So he turned his attention to new mission options, one of which was the evangelization of Africans. He was known for his capacity for adaptation.[5] Rhodes was interested in civilizing Africans through schools, churches, and clinics, and was willing to finance missions that carried out those activities.

Twelve years earlier William Booth had proven his agility of purpose by saving from demise his East London home mission, which he had founded in 1865. He had largely failed to win the urban poor, "heathen" as he termed them, to his Wesleyan version of Christianity. By the late 1860s he had opened mission "stations" beyond his East End mission halls. In the West End and in country areas he and his wife Catherine had begun their itinerant preaching to congregations quite unlike the East End Irish, Jewish, Italian, and Eastern European immigrants. In the English Midlands, Cornwall, and Wales they had converted thousands by using American techniques they had learned from evangelists James Caughey, Phoebe Palmer, and Charles Finney in the 1850s and early 1860s. In 1878, when their Christian Mission's growth ebbed for a second time, William had changed its name to "a salvation army" and had caught the imagination of an imperial age with military jargon, uniform, and music. As growth in the Salvation Army's membership declined again by the late 1880s the Booths paid increasing attention to overseas territories in North America, South Asia, Australia/New Zealand, and South Africa.

The Salvation Army, as it sought to find its mission in 1890, was only slightly more confused about its place in southern Africa than the established Christian sects that preceded its 1891 arrival in Mashonaland. Only Cecil Rhodes' BSAC, that had arrived on September 12, 1890, had a clear notion of what it wanted to accomplish—it sought wealth, by whatever means necessary. Cecil Rhodes' Pioneer Column in its trek to Mashonaland consisted of 200 young tradesmen, escorted by 350 police who were attended by 400 African Cape "boys." Rhodes had promised that each pioneer would receive 3,000 acres of land and fifteen gold claims. They raised the Union Jack over Fort Salisbury, named for the British Prime Minister,

---

5 Murdoch, "William Booth's Darkest England and the Way Out."

The Salvation Army Invades Mashonaland, 1891–95

thus claiming its possession for Queen Victoria. Three years later Dr. Leander Starr Jameson would lead nearly all of the white men of Mashonaland south to attack the Ndebele kingdom of Lobengula for a promise of twenty gold claims, 6,000 acres of land, and a share in the King's wealth, including 362,000 head of cattle.[6]

When the Salvation Army arrived at Fort Salisbury its officers joined missionaries of five Christian missions that had recently preceded them: the Roman Catholic, Church of England, London Missionary Society, Dutch Reformed Church of South Africa, and British Methodists. In 1859 the London Missionary Society's (LMS) Robert Moffat had begun work in Matabeleland. During the LMS's first three decades it did not make a single convert. The Ndebele and their (Zulu) king, Mzilikazi, had granted the LMS a site at Inyati in 1859, and in 1870 Mzilikazi's son Lobengula gave the LMS a second site at Hope Fountain. In 1895 the BSAC ceded the LMS a 24,000-acre farm at Dombodema. Thus land acquisition and friendship with Lobengula, not Christian converts, were the prime achievements of the London Missionary Society. Other missions would inherit the same traits.

The Roman Catholics had arrived in Bulawayo, Lobengula's capital, in 1879, but Jesuit Father Peter Prestage did not found the first Catholic mission until January 20, 1885, when he set up a station at Empandeni. Jesuit efforts also failed to produce a single convert. Mother Patrick's Dominican Sisters arrived at Fort Salisbury in July 1891, four months before the Salvation Army, to establish a hospital. In 1892 they established a convent chapel and school. That year the Jesuits established a mission station at Chishawasha near Salisbury. The Church of England (Anglican) missionaries were the last to arrive before Rhodes' pioneer column. In 1888 Bishop Knight-Bruce of Bloemfontein, South Africa, visited Matabeleland after long negotiations to gain King Lobengula's permission to do so.

After the BSAC set up Fort Salisbury in September 1890, several protestant missions arrived in Mashonaland in swift succession. South Africa's Dutch Reformed Church (September 9, 1891) set up a station at Morgenster. Two groups of Wesleyan origin, the British Methodists (September 29, 1891) and the London-based Salvation Army (November 18, 1891) followed the Union Jack into Fort Salisbury. Four American missions came in the wake of the British missionaries. In 1893 and 1895 the American

---

6. Todd, "White Policy and Politics 1890–1980," 116–17. "Ndebele" refers to the people and language of this kingdom in an area on the northern border of South Africa. The people are related to the Zulu and Ndebele people of South Africa from which they migrated in 1838. The British termed this area "Matabeleland" and they termed the area of the Shona-speaking dynasties of central Rhodesia "Mashonaland." The Shona are a diverse group made up of many tribes.

Board of Commissioners for Foreign Missions opened stations at Mount Selinda and Chikore. The Seventh Day Adventists founded a mission station at Solusi in 1894. The American Methodist Episcopal Church, led by Bishop Hartzell, opened the Old Umtali mission in 1898. Also in 1898, the Brethren in Christ Church founded its Matopo Mission. Other missions from various nations joined the scramble into Rhodesia in the late 1890s. They included the South African General Mission that opened a station at Rusitu in 1897, near the Mozambique border. In 1898 the Church of Christ (U.S.), the Presbyterian Church of South Africa, the Free Presbyterian Church of Scotland, the Church of Sweden, the Swedish Free Church Mission, the Free Methodist Church (U.S.), and the South African Baptist Missionary Society set up mission stations.[7]

C. J. M. Zvobgo has summarized two common understandings that missionaries in Mashonaland and Matabeleland shared between 1859 and 1898. First, they held that in light of the early experiences of the London Missionary Society and the Jesuits in Matabeleland, the missionary enterprise "had little chance of success until Ndebele power was broken, and that this could only be done by force." This caused missions to welcome the BSAC and its soldiers to Mashonaland in 1890. And second, "missionaries were indebted to C. J. Rhodes for grants of land on which they built their mission stations." This was "a situation to which no other territory in Africa could offer a parallel," according to C. P. Groves. By 1925 the BSAC had given 325,730 acres of land to church missions and the missions had purchased an additional 71,085 acres. Zvobgo pointed out that "much of this land was acquired without the permission of the African chiefs and their people."[8]

None of the missions succeeded in converting acquisitive rough white South African miners, whose interests were as material as those of the BSAC. They did not crave spiritual wealth. Thus most missions readily adopted work among Africans that the BSAC chose for them, particularly when large land grants and financial support accompanied their cooperation.

William Booth's *All the World* missionary magazine, edited by Major Susie F. Swift, an American graduate of the elite Vassar College, stated baldly that the Salvation Army did not want to be left "behind in these Colonial advances." Booth embraced the era's postmillennial progressive imperative to spread the gospel before Christ's triumphal second coming, an enthusiasm that meshed nicely with Britain's imperial colonizing agenda. Booth also shared the general nineteenth-century ignorance of, but fascination with,

---

7. Zvobgo, *The Wesleyan Methodist Missions in Zimbabwe, 1891–1945*, 2–4

8. Zvobgo, *Wesleyan Methodist Missions*, 5–6; Zvobgo quotes from Groves, *The Planting of Christianity in Africa*, iii, 103–4.

African culture. He had copied the title of his social scheme, *In Darkest England and the Way Out*, from H. M. Stanley's popular title, *In Darkest Africa*, published earlier in 1890.

While the missionary journal, *All the World*, pitied the poor bushman from whom white men had taken "the land of his forefathers," Major Swift held that Africans must "yield" to Western civilization's advances or "die." In a twist of logic she urged Salvationists to save "swarthy brothers and sisters of the Dark Continent" from "damning European habits" that "canteen keepers and brandy farmers" had brought to Africa. *All the World* also reported that other missions were inciting the Army to act in league with Christianity's imperial enterprise. Mr. Judd of the CIM [China Inland Mission] wanted to know if "China is not in *All the World*." He scolded that China had about one-fourth of the world's population, but no Salvation Army.[9]

So the Salvation Army's fallback mission program, as its London headquarters reported it, was to save Africans from heathen beliefs and from European vices. This was General Booth's charge to his Southern Africa commander. But Booth also wanted to move England's unemployed to British colonies in the Southern Hemisphere and Canada. For this scheme he asked Cecil Rhodes' BSAC to underwrite a "back to the land" program for London's unemployed in Southern Africa, particularly in the new colony of Rhodesia.

Already, by late 1891, Major John Pascoe, the Salvation Army leader in Mashonaland, realized that his missionary evangelist officers were failing to convert white sinners in the Masonic Hall billiard room that he had rented in Fort Salisbury. Wesleyan (British) Methodists were doing little better in the Masonic building's dining hall.[10] After a short period of "packed congregations" who heard the Salvationists sing and preach, white settlers proved not to be "of the class to which the Army's meetings appealed." Only out of desperation did Pascoe consider turning to an alternative enterprise of "converting the natives." But, he noted, this job was "too big for two or three individuals, however enthusiastic, to tackle." Nevertheless, he found that Africans were "fond of the white people" and so he "started to hold meetings amongst the natives."[11]

---

9. Mahlah, "Away to Mashonaland," *All the World*, June 1891, 468–70; Swift, "Editor's Diary," *All the World* (March 1892) 210.

10. Zvobgo, *Wesleyan Methodist Missions*, 25.

11. "Editor's Diary," *All the World*, March 1892, 210, gave a *Cape Town Argus* account of the first Salvation Army meetings in Fort Salisbury. "Historical Record," Salvation Army Archives, London, has an account of the Army's first years in Rhodesia. Other early accounts are in: Gale, *One Man's Vision*; James Johnston, M.D.; "Mrs.

While The Salvation Army went to Mashonaland to evangelize whites and then to find land for England's urban unemployed, it ultimately realized that it was succeeding in neither goal. Its ultimate success came from a desire that it had only vaguely considered in 1891—to convert Africans to Christianity.

When the British South Africa Company, prodded by the British government, proposed to give land and money to missions that worked with natives, missions found that they were in league with Rhodes' BSAC and the white settler bureaucracy that made up the Rhodesian governments until 1980. Within three days of the Salvationists' arrival at Fort Salisbury Dr. Leander Starr Jameson, Rhodes' BSAC administrator in Mashonaland, gave Major Pascoe a farm of 3,000 acres and two "stands" (lots) in Salisbury. Pascoe set out to choose the best land he could find in the Mazoe Valley north of Salisbury. It is unclear whether the BSAC meant the farm to be Pascoe's personal property, due him as his pioneer grant, or whether it was from the beginning Salvation Army land held in Pascoe's name for William Booth. The title deed may have made no distinction at the time. Booth held all Salvation Army property in his own name or in the name of a surrogate in countries the Army had "invaded."[12] The Army itself belonged to his family until 1929. But as the Army became incorporated in various nations after 1890, it held land as a national corporation. On March 11, 1892, Pascoe carefully chose land sixteen miles north of Salisbury in the Mazoe Valley. He announced that it was "grand country for the General's [social] scheme."

What gave Cecil Rhodes the right to distribute land that belonged to Africans? In 1888 Rhodes' colleagues, Charles Donnell Rudd and Rochfort Maguire, had negotiated a mining concession that King Lobengula signed, but later repudiated. The concession read: "I, Lo Bengula, King of Matabeleland and Mashonaland and other adjoining territories . . . do hereby grant and assign . . . complete and exclusive charge over all metals and minerals situated and contained in my kingdoms . . . ." A missionary, the Rev. C. D. Heim, interpreted for the negotiators as a trusted friend of Lobengula's, and signed the document as a witness. Heim wrote to the London Missionary Society that Rhodes' representatives promised Lobengula that "they would not bring more than ten white men to work in his country and that they would abide by the laws of his country and be as his people." Lobengula granted a mining concession, but Rhodes' plan was to use the document

---

Pascoe" in Boggie, *Experiences of Rhodesia's Pioneer Women*.

12. McKinley, *Marching to Glory*, 29–35, discusses an 1884 secession crisis in the United States that resulted from Booth's policy of holding overseas land through a surrogate.

as an opening wedge to a full-scale European ownership and settlement in Rhodesia.[13]

On January 1, 1890 Rhodes' BSAC asked Frank Johnson to organize the Mashonaland occupation. Johnson was a twenty-three-year-old to whom Rhodes offered £87,000 to choose 200 pioneers in the Cape Colony of South Africa to carry out this invasion.[14]

The British crown had chartered the British South Africa Company as a joint stock enterprise on October 15, 1889, on the basis of the mining concession Rhodes had received from Lobengula.[15] Now the British government prodded Rhodes to compensate Christian missions with land concessions for serving the humanitarian interests of the white settlers and Africans. This would allow the BSAC to focus its attention on profitable mining enterprises.

Throughout the colonial era the Salvation Army, like other Christian missions, lobbied for land grants and cash subsidies to run its schools and hospitals. The state would subsidize the Army's churches, since pastors would also be trained as teachers and receive teachers' salaries from the state. This was important income for a poor organization like the Army. The grants were first offered by the BSAC, and later by Rhodesian governments run by the white settler community. As a result the Salvation Army and other missions became part of the colony's governing apparatus that ensured domestic tranquility, the acquiring of BSAC profits, and the cultural enterprise that Rhodesians termed the cultivation of "western civilization" among the Africans. All of this would be done at the expense of such unfair treatment of Africans as forced labor in mines and on farms, and the denial of land ownership and of political and legal rights. Neither the Salvation Army nor Rhodesian governments down to 1980 sought the advice of Africans in matters of state or church polity. This paternalistic system assumed that Africans were not competent to run the state or church.

Did Africans respond violently to theft of their land and degradation of their culture? Did they hold both the Rhodesian state (BSAC and settler governments) and Christian missions responsible for the theft? That the African response in the 1890s has been largely unknown in the West is due to a filtering of information through BSAC and mission reports and a lack of interest in Africa by Western governments or academic and church historians. BSAC stockholders and British and American mission supporters would

13. Lapping, *End of Empire*, 450.
14. Pakenham, *The Scramble for Africa*, 374.
15. See Samkange, *Origins of Rhodesia*, for a full account of Rhodes' dealings with Lobengula, the Ndebele king. Also see Todd, "White Policy and Politics," 116; and Pakenham, *The Scramble for Africa*, 494-95, on Lobengula's death.

have been startled to find that Africans were ungrateful for what they saw as the West's humanitarian largess. This is not to say that all missionaries sided with the BSAC and Rhodesian settler regimes in their treatment of Africans. They did not. But financial and cultural ties that bound church and state in Rhodesia made missionary complaints against abuses the exception rather than the rule. Part of this was a false notion that missions did not function in the political arena, in spite of the fact that they did serve as the arms and legs of the imperial state system.

Few Salvation Army publications in the 1890s tried to imagine why Africans might attack its property or its missionaries. Few missionaries raised issues of land confiscation and denial of the vote with mission boards in Britain and America. Canaan Banana, Zimbabwe's first state president, a Methodist minister and historian, named several missionaries "who campaigned tirelessly for African advancement." These included Methodists John White and Herbert Carter, Anglican Arthur Shearly Cripps, United Methodist Bishop Ralph E. Dodge, Catholic Bishop Donal Lamont and Sister Janice MacLaughlin, and Anglican Bishop Kenneth Skelton. He also listed three he regarded as totally "co-opted by the colonial state."[16]

But on the whole churches chose to see the deaths of missionaries as being for the faith—that is "martyrdoms"—not as responses to theft of land or degrading of African culture. Nor did the secular media challenge what missions and governments did. One excuse given for not reporting abuses was that people at home would not comprehend the nature of African culture as anything other than "heathen." If a spirit medium told Africans to kill whites who had censured their religion, the report would portray "pagans" who had allowed "superstition" to cloud their minds. Missionaries, after all, had gone to Africa to destroy superstition and polygamous behavior. But as Banana asserted, a few missionaries did raise questions about white settlers' ill treatment of Africans.

The Salvation Army's Major John Pascoe, although he did not speak out publicly like his Methodist missionary friend John White, did sympathize with the Shona in the Salisbury area and held some European behavior and filthy language in contempt. He charged that the European "march of civilization" not only taught the Shona Christianity, but also "the oath." Salisbury's 500 white settlers consisted largely of publicans and BSAC officials. The rest of the white immigrants had gone prospecting. Pascoe found that it was "a disgrace the things [natives] have to tell about the treatment

---

16. Banana, "The Role of the Church in the Struggle for Liberation in Zimbabwe," in *Turmoil and Tenacity*, 198–99.

The Salvation Army Invades Mashonaland, 1891–95

received from the white men." Yet he also despised what he saw as the natives' "thieving and deceitfulness among themselves."[17]

Pascoe's private letters in 1892 to Salvation Army leaders in South Africa and London described the Army's Mashonaland work as "backward" and without "the right men, except for Captain Cass." They found the Shona language to be exceedingly difficult, unlike Ndebele, which Pascoe's officers found to be close to the Zulu spoken in their homeland, South Africa. But Pascoe argued that Roman Catholics, Anglicans, and Methodists were not doing much better, although, unlike the Army, they had made some progress. British Wesleyan Methodists, with whom Pascoe worshipped when no one showed up for the Army's services, had "eight ministers for the native work." Pascoe could not recommend any of his officers to do native work, either alone or in pairs. He did not specify their deficiencies, but he complained that "We cannot get any meetings at all." But when he attended a Wesleyan service he found that they did little better. He was one in a congregation of five. And by his estimate there were only "a dozen professed converted people in the town" of Salisbury.[18]

Even British South Africa Company Administrator Jameson's favorable attitude toward the Salvation Army did not raise Major Pascoe's hopes for success. There were "no prospects" for religious work in Salisbury, certainly not among the whites. Finally, on July 5, 1893 he wrote: "I have come to the conclusion that I had better resign." By then only Captains Cass and Crook at the Mazoe Farm remained in Rhodesia from the Army's original 1891 pioneers. After Pascoe resigned from the Army's ranks he ran a business in Salisbury, Pascoe & Sons, Building Contractors. In 1906–7 he served as Mayor of Salisbury. He died there in 1928.[19]

Yet in spite of Pascoe's loss of personnel and purpose, Salvation Army leaders in London in late 1893 shared the British public's excitement over the Rhodesian colony's defeat of the Ndebele's rising of that year. When

---

17. Thompson, *Delayed Harvest*, 27, quotes Pascoe's remarks from *All the World* (April 1893).

18. "Letters Written by Major John Pascoe" (London: Salvation Army Archives) to Commissioner Thomas Estill, May 8, July 26 & 31, Aug. 14, & Sept. 11, 1892; and to Commissioner Frederick Booth-Tucker, the Army's Foreign Secretary in London, on Apr. 28, 1892. For hopeful reports about the Army's Mashonaland enterprise see Captains Robert H. Scott and D. Crooke, South Africa *War Cry* (1891–92). Thompson, *Delayed Harvest*, 21–26, claims that by 1892 reports to the South Africa *War Cry* and *All the World* in London were dwindling.

19. "Letters Written by Major John Pascoe" to Commissioner Thomas Estill (Sept. 19, undated, Oct, 10, 1892, Nov. 10, Dec. 12, 1892; & Jan 15, Feb. 5, Apr. 9 & 29, & July 5, 1893. A July 5 letter contained his resignation according to Thompson, *Delayed Harvest*, 30.

the BSAC, representing Britain's imperial government, routed the Ndebele natives, at least that was their interpretation, General Booth saluted "the aggressive and daring Cecil Rhodes and the sagacious and far-seeing Sir Henry Loch." Booth would soon ask for more funds and land from Loch, the British High Commissioner in South Africa. Booth's eldest son and Chief of Staff, Bramwell, met Rhodes twice and recalled that no one except his own father had "made such an impression upon me as did Cecil Rhodes. . . . His whole presence spoke of personal force, of faith in ideas, and of iron self-reliance." Passion for adventure and lack of interest in administrative detail marked both William Booth and Cecil Rhodes. Fortunately Booth had a son who took care of administrative details while he dreamed imperial dreams.

The British South Africa Company's imperial designs were matched by those of William and Bramwell Booth. The Salvation Army joined the cheer that went up from Anglicans, Methodists, the London Missionary Society, and Jesuits, who saw Chief Lobengula's defeat as a victory for Christian expansion, according to Prof. C. J. M. Zvobgo.[20] Recent historians of Rhodesia/Zimbabwe have not been kind to Rhodes or Loch or Jameson or their sycophants in the war against Lobengula.

D. N. Beach, Professor of History at the University of Zimbabwe, claimed that the Rhodesian state and the Christian missions developed a myth about Ndebele-Shona relations at the time of the 1893 BSAC-Ndebele war that for a long time was held to be historical fact. Acknowledging that there were Ndebele raids to steal Shona cattle and murder of Shona tribesmen, Beach attacked the myths that BSAC administrators and missionaries shared when they accused the Ndebele state of being "a crude system of 'savagery.'" Beach claimed that this myth ignored the Shona's counter raids against the Ndebele. He asserted that the missionaries' reason for spreading the myth was their desire "to gain support for missions to save the souls of the 'savage' Ndebele." For the BSAC, the myth provided a rationale for the company's conquest of the Ndebele. In place of the myth, Beach offered a history of a complex Ndebele and Shona religious and political system about which the BSAC and missionaries knew little. Yet the missions' informal support for alliances between the BSAC and the Shona in 1893 had "profound effects on the subsequent history of the southern Shona, as Shona raiders struck deep into the Ndebele kingdom."[21]

---

20. *Darkest England Gazette*, 11 Nov. 1893, 7; Bramwell Booth, *Echoes and Memories*, 147–48 On missionary support for the 1893 BSAC rout of the Matabele see Zvobgo, *A History of Christian Missions in Zimbabwe*, 6–10. On the 1893 war see Glass, *The Matabele War*, 1968.

21. Beach, *War and Politics in Zimbabwe*, 15–18, 37.

The Salvation Army Invades Mashonaland, 1891–95

The Shona were a loose collection of dynasties that included a majority of Africans who lived in what Cecil Rhodes renamed Rhodesia. In 1893–96 the Shona were anxious to seal alliances between their numerous dynasties in order to defend themselves against each other and against the Ndebele, a more centralized nation whose area around Bulawayo, situated between South Africa and Mashonaland, was known to white settlers as Matabeleland. To accomplish their goal of creating defensive alliances, the Shona allied with missions and with the British South Africa Company.

British and South African Afrikaner groups who were competing to gain mineral, land, and trade rights along the Rhodesia-South Africa border, were looking for allies in 1893. Before 1893 none of the agreements between the whites and Shona had led to a major anti-Ndebele coalition, even though the treaty-making season that had such aims in mind had begun in 1888–90. The Rhodes-Rudd Concession of October 1888, and the 1890 Afrikaners' Adendorff Concession, had tried to reduce Ndebele King Lobengula's hegemony in Rhodesia. The Dutch Reformed Church, the London Missionary Society, and missionaries of Anglican and Wesleyan churches served the BSAC and Afrikaner parties as messengers during five years of negotiations.[22]

The 1893 BSAC-Shona-mission alliances ultimately led to the 1896–97 Ndebele-Shona rising. Many of the BSAC-Shona alliances, as well as those between the BSAC and Christian missions, carried over into this conflict. Beach argued that when the BSAC began the war against the Ndebele in March 1896, "a considerable number of people [mainly Shona tribesmen] chose to fight on the side of the colonial government."[23] In fact, more Africans collaborated with the whites, or were neutral, than were resistance fighters who sought to oust the BSAC, settlers, and missions from their land, this in spite of the fact that the BSAC Native Department angered Africans when it tried to collect a new hut tax in order to force Africans to work in mines and on farms. It also began to interfere in African internal affairs. Yet Africans in Mashonaland around Fort Salisbury and in Matabeleland around Bulawayo were unable to form an alliance against white colonizers.

As for Christian missions, Beach argued that in the 1880s and 1890s "a number of Shona rulers found them valuable, but the reasons for the interdependence are often unclear." Beach found it odd that the Shona "should have committed themselves so early to the white side, at a time when the central Shona rising seemed to be succeeding." Without knowing it, Shona who sided with missions "were completing the chain of collaborating

22. Beach, *War and Politics in Zimbabwe*, 55–59.
23. Ibid., 70–71, 77f.

territories that ran all the way from the upper Save [river] to the lowveld." Thus Shona collaboration with the BSAC and missions did them no good. In fact it was "not surprising that many of the descendants of the collaborators of 1896 were strongly nationalist from the 1950s onwards," apparently trying to make amends for past actions.[24]

When Thomas Estill, the Salvation Army leader in Southern Africa, left for a new appointment in Australia in 1894, after Lobengula's defeat but before the combined Ndebele-Shona uprising in 1896–97, he left a memorandum concerning the Army's future work in Rhodesia. "I do not think there is much to do among the Europeans, as there are only some 1,500 in the whole country, but I think the present is the time for us to make a mark upon the natives." Such was the optimism after Logengula's 1893 demise, although Salvation Army forces were disintegrating from mass resignations. Most churches were adopting this native strategy. Major Pascoe had come to the same conclusion prior to his resignation as the Army's leader in Rhodesia.

Commissioner Estill's strategy, as one may expect, depended on the Army's ability to gain "privileges and concessions" from the BSAC. The Salvation Army had surveyed its 3,000-acre farm in the Mazoe Valley and had secured a clear title deed to the farm from John Pascoe. Estill sent Adjutant Taylor from Swaziland to succeed Pascoe as the Army's commander in Salisbury. Taylor took along Captain Charlotte Ada Griffin, aged thirty-seven, to wed the farm manager at Mazoe, Captain Edward Cass, aged twenty-nine. The wedding took place at John Pascoe's home. Pascoe's friend, Wesleyan Methodist missionary John White, officiated.[25]

Such was the situation for the Salvation Army and the general state of affairs in Rhodesia on the eve of what became known as the First *Chimurenga* (rising) of 1896–97, the first general African war of Shona and Ndebele dynasties against the British in Rhodesia. This *Chimurenga* would also be the occasion for the first test of Salvation Army mission strategy. Would the Army continue to work among only white settlers, a work that all but one of its pioneer missionaries had abandoned, or would it decide to work among Africans? What inducement would lead the Army to this strategic decision? Who would lead this new advance after the first independence war?

---

24. Beach, "The Initial Impact of Christianity on the Shona"; Beach, *War and Politics in Zimbabwe*, 86–87.

25. Thompson, *Delayed Harvest*, 32.

Chapter 3

The First *Chimurenga* (1896–97) and the Death of Captain Cass

> Universalizing discourses of modern Europe and the United States assume the silence, willing or otherwise of the non-European world. There is incorporation; there is inclusion; there is direct rule; there is coercion. But there is only infrequently an acknowledgment that the colonized people should be heard from, their ideas known.
>
> —Edward Said[1]

On the afternoon of Monday June 15th, 1896, a news flash came through Mashonaland's telegraph wires that Chief Mashayamombe's Shona warriors had attacked the Beatrice Mine and J. C. Hepworth's farm on the Zwenzwe River.

Remnants of the Ndebele nation, after the British defeat of King Lobengula and his subsequent suicide by poison in 1893, had begun to slowly recover in 1894–95.[2] In March 1896 the war began in the South in Matabeleland. In June it spread northward to Mashonaland, the location of the Salvation Army's Mazoe Farm (later renamed Pearson Farm) and its work among Shona-speaking people. It was in the Mazoe Valley that the Salvation

---

1. Said, *Culture and Imperialism*, 50.

2 Ranger, *Revolt in Southern Rhodesia*; and Beach, *War and Politics in Zimbabwe*, chapters 3–5, provide superb histories of the resistance to white rule in Rhodesia known as the First Chimurenga. Zvobgo, *A History of Christian Missions in Zimbabwe*, chapter 2, provides a solid history of the role of Christian missions during the rising.

Army's missionary farm manager, Captain Edward T. Cass, became the Salvation Army's first "martyr" in Africa.³

Captain Edward Cass

Ndebele and Shona leaders gave five reasons for their *Chimurenga*. First, the British South Africa Company, white settlers, and Christian missionaries had forced them off their land so that Cecil Rhodes could make enormous land grants in 1893 to soldiers, settlers, and missions. Second, by chibaro (forced labor that was tantamount to slavery), the BSAC coerced Africans in need of cash to pay taxes, work on farms, in mines and as porters. Third, the "native police" on whom the BSAC depended after it removed all but forty of its own soldiers in 1895, behaved brutally in collecting the hut tax and in exacting forced labor. Fourth, the collection of the hut tax had led to confiscation of as much as 80 percent of Africans' livestock. It was by the number of their cattle that Africans calculated their wealth. And fifth, crop and cattle scourges, as well as a plague of locusts and the rinderpest cattle disease, had robbed Africans of their livelihood. As for missionary involvement in the First Chimurenga, historian Elizabeth Schmidt found that "there was much resentment over the fact that the BSAC government

---

3. In 1906, in South Africa, the Salvation Army's second "martyr," Lieutenant Sifalafala Ngcobo, a Zulu, was killed with knobkerries and assegais in the Nkandla Forest during the Bombata Rebellion. See Tuck, *Salvation Safari*, 34–35.

The First *Chimurenga* (1896-97) and the Death of Captain Cass

allowed missionaries to keep their herds," while at the same time a Jesuit missionary was helping the BSAC slaughter African-owned cattle.[4]

It was in this context that a party of Shona killed a Salvation Army officer, a member of the Army's pioneer party, Captain Edward T. Cass. This incident led white Rhodesians and Salvationists in London, to weave a "martyrdom" story into Rhodesia's pioneer mythology. From 1896 to 1980 the Army and the white Rhodesian state were to a large extent inseparable in their histories and sympathies.

Overall, W. D. Gale estimated that during the 1896-97 Chimurenga, Africans killed 119 whites as well as an unspecified number of "Colonial natives." Other estimates ran as high as 450 whites killed, about 10 percent of the settler population. The number of Africans who died in the fighting is unknown.[5] Not until later would white scholars who studied Shona and Ndebele literature and oral tradition discover that the African mythology surrounding this event was equal to that developed by the whites.

On Tuesday June 16, 1896, Salvation Army Captain Edward T. Cass was working with other white settlers to install new equipment at Alice Mine.[6] Why was Cass, a missionary, working at the mine? Given the problem that John Pascoe had had living on his Salvation Army allowance prior to his resignation, one may suspect that Cass was earning a few extra shillings to support his new wife. But from Army records we know that Mrs. Cass had returned a £5 note that the Army's South Africa headquarters had sent to them in February 1896. She enclosed a note that claimed headquarters needed the money more than she and her husband did.[7] This almost certainly indicates that Cass, like Pascoe in 1891-93, was being well cared for by outside income, something churches refer to as a "tent-maker" livelihood in which ministers earn their keep in an auxiliary occupation much as St. Paul had done in the first century of the Christian era. The Army forbade

---

4. Schmidt, *Peasants, Traders, and Wives*, 36–39. Judge Joseph Vintcent, Acting Administrator for Mashonaland, listed African grievances as: BSAC and settlers taking of land and cattle; compulsory labour in mines; rough treatment; and "evil circumstances" such as starvation, drought, locusts, and rinderpest. Zimbabwe National Archives, Harare, LO 8/2/1, 8/3/1.

5. Gale, *One Man's Vision*, quoted in Thompson, *Delayed Harvest*, 40. Thompson quoted magazines that reflect a white settler mythology of the war. *The Wide World, Blue and Old Gold*, and *The Outpost*, regimental magazine of the BSAC Police, had published the white settler myths in 1953. *Delayed Harvest* had put the white death toll at 450, "ten percent of the European population had lost their lives."

6. Zimbabwe National Archives records show that the Alice Proprietary Mines Ltd. opened in 1890 and operated till 1923. See A 3/6/1–10 (1890-1923) and A 1/7 (1890-91).

7. "Chief Secretary's Notes," *The War Cry*, South Africa (15 Feb. 1896).

its officers to take jobs outside their regular work, but its missionaries were beyond headquarters' scrutiny.

An urgent telegram arrived at Alice Mine from Dan Judson, Inspector of Telegraphs at Salisbury, twenty-seven miles away, giving them the ominous news of the extent of the Shona rising. The message caused mine manager J. W. Salthouse to begin to "fortify the position" and to wire Fort Salisbury to request a conveyance to take the three women who lived in the vicinity of the mine to the fort. A return telegram told him that the Shona had killed Tate and Koefoed and four laborers at Beatrice Mine.[8] Salthouse had already heard of the killings in the area close to Mashonongombi's Kraal near Hartley. Spirit mediums Kaguvi and Nehanda, the latter living not far from Captain Cass in the Mazoe Valley, were implicated in the rising.[9]

BSAC Administrator L. S. Jameson had left Salisbury in a dash to attack the Boers in the South African Transvaal colony just before the Shona had struck their deadly blow in Mashonaland. Dr. Jameson had taken most of the white police with him, as well as the cache of BSAC arms and ammunition. Salthouse asked Acting Administrator Vintcent for advice in the dire circumstances of having inadequate defense forces at Salisbury. The Mine Manager was responsible for nine men and three women in the undefended area of Alice mine.

Salthouse told Captain Cass to bring his wife to the mine from the Salvation Army's Mazoe Valley Farm nine miles away. Cass returned with his wife at dawn on June 17 to join James Dickinson, the Mazoe District Acting Mining Commissioner and his wife; his assistant H. Spreckley; Archer Burton, Manager of the Holton Syndicate store; and T. G. Routledge of the telegraph office. John Pascoe, the former Salvation Army leader, had also been helping to erect the ten-stamp battery at the mine along with Stoddard, William Faull, and Fairbairn. A "Cape boy" named George and about a dozen Shona completed the group in the area of Alice mine.

Early on June 18, J. L. Blakistone of the African Transcontinental Telegraph Line, H. D. Zimmerman (later named Otto Christian Rawson), the owner of a Salisbury general store, and a "Cape boy," arrived with a wagonette sent by Judge Vintcent to take the wives of Cass, Dickinson, and Salthouse to Fort Salisbury. Ahead of the party of women that left at noon, Captain Cass and James Dickinson had gone to the Army's farm to pick up papers and prepare dinner for the women. Apparently they regarded the farm as a safe haven, possibly due to the presence of BSAC Native Police

---

8. Beach, *War and Politics in Zimbabwe*, 105–7, gives an account of the Beatrice Mine incident.

9. Ibid., 103–7

The First *Chimurenga* (1896–97) and the Death of Captain Cass

who were stationed there. About five miles from Alice Mine men in the first group to leave the mine after Cass and Dickinson heard a shot.

John Pascoe ran forward and saw Shona natives clubbing Captain Cass to death with knobkerries (clubs). Pascoe later assured the new Salvation Army leader in South Africa, Commissioner Ridsdel, that "strange natives" had taken Cass's life, "not those among whom he had been working." The Shona warriors also killed James Dickinson and William Faull. Pascoe and his group rushed towards the mine to turn the women's wagonette around. They barely succeeded in sending the women back to the mine before the Shona warriors caught up with them. They all returned safely to the mine where they scrambled up a kopje (hill) and built a hut out of rocks.[10]

Blakistone and Routledge volunteered to go to the telegraph office to wire the acting administrator at Salisbury for more help. They arrived at the office and sent their message, but on their return trip to the laager they were shot and killed. A Blakistone-Routledge Memorial Commission later (1929-36) erected a memorial at Mazoe to herald the valor of the Mazoe Patrol.[11] The six survivors spent the night under fire in a hut. A later version of the embellished Rhodesian tale of courage claimed that a Basuto warrior[12] spent the night "shouting in English what he intended to do to the women when the men were all killed."[13] At dawn on June 19 rescuers arrived. Shona warriors wounded one as they charged into the laager.

Only after thirteen more horsemen arrived on Saturday 20th, commanded by Inspector Randolph Nesbitt, did the party of about thirty start out at 9:30 a.m. for Fort Salisbury.[14] Sheets of iron on the wagonette protected occupants from constant fire from the Shona warriors who hid in the tall grass on either side of the road. Two more men were killed, but due to the natives' obsolete weapons most of their shots went awry. Pascoe, in an exposed position on the roof of the wagonette, shouted intelligence about

---

10. Thompson, *Delayed Harvest*, 39–52, used as his historical sources: H. D. Zimmerman, the only living survivor; Hugh Pollett, who got his information from Fairbairn; the *African Review*, London, 12 Sept. 1896; the *Rhodesian Digest*; and the *Herald* (24 June and 7 July 1897). At the time he compiled his history Colonel Thompson was the Salvation Army's Territorial Commander in Southern Rhodesia.

11. Baxter and Burke, *Guide to the Historical Manuscripts in the National Archives of Rhodesia*, 38; Archives ms. (BL 1/1/2–4).

12. This is a strange reference, since Basutoland (now Lesotho) is in South Africa.

13. Thompson, *Delayed Harvest*, provides several Rhodesian myths surrounding what became known as the heroic Mazoe Patrol.

14. Inspector Nesbitt received the Victoria Cross for leading the Mazoe Patrol rescue. He became Native Commissioner at Goromonzi. Lt. Dan Judson, Intelligence Officer of the Salisbury Field Force, assisted him. He retired as Postmaster General. Baxter and Burke, *Guide to the Historical Manuscripts*, 242.

the enemy's locations to the driver. They arrived at Salisbury about 9 o'clock that night. Salvation Army historian Colonel Victor Thompson wrote that Hugh Pollett, a member of the Mazoe Patrol, claimed that Cass's body was respectfully covered with grass and bushes in a consideration of his work as a missionary.[15] Others gave gruesome reports of the body's dismemberment. The South Africa *War Cry* and other Salvation Army journals announced Captain Cass's "martyrdom" for "those whom he came to bring light and life." Cass's Salvationist comrade, John Pascoe, testified that Cass had "lived for the natives" as "a lovely example of Christlikeness." While there is no reason to doubt these adulatory statements in Salvation Army journals, the Army in England, not surprisingly, failed to tell the African side to the story.[16]

Survivors of the party who took refuge at the Alice Mine and of the relief forces sent to escort them to safety. Mrs Cass third from left in front row. Major John Pascoe seated atop the wagon. (By permission, Zimbabwe National Archives.)

15. Thompson, *Delayed Harvest*, 41–42, quotes Hugh Pollett in *Rhodesian Digest*, 1953. Hugh Pollett, a member of the Mazoe Patrol, likewise claimed that Cass's body was respectfully covered with grass and bushes, a consideration of his work as a missionary.

16. Edward Joy, and Harold H. Rawson (Mazoe Patrol survivor), "Martyred by the Matabele: A Thrilling Story of the '96 Rising," *The Christmas War Cry* (n.d.) 9–10, by arrangement with the *Rhodesia Herald*, confuse Matabele with Shona and discuss the event as an element of settler mythology. M. D., "From Battle and Murder, and from Sudden Death," *All the World*, Jan. 1897, 29–32; Cyril Barnes, "Martyr in Mashonaland," London: Salvation Army Archives; and, *One Man's Vision*, provide Salvationist and white settler views of the Cass killing, but no historical analysis.

The First *Chimurenga* (1896–97) and the Death of Captain Cass

Cass had lived close to and had worked with white settlers who had taken Shona land. The Shona may well have found it difficult to tell whose side Cass and the Salvation Army favored in the African struggle to retrieve their land. Indeed there is reasonable evidence that the Army's Mazoe Farm was the home of the BSAC's Native Commissioner and was a post of the BSAC Native Police, according to a statement Cass's wife later gave to the Army's War Cry in London.

The Salvation Army erected a monument to Captain Cass's memory beside the road where he died, near the Mazoe Valley farm he had managed. In addition to this landmark the Army later renamed the Mazoe farm for William Pearson, a British Salvation Army leader who had never visited Shona territories. This new name and the Cass monument converted a rural African place with its own religious meaning and spirit mediums, and turned the landscape into an English Christian shrine.

Cass Memorial beside road in Mazowe Valley

Terence Ranger has studied Anglican transformations of African sites into English Christian shrines. He concludes that Anglican consecrations placed English names on the African landscape at the white settler missions as an intricate part of the colonizers' attempts to "convert" an African "heathen" scene, as well as the people themselves so that they conformed to a European countryside.[17] It is true that the subjects of Ranger's studies were Anglicans and Roman Catholics for whom sacramental transformations had more meaning than they might have had for non-sacramental Salvationists. But the Salvation Army, by naming sites for English settlers and officers in London who had never visited the colony, was as assertive of white superiority as its high church contemporaries in altering the landscape to conform to what they deemed to be the values of Christian, Western civilization.

When the Salvation Army opened another mission in Chiweshe in 1923, they changed its African name "Nyachuru" to the name of another English Salvationist who had no connection with Africa, Henry Howard. A Canadian Salvationist missionary objected to the change, proposing that they at least connect the name to a missionary who had served in Rhodesia. Add to this rechristening of land the Army's ritual English use of British uniforms, flags, processions, brass bands, and a native "march past," a parade stand on which a white Salvation Army leader stood on great occasions to receive the Africans' salute, and you find more than a little bit of Britain in darkest Africa. All of these material symbols marked submission of Africans to an allegedly superior Western culture. And they allowed missionaries to enjoy a bit of their homeland's material culture when they served overseas.

With independence in 1980, Africans, like their contemporaries in India, began renaming cities, streets, and memorials, to restore their African significance. Thus the capital city, Salisbury, became Harare, and Rhodesia became Zimbabwe, but most of the Salvation Army's Europeanized terrain continues to bear English names. South Africa has begun a similar exercise in re-africanizing its landscape by altering English and Boer names to place names that revert to pre-colonial times.

Generally speaking the Salvation Army denies that it indulges in sacerdotal exercises of sanctifying places and objects, including monuments or banners or clerical garb, or of making pilgrimages to holy shrines, or even of recognizing sacrifices for the faith as martyrdom. Yet the Army's official literature referred to Edward Cass as a martyr and the Army built a monument at Mazoe so that pilgrims could recognize his heroism. In Africa the Army has, as often as not, placed British artefacts and names on a plane above customs held sacred by the Shona and Ndebele people. Colonel William J. Pearson had no association with Rhodesia when the Army renamed Mazoe Farm in his honor so it is not surprising that in the African mind, placing his name on the site had no effect. Africans had their own reason for holding the Mazoe landscape as sacred, quite different from the one the Army intended in 1897.

17. See Ranger, "Taking Hold of the Land."

The First *Chimurenga* (1896–97) and the Death of Captain Cass

The Mazoe Valley was the home of Nehanda Nyakasikana, the spirit medium of the Hwata people. Nehanda had a spiritual influence on Shona warriors involved in the First Chimurenga in which Cass was killed. At the end of that war in 1897, the BSAC executed her, confiscated her land, and moved her Hwata people to the crowded Chiweshe Native Reserve. At the time of the Second Chimurenga in the 1970s Shona Patriotic Front leaders revived the memory of Nehanda as a hero of African nationalism as Shona soldiers fought once again for the liberation of African land. African Salvationists at the time of independence in 1980, some of whom were Nehanda's descendants, complained about the Army's sale of "Pearson" and "Usher" Farms to white commercial farmers. These farms had sacral meaning for Africans quite apart from whether or not they were profitable, the reason given by the Army's leaders for the sale. In Shona minds the Mazoe Valley Farm had survived as an African landscape whose land they would once again control following a second Chimurenga, a rising that they would win. When they did not redeem this land for African use they emphatically expressed their disappointment in a protest march.[18]

Nehanda Nyakasikana (c.1840–98) as a prisoner after the Chimurenga. (By permission, Zimbabwe National Archives.)

Neither the BSAC nor the British or Rhodesian governments offered official honors for Edward Cass, although they honored the valor of several

18. Matsvetu, in oral history interview in Chiweshe by the author, August 1998.

BSAC functionaries who lost their lives as members of the Mazoe Patrol with monuments or military honors. Nonetheless the Rhodesia Herald praised Captain Cass as an "agriculturalist" missionary who was "a sturdy champion for native grievances" and who was "conversant in many of the Kaffir [African] dialects." The report claimed that Cass spoke Shona "as well as the Mashonas themselves."[19] If this was the truth, then it is a pity that so much Rhodesian myth obscures it. The Salvation Army held a curious position in Rhodesia. It was in but not quite of the white Rhodesian settler community, at least when it came to being part of a memorialized cultural landscape. Yet it refused to become African in most of its pageantry or in naming its memorials and martyrs.

Edward Cass's wife Ada gave an interview to the Salvation Army's international *War Cry* when she went to London after her husband's death. Although she had been in Mashonaland only briefly prior to Edward Cass's killing she reflected what Professors David N. Beach and Terence Ranger saw as the white settler's myth that "peaceful" Shona lived "in daily fear of their fiercer neighbors, the Matabele." The Shona, according to this Rhodesian view, had been "overawed by the Matabele into fighting the white man." Mrs. Cass believed that iron, gold, and copper "will doubtless be found in enormous qualities" [sic] and claimed that the "Zimbalye" [sic] ruins were a "weird spot" where Solomon had allegedly extracted much of his wealth. She said the Army's work was doctoring, settling disputes, and visiting native kraals (villages of twelve to fifty huts) to conduct evangelistic meetings. The paternalistic white missionary would civilize the primitive African.

But Ada Cass's most newsworthy claim was the attestation to Salvation Army integration into the white settler mentality. For the first time she revealed that fourteen BSAC "native police" and Native Commissioner H. H. Pollard lived at the Army's Mazoe Valley Farm.[20] In spite of the Army's joining hands with white settlers who had taken African land she found it hard to understand why Africans "rebelled, set on her husband, and 'cut off his hands and feet.'"[21] She was the only person who referred to the mutilation of the body of Edward Cass, at least in documented evidence available to me. Other reports indicated a reverence for his body and a gracious burial

---

19. *The Herald*, 7 July 1896, quoted by Thompson, *Delayed Harvest*, 44.

20. Letter, "To the Intelligence Officer, Salisbury, 18 Sept. 1896," at the Zimbabwe National Archives, states that Pollard was "missing." A telegram of 29 June stated: "Zambesi boy overheard Mashonas discussing how to kill Pollard. All Pollard's cattle stolen. Pollard escaped to Chibongas' kraal." D. N. Beach, in a letter to the author, said that he had no knowledge of a native police post at the Farm.

21. "Life in Mashonaland: SA Settlement Occupied by Rebels, Short Talk with Captain Mrs. Cass," London *War Cry*, 27 Feb. 1897, 3.

The First *Chimurenga* (1896–97) and the Death of Captain Cass

by Shona warriors. Could it be that in her simplicity she told the truth and others had chosen to invent yet another myth? If Ada Cass's testimony that the Mazoe Farm was a police station for the Native Police is true, and it is fair to think that she knew who was living at the farm where she resided, then a shadow falls across the Army's claim of political neutrality in 1896. It would repeat the claim in 1978 in spite of contrary evidence.

Major Misheck Nyandoro, a Shona Salvation Army officer-historian who wrote the official history of the Army in Rhodesia-Zimbabwe, points to a close relationship between the Army's pioneers and other white settlers as the reason why natives suspected that they shared similar interests, and many of these interests were antithetical to the African desire to recover their land and liberty. Nyandoro, writing in the wake of the 1970s liberation war, lists several examples of poor relations between white settlers and Africans. He then asserts that Captain Cass, the Army's martyr, because of his associations with other settlers, was viewed by Africans as a man who "betrayed himself" because he "identified himself with the enemy" in the 1896 rising.[22]

Thus Captain Cass's death was a tragic tale of a tangled web of relationships in which Salvation Army missionaries, not unlike their fellow missionaries in other Christian denominations in Rhodesia, lived in a white settler community of shared interests. M. F. C. Bourdillon, has claimed that expatriate "missionaries saw nothing wrong in using colonial power to gain ownership of land and greater control over the people they claimed to be serving." He argues that "well-established, formal churches, often working in conjunction with political powers," were frequently "influenced by the point of view of those people." The Salvation Army cannot be described as a "well-established, formal" church; rather it was a mission whose interests were closely tied to the poor rural Africans it served. Nevertheless, according to Bourdillon, Western missionaries "largely shared the assumptions of superiority with colonial powers, believing that they were on a civilizing mission to Africa."[23] Many white Salvationists proved to be no exception to the rule.

Missions, settlers, and British South Africa Company officials, worked hand-in-hand to promote their own social, economic, political, and cultural interests by appropriating Shona and Ndebele property, labor and cattle, power, and treasured sacred landscapes. Salvationists helped white settlers in construction, mining enterprises, and social services. By providing housing for fourteen BSAC native police and a Native Commissioner they raised

22. Nyandoro, *Flame of Sacred Love*, 11–20.
23. Bourdillon, *Religion and Society*, 265–68.

questions about the Army's right to claim that Salvationists were servants of the native. And they even commented on whether or not they could correctly term Captain Cass a "martyr" when he shed his blood while on a mission to convert Africans to Christianity.

Like other missions the Salvation Army linked itself to Cecil John Rhodes' mercenary venture almost immediately upon their arrival in Fort Salisbury in 1891. Salvationists accepted land and financial grants Rhodes took from taxes he illegally levied against Africans, according to the charter the British government had given to his British South Africa Company. Ranger claims that the British government tried to rein in Rhodes and the BSAC's administrators who violated native rights and confiscated their land. The result was that the BSAC tied itself all the more closely to settler interests and detached itself from responsibility for assisting Africans.[24] Is it unreasonable to view the Salvation Army as Rhodes' accomplice? Or is it unfair to see William Booth as benefiting from Rhodes' imposition of an English landscape and culture and rule on Africa in the name of Jesus of Nazareth?

Colonel Victor Thompson, the Salvation Army's territorial leader in Southern Rhodesia in 1957, and a careful historical researcher, expressed surprise when he found an 1896 account of Cass's "martyrdom" in the Army's *All the World* missionary magazine. The author of the article had credited the heroic Cass with conveying "women and children [to] safety" at a time when he was already dead. Thompson found it "hard to understand how this apocryphal [tale] . . . got to London." But he then found "similar stories" that the Army's press had invented to make the case for Cass's "martyrdom." In fact, there were no children in the Mazoe episode, but an Army writer apparently made them up under literary license for the purpose of using them as a device to increase Cass's chivalry claimed by Salvationists and Rhodesia's white settler community. They added another item to the catalogue of heroic myth. Thompson claimed that myths about Cass's death came from an alleged African eyewitness, Major Cyrus Soko, and that they could be found in such sources as Noel Hope's "Lucy in Lion Land" and in "Tit-bits," published in the London *War Cry*.[25]

Such Rhodesian myths reveal how white settlers, including missionaries, regarded Africans in the 1890s. But Rhodesia was not the only locale for which white Salvationists in England and Rhodesia adopted a mythology in the late 19th century. *All the World* also spoke disparagingly of Roman

---

24. Ranger, *Revolt in Southern Rhodesia*, 58–60.

25. Thompson, *Delayed Harvest*, 44–45; and Noel Hope's *Lucy in Lion Land*, and in "Tit-bits," *The War Cry*, 24 Oct. 1896, 8. (*Pace* Thompson, the article is headed "Under One Flag" and found on page 12 of that issue.)

The First *Chimurenga* (1896–97) and the Death of Captain Cass

Catholics in "South Ireland" as "the nearest missionary ground to Great Britain" where "superstition" abounds and where the Salvation Army must "expect the stone from the unseen hand and the blow from behind as their almost daily portion."[26]

Anthony J. Chennells explored the white Rhodesian capacity for self-delusion in the 1890s. For his study Chennells noted that the Rhodesian "occupation of Mashonaland in 1890, the invasion of Matabeleland in 1893, and the repression of the risings of 1896 and 1897, were often repeated in novels and amateur histories about the period." They "were made to run into a single heroic action where Rhodesians defined themselves and what the [British South Africa] Company claimed to be their civilized mission, in a continuous battle against the forces of cruel disorders appropriate to the heart of Africa."[27]

But there was, running alongside the white Rhodesian mythology, an African story of which white settler mythmakers were unaware and would not fathom since it was embedded in African culture. And there were only a few missionaries who reminded European settlers that their theft of African land was reason enough for the violent reaction of Ndebele and Shona warriors. When they looked backward from the 1970s, Africans would describe the 1893 and 1896–97 risings as their First Chimurenga—hence the importance of the myths around Captain Cass's death that enlighten the historical context of both the First and Second Chimurenga for whites. In this light the actions of 1970s African "terrorists" as whites called them, or "freedom fighters" as Africans would name them, in the Second Chimurenga may make more sense.

While Ranger does not discuss the killing of Edward T. Cass in his history of the 1896–97 rising, he does describe the first Mashonaland rising of those years as the "most spectacular manifestation of resistance in East and Central Africa." Ranger holds that Rhodesian whites at the time did not think that the Shona "had any sense of religion or possessed any religious organization." Missionaries, like the British South Africa Company government administrators who supported their work, regarded Africans with "contempt and dislike." Resident Magistrate Marshall Hole's view was that the Ndebele cowed the Shona into "a condition of abject pusillanimity" and made them "incapable of planning or any combined or premeditated action." The rising of 1896–97 proved that the British South Africa Company and the missionaries were mistaken.

---

26. "Where the Shamrock Grows," 139.
27. Chennells, "White Rhodesian Nationalism—The Mistaken Years," 124.

Quite the opposite was true. Ranger argues that the Shona had a well-developed religious system, and that Europeans "widely overstated" Shona subservience to the Ndebele. Ranger finds that Shona political development in the early nineteenth century provided complex hierarchies of which Europeans had little knowledge. Internecine nineteenth-century warfare did not destroy the authority of the paramount chiefs nor did it disrupt the long-established Shona system of trade. Neither did the wars destroy the religious system centered on a high God, Mwari, or the system of spirit mediums that focused on the power of the dead to mediate between the divine and the living realms. What missionaries saw as African depravity was in fact the Shona's capacity for "steady passive resistance" to the British invasion that turned into "an armed attack upon the missions and their few converts as well as upon all other whites" in 1896. Ranger claims that the missionaries' failure to find converts among the Shona is proof of Shona "passive resistance" to the whites' cultural aggression.

As one Jesuit missionary put it in 1896, it was their strong religious tradition that caused Africans to be unwilling to become Christians. In the six previous years Roman Catholic missionaries had baptized only two Shona converts. Likewise, their lack of success among the Ndebele had made the missionaries "natural, if qualified, supporters of Rhodes" in his desire to overthrow Lobengula in 1893. On that occasion, the whites' successful use of violence delighted both the British South Africa Company and Christian missions. Each was convinced that destruction of the African military and cultural system would open the way to "civilizing" programs. Lord Grey, the BSAC administrator in 1896, recognized an African desire to retain independence. But against this desire the BSAC, white settlers and missions became allies against the Shona and Ndebele, with only a few missionary dissenters to openly oppose the suppression of the First Chimurenga.[28]

By 1896–97, British South Africa Company Reports had officially classified the Salvation Army as a "religious body with a place of worship that held more or less regular services." The Church of England was the largest Christian denomination with eight main stations, twelve out-stations, 2,942 white members, 1,096 African members, twelve white clergy and nine "others." The Report indicated that the Salvation Army's farm in the Mazoe Valley had 5,000 acres, 2,000 more than had been previously reported. The Army also owned stands (small urban plots) at Tuli and Umtali.[29] Between 1898 and 1900 more missions had joined the "scramble" into Rhodesia, undeterred by the 1896–97 Chimurenga. Seventh Day Adventists, more

---

28. Ranger, *Revolt in Southern Rhodesia, 1896–97*, xii, 3–27.
29. British South Africa Company Reports, 1896–97.

The First *Chimurenga* (1896–97) and the Death of Captain Cass

Presbyterians, the American Foreign Mission, the General Nonconformists, and the Union of Hebrew Congregations joined missions that had arrived in Mashonaland before the 1896–97 war.

But the Salvation Army was forced to close its failed mission to white settlers and the Shona in 1896. Salvationists did not reopen their work in Mashonaland until 1901. By that time, the British South Africa Company had convinced the Salvationists that their mission to Africans must override their earlier aim of converting white miners from South Africa to Christianity. New financial inducements persuaded the Army to follow the BSAC's program. While it continued to operate social services for whites in cities, hereafter its rural programs in education and medicine would focus on Africans, and before long its membership was almost totally African.

Chapter 4

Rhodes and Booth
"Wholesale Salvation," 1901–8

"When ye get among th' Chinee" . . . says [the Emperor of Germany], "raymimber that ye ar-re the van guard iv Christyanity" he says, "an' stick ye'er bayonet through ivry hated infidel you see" he says. "Lave him understand what our western civilisation means. . . . An' if be chance ye shud pick up a little land be th' way, don't lave e'er a Frinchman or Roosshan take it from ye."
—Finlay Peter Dunne, *Mr. Dooley's Philosophy*[1]

Probably Cecil Rhodes' version of social imperialism, which thought primarily of the economic benefits that empire might bring . . . to the discontented masses, was the least relevant. There is no good evidence that colonial conquest as such had much bearing on the employment or real incomes of most workers in the metropolitan countries, and the idea that emigration to colonies would provide a safety-valve for overpopulated countries was little more than a demagogic fantasy.
—Eric Hobsbaum, *Age of Empire*[2]

Although after Cass's death in 1896 the Salvation Army closed its work in Mashonaland, William Booth still nurtured his dream of opening a

---

1. Dunne, *Mr. Dooley's Philosophy*. New York: 1900, 93–94, cited from Hobsbaum, *The Age of Empire*, 56.
2. Hobsbaum, *The Age of Empire*, 69.

Rhodesian land colony settlement for white settlers taken from England's unemployment rolls. By June 1901 the General was working hard in London to get Cecil Rhodes' British South Africa Company and the British government to provide financial support for his "Darkest England" scheme in Rhodesia. He continued his strenuous campaign from 1901 to 1908.

Meanwhile, in 1896 the Salvation Army opened a white corps in Bulawayo, Matabeleland. The Mazoe Valley Farm near Salisbury reopened in 1901 when the Army appointed Staff Captain and Mrs. Frank Bradley with Adjutant and Mrs. Mbambo Matunjwa from South Africa to take charge of the farm Captain Cass had managed. In 1904 the Army appointed Lieut. Colonel Johnston as Provincial Commander in Matabeleland. He would also run the "commercial side" of the Mazoe Farm after 1906. In 1908 Captain and Mrs. Ben Muhambi became the first African officers in Matabeleland, and two African officers began operations in Salisbury's Shona townships in 1909.[3] The Army had shifted from saving white miners to evangelizing Africans who lived in native reserves.

Cecil John Rhodes portrayed on stamp to mark 50th anniversary of Pioneer Column. (Image courtesy of Alan MacGregor, Simon's Town, South Africa.)

3. "Historical Survey, The Salvation Army, Southern Rhodesia," London: Salvation Army Archives, n.d.

Between 1891, when William Booth first met Cecil Rhodes in South Africa, and 1908, when he finally realized that the BSAC would not respond to his pleas for financial grants and land, the General's quest for support from the BSAC and the British government had become an obsession. In 1902 Booth recalled his first meeting with Rhodes. Rhodes was then Premier of the Cape Colony and Booth was making his first visit to the colony. After they discussed Booth's dream for "an Over-the-Sea Colony," Rhodes had promised him, "I can give you whatever extent of land you may require" in Mashonaland. At their next meeting in South Africa in 1895 Booth claimed that Rhodes had "renewed his offer of land in Rhodesia."[4] But Booth later found out that subsequent problems in the BSAC made the promise hollow.

Booth called his 1890 Darkest England social reform program "wholesale salvation." In three steps he would move Britain's unemployed from city workshops to farm colonies in England and then to overseas settlements in British colonies. Instead of retailing salvation by winning converts to his Wesleyan form of Christian faith, he would evangelize the masses through an imperial social program that would put thousands of emigrants under the mentoring supervision of Salvation Army officers.[5] W. T. Stead, Britain's leader in "yellow" journalism, as well as Rhodes' friend and fellow imperialist, became Booth's amanuensis in putting the Darkest England plan in book form in 1890. His book's title, *In Darkest England and the Way Out*, mimicked *In Darkest Africa*, the title of Henry M. Stanley's best-selling report of his journalistic adventures in Africa published earlier that year.[6]

Booth's second partner in developing his social scheme was a Salvation Army officer and socialist, Frank Smith, later a leading light in Britain's Independent Labor Party with his friend Keir Hardie.[7] After Smith resigned from the Salvation Army in 1891, he became a member of the London County Council, and in 1929, a Member of Parliament. Smith's life-long quest for social justice began in 1884 when had read Henry George's 1879 book, *Progress and Poverty*, on his way to take charge of the Salvation Army in the United States following a schism. Smith became George's life-long devotee. George proposed that governments adopt a single tax on land values. That tax would place a heavy duty on the value of unused land that

---

4. "The Founder and Cecil Rhodes," *The War Cry*, London (4 July 1953, extracts from a March 1902 article).

5. See Murdoch, *Soldiers of the Cross: Susie Swift & David Lamb* for more on the Army's social programme, including its post-World War I Emigration Scheme for overseas settlements.

6. Booth, *In Darkest England and the Way Out*; Charles M. Stanley, *In Darkest Africa*.

7. Murdoch, *Frank Smith: Salvationist Socialist*.

would cause speculators to sell their excessive holdings, thus freeing up the land for the use of the nation's landless poor. The end result of the sale of unused land would be the formation of land cooperatives by the masses that would increase production, secure justice in wealth distribution, benefit all classes, and "make possible an advance to a higher and nobler civilization."[8] According to George, the availability of land would create social justice and opportunities for the masses in America and Britain, including Ireland.

In 1887 William Booth replaced Frank Smith as the Army's commander in America with his second son Ballington. Smith gave his poor health as the reason for his request to return to England. Between 1888 and 1890, Smith served as Booth's private secretary. He travelled with the General on his frequent tours of Britain. Smith also travelled to Europe and Ireland to collect material for the social reform program that they were planning.

In the 1890 book Booth acknowledged the contributions of neither Frank Smith, the ideologue of the social scheme, nor of W. T. Stead, its writer (apart from his reference to "valuable literary help from a friend of the poor . . .").[9] It is reasonable to discount Booth's contribution as author on two grounds. First, he had never been a social reform thinker; he was heart and soul an evangelist. And second, at the time the book was being written his wife Catherine was dying a painful death of cancer, leaving him no time or energy for social scheming.[10] But most importantly he had on his staff Frank Smith, a skilled social reformer, and Suzie F. Swift, a Vassar graduate and editor of the Army's missionary magazine, *All the World*, who claimed a role in drafting the book's outline.

For the ideas behind urban workshops, the first stage of the Darkest England scheme, Frank Smith passed to the Booths, Swift and Stead, Count Rumford's late-eighteenth-century ideas for handling urban beggars in Bavaria. Rumford had "served with considerable distinction" as an "American officer" in the Revolutionary War. After the war he had settled in England and then moved to Bavaria to take command of its army. There he set up Houses of Industry (urban workshops) where, beginning on New Year's Eve 1790, he had compelled beggars to work. He found that when he treated them with justice and kindness, offered them clean and orderly surroundings, and provided them with satisfactory yet inexpensive provisions, the beggars responded with hard work. Best of all for the cost-conscious Booth, Rumford's program was self-sufficient. That Rumford used a military approach to solve the problem of unemployment was particularly appealing to

8. Henry George, *Progress and Poverty*, xxix.
9. Booth, *Darkest England*, preface.
10. Murdoch, "Frank Smith, M.P."

Booth.[11] Smith picked up the term "elevator" either from Edward Bellamy's 1888 book, *Looking Backward, Looking Forward*, or in earlier French socialist literature.[12]

By 1890 Smith was already implementing the workshop plan in London's "elevators," possibly the best indicator that he was the genius behind the plan. The idea of setting up urban "colonies" (workshops) was to provide work for the unemployed as a first step in their rehabilitation. Workers would salvage furniture and clothing from the emerging middle class, repair them, then sell them to support the Salvation Army rehabilitation program. Booth assumed that a large part of the problem was drunkenness and other aspects of "sinful" living. He would deal with these problems through personal redemption from sin as a part of rehabilitation.

Smith picked up ideas about the second phase of Darkest England's three-step system, farm colonies in England to train the urban unemployed before sending them overseas, from E. T. Craig, a disciple of Robert Owen. Although Craig's 1831 co-operative experiment at Ralahine, Ireland, failed in 1833, it was nonetheless a model worth imitating. Under an agreement with a wealthy Irish landowner, John Scott Vandeleur, Craig induced unruly, insubordinate peasants to join in a cooperative experiment in order to increase production and improve their living standard. All profits, after rent was paid to Vandeleur, belonged to the peasants. Craig forbade intoxicating drink and tobacco. The Salvation Army adopted this rule in its city workshops and on its farms, and also the Owenite tradition of providing physical and moral training. Later reformers saw Craig's Irish cooperative as the one successful Owenite experiment. Unfortunately, the gambling debts of Vandeleur, the estate owner, led to the closing of the cooperative, not any deficiencies in the work of the peasants.

When William Booth established his farm colonies, Craig's Ralahine was the format he followed, although Booth was in no sense a descendant of the secularist Robert Owen. The willingness of Booth and Smith to embrace and adapt ideas from heterodox sources, and to go beyond the boundaries of their evangelical Christian traditions to find ideas that would attract a long list of financial subscribers, was an imprint that remained on the Salvation Army through the twentieth century.[13] This second step in the Darkest

---

11. Booth, *Darkest England*, Appendix: "How Beggary was Abolished in Bavaria by Count Rumford," xviii–xxii.

12. Murdoch, "Rose Culture and Social Reform."

13. Booth refers to Ralahine in the Appendix to *Darkest England*, xxiii–xxiv. On Ralahine see Vincent Geohegan, "Ralahine: Ireland's Lost Utopia," paper presented at Utopian Thought and Communal Experience Conference, New Lanark, Scotland, 1988; Garnett, "Robert Owen and the Community Experiment"; Darley, *Villages of Vision*,

England plan, to move the urban unemployed to farms in England for training in agricultural skills and moral reformation, had significant success, but only as part of the third element.[14]

The third stage of Darkest England's ideas, and the one of greatest interest in this study, would move England's unemployed, after training in farming skills, to "vacant" lands in Britain's overseas colonies—Canada, Australia and New Zealand, and Southern Africa. It was for this phase Booth asked Cecil Rhodes and others for help in moving thousands of England's urban poor to Rhodesia's vast, allegedly "uninhabited" lands. Besides solving England's problem of urban unemployment, Booth had a vague notion that he would also elevate the "criminal and submerged classes of Africa." There is no record that Booth ever spelled out who these "criminal and submerged classes" were, white or black. He hoped that Rhodes, who shared his dream of white emigration to Southern Africa, would also make this Salvation Army imperial scheme part of his last will and testament.

In 1889, Booth acknowledged the English source for the first step in the three-part emigration plan he was about to publish. It was Reginald Brabazon, 12th Earl of Meath, a member of the Church of England. Booth mentioned his debt to Meath in a speech published by the *Times* of London, saying that Meath's pamphlet on poverty expressed his ideas exactly. The context of the speech was the opening of a second shelter for unemployed men at Clerkenwell in London. For three pence the men would receive supper, a "homely talk on salvation" and bed and breakfast. Unlike the common lodging house, the men would find shelter in an atmosphere that was free from "vile, demoralizing associations." And Booth promised the men would not need to do something "religious in return."

Lord Meath's book, *Social Arrows* (1886) also provided Smith and Booth with ideas for the third part of their Darkest England plan—the creation of overseas farm colonies for England's urban unemployed. Meath had pressed for state-directed colonization of the unemployed in "Greater Britain." *In Darkest England* (1890) offered the Salvation Army as the state's agent in selecting, preparing, and transporting poor but willing settlers who wanted to relocate in Britain's empire. Booth agreed with Meath that British

---

1975, 84–85, 105; and three books by E. T. Craig, *Cooperative Society Illustrated* (1880); *History of Ralahine and Cooperative Farming* (1882); and *An Irish Commune* (1919).

14 See Murdoch, *Origins*, 162–63. There are a few farm colony remnants, but they are not being used as launching pads for emigration to overseas colonies. See: Murdoch, "William Booth's In Darkest England and the Way Out" (http://www.wesley.ncc.edu/theojrnl/25-6www.wesley.ncc.edu/theojrnl/25-6); and "Anglo-American Salvation Army Farm Colonies, 1890–1910." See also Haggard, *The Poor and the Land*, and Spence, *The Salvation Army Farm Colonies*.

colonies would not be willing to accept London's idle, vicious paupers, but that the urban poor could improve their work habits and their character on farm colonies in England prior to emigration. Meath also set out a plan for processing emigrants for an overseas colony. Character was more important than agricultural training. A government program to move emigrants to the colonies had failed because it had not followed this character-building plan. In addition, children without families could be trained on model farms in England to be apprenticed to colonial farmers.[15]

There is no suggestion that Meath had much affection for General Booth. In an 1884 article he excluded the Salvation Army from a list of charitable organizations that deserved the support of "men of leisure."[16] Meath was the President of the Church Army, a Church of England imitation of the Salvation Army and potentially its principal rival. In 1882–83 William and Bramwell Booth had been negotiating a merger with a committee appointed by the Archbishop of Canterbury, but the Booths had declined the invitation to make the Salvation Army an urban evangelical branch of the state church.[17] By the mid-1880s Meath's Church Army had its own plans for social reform that competed with Booth's program.

Meath led two other competing social reform groups as President of the Social Service Union and the British Institute of Social Service, inspired by Booth's friend J. B. Paton.[18] Meath may have indirectly critiqued Booth in 1904 when he attacked a "great religious Nonconformist leader" who had failed to mention 22 German Labor colonies in existence in 1890 when he was recommending such colonies for England. Had Booth or Frank Smith done this out of ignorance of what had occurred in Europe or out of a desire to "claim credit for an idea which was not novel," as Meath claimed?[19] Booth often found that religious, labor, professional social workers and philanthropists were his most ardent foes in the field of social reform.

Unfortunately for William Booth, Cecil Rhodes did not mention the Salvation Army emigration scheme in his will. Instead, Rhodes authorized

---

15. Brabazon (Earl of Meath), *Social Arrows*, 112, 116, 133, 137, 189, 220–21, 133–35. Meath, ed., *Prosperity or Pauperism?*

16. Earl of Meath, *Brabazon Potpourri*, 22.

17. Murdoch, "The Salvation Army and the Church of England, 1882–1883," provides the story of why these negotiations failed. See also Eason, "The Salvation Army and the Sacraments in Victorian Britain."

18. Booth's sons, Ballington and Herbert, had attended J. B. Paton's Theological Institute in Nottingham. When William Booth was looking for a denominational affiliation outside the Methodist New Connexion in 1864, he consulted Paton about a place with the Congregationalists (Independents). See Murdoch, *Origins*, 34, 37.

19. Meath, *Brabazon Potpourri*, 269.

the use of his fortune to form a "Secret Society" to extend "British rule throughout the world." His "system of emigration from the United Kingdom" was on a grander scale than Booth's. He would occupy "the whole continent of Africa, the Holy Land, the valley of the Euphrates, the Islands of Cyprus and Candia [Crete], [and] the whole of South America." Thereby Rhodes would "render wars impossible and promote the best interests of humanity." From the 1840s on, colonial reformers like Edward Jenkins had called for what amounted to a revival of mercantilism. They would: 1) find work for the poor in the colonies; and 2) use them to provide a market for British manufactures, thereby providing employment opportunities in Britain. Booth and Smith were reinventing a fifty-year old idea in their overseas colony plan, but updating the scheme to fit late-nineteenth-century imperial designs.[20] But in death in 1902 Rhodes provided no money for the Salvation Army imperial scheme.

Henry George, Robert Owen, Count Rumford, E. T. Craig, German farm colony advocates, the Earl of Meath, Cecil Rhodes, and W. T. Stead are a sampling of the imperial and social ideologues whose ideas were taken up by William Booth and Frank Smith. Others also contributed to planning the Army's social services in the late 1880s and early 1900s. While subordinate Salvationists dug out ideas from the social reform literature, Booth put his imprimatur on the ideas and placed his reputation behind their implementation. William and Bramwell Booth, Frank Smith, Susie Swift, and W. T. Stead incorporated the reform measures into *In Darkest England and the Way Out*, drawing the attention of leading reform critics in reviews in nearly every major journal. Booth raised over £100,000 within four months of the book's release in October 1890 and Frank Smith began to put the plan into effect in England.

While the last two aspects of Booth's utopia, the farm and overseas colonies, lasted in their intended form only until about 1914 in England, North America, and Australia/New Zealand, their life-span has been considerably longer. Urban workshops—now called Adult Rehabilitation Centers in the United States—continue to be the major element of the Army's social services into the twenty-first century as they work with the homeless, the addicted, and those released from prison. More important, the effect of the Darkest England scheme was to turn the Salvation Army away from a single emphasis on urban evangelism toward a dual program of spiritual and social reformation by 1890.

Booth's official biographer, Harold Begbie, argued that in 1898 the Salvation Army's General had seen the unpredictable Cecil Rhodes as "a man

---

20. Pakenham, *The Scramble for Africa*, 376–77; Porter, *The Lion's Share*, 81.

who might either plunge [Britain] into war or make an end of a very dangerous tension [in Southern Africa] by reasonable and conciliatory diplomacy." This was just before the Boer War broke out in South Africa—a war which Booth regarded with horror, although he sent Staff-Captain Mary Murray to minister to the troops engaged in it. The occasion for Booth's comment was a May 1898 visit by Rhodes and Charles Loch of the Charity Organization Society to the Salvation Army's Hadleigh Farm Colony in Essex on the Thames River estuary east of London.[21] Salvation Army reports indicated that Rhodes was "immensely impressed" with the farm that represented the second stage of Booth's plan to rehabilitate the urban unemployed and prepare them for an overseas colony.

On the train back to London Booth and Rhodes had a serious discussion. Booth, ever an evangelist to the heathen, gave this recollection of their talk. He had asked Rhodes, "How is it with your soul?" Rhodes responded, "It's not quite so well with my soul as I could wish." "Do you pray?" "Sometimes, not quite so often as I should." "Will you let me pray with you—now?" Rhodes agreed and they knelt down in the coach. Booth asked God to guide Rhodes and save his soul. When Rhodes died in 1902 at age forty-eight, Booth wrote in his diary, "I wonder whether in our several interviews I did what I could for his soul?"[22]

British governments and religious leaders made small distinction between African natives and what Booth termed Britain's "submerged tenth." The "heathen," home-grown and foreign, needed saving and civilizing; this was the task of Christian missions at home and abroad, by whatever means they devised. With a call to "lift them in pity from sin and the grave," missions did not always sense a call to develop a personal attachment to the African poor any more than middle-class Christians mixed with the poor of London's East End. Social reformers seldom associated with beneficiaries of their arms-length largess. As in the social distance between London's social workers and its poor, missionaries and their African charges lived lives apart, in distinct neighborhoods and in separate churches and schools. Missions and the BSAC engaged in paternalistic and authoritarian management of those under their control. This was an aspect of Britain's consciousness of imperial prowess. Missionaries from North America and elsewhere shared in this Anglo-imperial mission culture.

Historian Bernard Porter defines the 1890s "new imperialism" of British leaders Chamberlain, Rosebery, Curzon, Milner, and Rhodes, as

---

21. Sandall, *The History of The Salvation Army*, vol. 3, 136–43, provides details on the beginning of Hadleigh and other farm colonies.

22. Begbie, *The Life of General William Booth*, II, 140, 188, 209–10, 231–32, 298, discusses Booth's associations with Rhodes.

an idea based on what Rosebery termed "an Imperial Race—a race vigorous and industrious and intrepid." Victorian imperialists were Darwinian in that they believed that "the survival of the fittest is an absolute truth in the conditions of the modern world. . . . England must have better schools, improved social reform, military conscription, and no political division, if it is to carry out its imperial mission in its colonies."[23] The old imperialism, before the 1877 designation of Queen Victoria as Empress of India, had wanted to regenerate Africa by use of "the Bible and the plough," thereby undercutting profiteers in human flesh by implementing "commerce based upon Christian standards and Western commodity."[24] For Cecil Rhodes and William Booth the new imperial scheme would result in a British-Christian world, with no distinction between what it meant to be British and what it meant to be Christian.

General Booth frustrated his commanders in the colonies, including his children who served in America, Europe, India, and Australasia, with his autocratic rule from London. As the British increased central control over colonies, including Cecil Rhodes' domination in Southern Africa, William and Bramwell Booth tightened their mandate over the Army's imperium. In North America, Europe, and Australia there were problems between 1884 and 1904 over issues of centralized control from London. There were also schisms that have not gained the attention of the Army's official historians. The final episode of authoritarian rule came with the deposition of General Bramwell Booth, William's eldest son and successor, by a council of the Army's international leaders in London in 1929.[25]

As with Cecil Rhodes' last testament that aimed to bring the world, even the United States, under Britain's Union Jack, General Booth proposed to move London's poor to Southern Africa under London's rule. In 1895 Rhodes claimed that "in order to save the 40 million inhabitants of the United Kingdom from a bloody civil war we colonial statesmen must acquire new lands to settle the surplus population to provide new markets for the goods produced by them in the factories and mines. . . . If you want to avoid civil war, you must become imperialists."[26] Thus, as people of their era, nearly all merchants and missionaries were imperialists and continued

23. Porter, *The Lion's Share*, 23–24; 45; 64.

24. See Thomas, *Rhodes*, 102ff, for his discussion of the transformation of the imperial enterprise based on speeches made at London's Exeter Hall in 1840 by missionaries and humanitarians.

25. Moyles, *The Salvation Army and the Public*, Essays 5, 7, 10; Murdoch, *Origins*, 115–45; McKinley, *Marching to Glory*, 29ff and 97ff; Larsson, *1929: A Crisis that Shaped The Salvation Army's Future*.

26. Porter, *The Lion's Share*, 129–32, quotes a missionary at the Exeter Hall meeting.

to be imperialists, albeit with slowly changing attitudes, until the scramble out of Africa began in the wake of World War II in the late 1940s and 1950s.

This gradually brought to a close of what was, as historian Eric Hobsbaum put it, "the classic age of massive missionary endeavor." But he argued that "missionary effort was by no means an agency of imperialist politics," in that missionaries were often at odds with the British South Africa Company and British colonial social policy. Yet, he continued, there can be no denying that colonial conquest opened the door to Africa for European and North American Christian missions, and that "the success of the Lord was a function of imperialist advance." Efforts of church and state mingled in that both ventures were "done by whites for natives," and were "paid for by whites."[27] State and church were paternalistic operations financed by state and commercial interests as well as mission funds.

In 1906 William Booth began two and a half years of intensive lobbying of the British government and the British South Africa Company (BSAC) to gain financial support for his plan to settle the English urban unemployed on Rhodesian soil. Costs would include transportation and the building of farm colonies. By his calculation Booth needed £100,000 from the British government and £150,000 from the BSAC and an unnamed group to colonize "Britain's surplus population."[28] In January 1906 he welcomed news that the opposition to his plan by certain members of the BSAC board was fading.[29]

Booth then turned to the new Liberal Party government that had replaced the Conservatives in December 1905. Liberals were generally friendlier to nonconformist churches like the Salvation Army while Conservatives favored the establishment's Church of England. Booth met Herbert Gladstone, the new Home Secretary, and Winston Churchill, a Colonial Office Undersecretary. Former Liberal Prime Minister Lord Rosebery assured Booth of his sympathy and the sympathy of the Rhodes' Trust. Booth also visited Dr. Buckle, editor of The Times, from whom he gained a promise of support.

Booth asked Captain Wise of the BSAC not to start a competing emigration scheme such as the one contained in Rhodes' will. Colonial Secretary Lord Elgin was cordial, but said that he had no money for the project. In March Booth saw his friend John Morley, Secretary of State for India, who promised help for "our Indian hospitals and Village Banks," but he had

27. Hobsbaum, *The Age of Empire*, 71.

28. Chennels, *White Rhodesian Nationalism*, 123, discusses the popularity of such schemes at this time.

29. Stead told Booth that John Burns had opposed the scheme because of unspecified "slanders" he had heard.

no control over the government's Africa funds. In May Booth explained his plan to Prime Minister Henry Campbell-Bannerman who said that he was appalled that the Salvation Army was doing great work with "limited resources, while organizations with so much wealth and power" were "spending their strength on useless contention." But he offered no "practical help in the shape of money."

In September 1906 Booth took courage when Dr. Leander Starr Jameson, the former BSAC administrator in Rhodesia who had spent time in jail as a result of his unauthorized raid on the Boers in 1898, and then had served as the Prime Minister of the Cape Colony, said that he was "anxious for the success of the R[hodesia] Scheme." Booth's hopes rose again when he heard that the BSAC "had accepted our proposals for the contract and [had] given us some of the privileges we asked for." The *Mining World* reported that "the Rhodesian market [gets] firmer at the very mention of a proposal to extend [Booth's] works to that territory." That tribute was based on "the fascinating influence of [Booth's] personality and the immense power for good he wields over men and things."[30] St. John Ervine, Booth's best biographer, claimed that the General saw colonization as the "most natural outlet for the over-plus population of this country," and contended that Rhodesia was "the most likely, if not the only possible country, for such a scheme to be tried with the possibility of success."[31]

On August 23, 1907 the *Rhodesia Herald* reported that the BSAC had offered General Booth a "large tract of land" and "a large sum of money" for his plan, which would cost £250,000. The editor found it "unlikely that the promised cooperation of the Chartered Co. is inspired by [Booth's] spiritual aim." Rather, with reasonable insight, the paper concluded that the grant resulted from a merging of the imperial designs of the BSAC and the Salvation Army. The editor did not altogether trust Booth and proposed an alternative plan, that the BSAC should float a loan on its own behalf if its aim was to provide jobs. The *Herald* reported that the Salvation Army and the Canadian government had set up a special commission to work out a colonization scheme that would send 1,450 settlers to ten Canadian townships, but this was "only a drop in the bucket of the Army's requirements."[32]

South African and Rhodesian whites already viewed the BSAC and the British government as meddlers in colonial affairs about which they knew little. The *Rhodesia Herald*'s editorial page carried a letter to the editor of South Africa's *Die Volkstem* that opposed Booth's plan on grounds

30. Begbie, *Life of General William Booth*, 2, 331–35.
31. Ervine, *God's Soldier*, 2, 791–94.
32. *Rhodesia Herald*, Aug. 23, 1907, and Sept. 6, 1907.

that the new emigrants, once settled on the Salvation Army's Rhodesian farm colonies, would leave the colony to flock to gold fields and become a nuisance. The *Kimberly Advertiser* preferred that the BSAC send settlers to Rhodesia from South Africa, which at the time was suffering from an economic depression. The *Advertiser* reasoned that South Africans had qualities that would be invaluable to Rhodesia, whereas Booth's poor urban migrants would run from adversity, die from malaria, gravitate to towns, and intensify Rhodesia's unemployment problem. It concluded that new colonies had a right to a better class of men than that of England's surplus slum populations.[33]

Nothing came of the BSAC offer to fund Booth's emigration scheme. The BSAC announced in January 1908 that "neither large monetary assistance nor free land will be forthcoming." South Africa was on the verge of concluding a plan of Union in 1907–8, between the former Boer and British colonies, which would detach South Africa politically from Britain's colonial control. This would initiate what Thomas Pakenham calls the beginning of the decolonization of Africa so far as white control was concerned.[34]

In this unsettled era, the *Rhodesia Herald* reported on January 18, 1908 that General Booth was "terribly disappointed at the lack of enterprise by the Company." But on February 28 the *Herald* rumored once again that a settlement had been made after all. The BSAC would provide millions of dollars for Booth's "efficient organization" to solve Britain's unemployment with a plan to colonize Rhodesia with white settlers. The BSAC would ask British Foreign Secretary Sir Edward Grey for a government charter to turn Rhodesia into a "flourishing industrial nation."[35] But surely Booth's request would be a minor concern of the British foreign ministry at a time when Britain was considering withdrawal from its colonial chores in South Africa.

In April 1908, over two years after William Booth recommenced his exhausting campaign to garner financial aid from the British government and the BSAC, his solicitor received news from the BSAC that their board definitely would not provide money for his Rhodesia Scheme. The General lamented that he had wasted "two years and five months spent in anxious negotiation, and more money than I like to calculate spent in the inspection

---

33. "Salvation Army Settlers," *Rhodesia Herald,* April 10, 1908, 4; "Salvation Settlers," *Rhodesia Herald,* April 17, 1908, 4.

34. Pakenham, *The Scramble for Africa*, 665–7.

35. "Salvation Settlers," *Rhodesia Herald,* Jan. 17, 1908, 4; "Salvation Settlement," *Rhodesia Herald,* Feb. 28, 1908, 3; Begbie, *Life of General William Booth*, 2, 331–35, 359, 361–70, 372–73, 379–80, discusses Booth's Rhodesian Colony Scheme at length.

of the country, drawing up legal documents and other matters. It may turn out useful in the future; but I don't know—God's will be done."[36]

Booth issued a public statement on May 22: "I regret to say [that] owing to [the] inadequate response of the British South Africa Company shareholders to [our] appeal for fresh capital [the] undertaking must be abandoned." He had hoped for millions of acres and large amounts of capital. He had intended to experiment for two years to prove that the scheme worked before he launched the full program. The Army's Chief of Staff, his son Bramwell, said diplomatically that the BSAC "are as acutely disappointed as we are at the temporary abandonment of the scheme." Nevertheless, he argued that "The great hope for the future of Rhodesia lies in obtaining a good white population."[37] No doubt sending a "white population" to Rhodesia was the sentiment of the day, but the BSAC was likely having second thoughts on who should administer the plan.

In spite of the fact that General Booth shared the racial sentiments of the British government and BSAC, his plan to provide white settlers from London's slums to enhance white settler control in southern Africa was not accepted by either funding source. The BSAC gave no reason for rejecting his scheme apart from a lack of money. Did they believe that the Salvation Army was incapable of carrying out the plan administratively? Were they concerned about the quality of the emigrants from London's East End? Were they worried about the reaction of white settlers already in South Africa and Rhodesia to a scheme that was under the control of missionaries, whom they possibly saw as religious fanatics? Did they know that Booth's Scheme was the product of Frank Smith's planning? Smith had resigned his Salvation Army post and was by now a Fabian and a socialist member of the London County Council. Was it the Church of England, speaking for itself or the Charity Organization Society and other conservative organizations that blocked Booth's ambition? Certainly Booth had many detractors by 1908, yet in spite of what his detractors might have been saying, by that spring the Salvation Army was running farms at Rondebosch and Talagourria in South Africa and at Pearson (formerly Mazoe) near Salisbury in Rhodesia. But William Booth's hope of spreading his grand imperial plan in Southern Africa was now nearly dead in spite of his blind hope for a resurrection.[38]

Four months later, in September 1908, the seventy-nine-year-old William Booth arrived in Southern Africa for a tour that included his visit to

36. Begbie, *Life of General William Booth*, 2, 358–59.

37. "Salvation Settlers," *Rhodesia Herald*, May 22, 1908, 4.

38. "Salvation Army," *Rhodesia Herald*, May 22, 1908, 7; "Town Council Report," *Rhodesia Herald*, June 12, 1908, 3.

Rhodesia. He reasserted his goal to send England's unemployed to Southern Africa. A farm settlement run by Salvation Army officers would find a place where white people who were content with essentials would live decently. He would send 4,000 British settlers to Rhodesia at a cost of £400 per family. Sensitive to South African public opinion, he allowed that some of the settlers might be from South Africa. Settlers would pay off loans for their property on an installment plan as they had done at the Army's land settlements in India, Australia and North America.

Booth told the media that the Salvation Army was working in fifty-three countries with 1,000 trained officers. It fed 200,000 and sheltered 22,000 "wretched creatures" every week. The *Rhodesia Herald*'s editorials now thought better of the General than they had earlier in 1908. Now he was the "grand old man of the Salvation Army," whose "fierce energy had caused the Army to work with the poor with honest purpose." Apparently his charismatic presence was modifying the editor's earlier opposition.

Booth had no message for black Africans to encourage their economic well-being or their human rights. Instead he advocated that the African "character must be made good." They must "not simply be taught to read and write and calculate." He shared the well-accepted notion that the Africans' role would be that of unskilled laborers, as it was in other white-dominated nations.

As for southern African governments, Booth brandished his autocratic formula for maintaining an orderly civilization. "What South Africa needs is strong government, but strong government has gone out of fashion."[39] In fact, paternalism remained much in vogue as the best way to deal with Africans, at least until 1960.[40] A Plan of Union for South Africa would increase apartheid (racial separation) in the Cape Colony where there had been limited liberal rule before the British negotiations with the Boers (Dutch-speaking people of the Transvaal). If any population proved difficult for the British to control it was the Boer settlers who had preceded them to Southern Africa. Was this was the population that Booth had in mind for discipline?

At Booth's first stop in Rhodesia in October he met a small group of the Army's white and African converts at Woodleigh Farm. The train that

---

39. "'General' Booth," *Rhodesia Herald*, Sept. 3, 1908; "'General' Booth," Sept. 4, 1908, 11; "'General' Booth," Sept. 18, 1908, 3; "'General' Booth," Sept. 18, 1908, 7.

40. Even the most liberal missionary teachers dealt with Africans by caning and other forms of harsh discipline during the 1950s, according to Ruth Weiss (with Jane Parpart), *Sir Garfield Todd and the Making of Zimbabwe*, 103. While Todd served as Prime Minister in the 1950s he returned to his mission school on weekends to administer discipline.

the BSAC provided for him stopped briefly at Leighwoods railway siding. James Usher, a Salvationist who owned the Woodleigh Farm, had arrived in Bulawayo (the Matabeleland capital) in 1894. In 1899 he had married the Army's local Corps Officer, Captain Jessie Stuart Rogers, whom the Army had appointed the previous year. In 1902 the Ushers attended the funeral of Cecil Rhodes and his burial in the Motopos hills, south of Bulawayo, a possible indication of their social standing and identification with the white BSAC government.[41]

On October 1 the General addressed a packed civic reception at Bulawayo's Grand Hotel at which the Mayor presided. He described the success of his colonizing venture in Canada as proof that he would not use Rhodesia as a dumping ground for England's urban refuse.[42] On October 8 Booth arrived at Salisbury's train depot to be greeted by "all classes"—although reporters listed only white celebrities of social rank: "prominent residents and business men." Booth told the cheering crowd that they knew "little of poverty here in Salisbury." Nevertheless, even here some had "slipped down in the battle of life" and needed "spiritual assistance." Booth lodged with the BSAC Administrator, Sir William Milton, who presided at his Drill Hall lecture. Attorney General Tredgold, Marshall Hole, Mayor Ross and Salisbury's city councilors were in the audience. Booth drew a word picture of London's East End, a "continent of misery and crime," where in 1865 he had begun his mission to "alleviate that ocean of misery" by rescuing more than just the "vicious and criminal classes." Again he was responding to criticism that his Darkest England scheme would dump Britain's slum dwellers on African soil.

When Booth returned to Cape Town to prepare to leave for home he called his colonization scheme the most exciting project "since Moses led the Israelites out of Egypt." If he found support he could fit "all of Britain's unemployed" into South Africa. Dr. Jameson, who had just concluded a four-year term as Prime Minister of the Cape Colony, had provided the Booth party with a railway car for his trip to Rhodesia and had given substantial grants to the Salvation Army's Rondebosch Social Farm for ex-convicts established in 1893.[43]

41. Paton, '*Mzilikazi*': *A Biography of Lieut. Colonel John Tudor Usher*, 4–22.

42. "'General' Booth: Arrival in Salisbury, A Hearty Welcome," *Rhodesia Herald*, Oct. 9, 1908, 4; "The General's Story, 43 years of Work, Colonization Schemes," *Rhodesia Herald*, Oct. 10, 1908, 4.

43. "General Booth, Another Lecture," *Rhodesia Herald*, Oct. 16, 1908, 7, no longer placed General in inverted commas, a practice *The Times* of London employed to take note of Booth's self-imposed title (actually a brief form of "General Superintendent," the title Booth had used in his Christian Mission, 1865–78. See the *Church Times'* sarcastic

But by the fall of 1908 Booth had failed to gain support for his plan to develop a farm colony for white settlers in Rhodesia. Neither the British government nor the British South Africa Company would offer land or money. His hopes to turn Rhodesia into a settlement for England's unemployed were dashed. Now he would have to find other means of building his Christian imperium in Southern Africa. Conceivably he would expand work that the Army was already doing by following the lead of other missions in "civilizing" and "Christianizing" the Africans, using funds from the BSAC government.

---

comment of July 23, 1897. See also "South African News: General Booth Leaves for England," *Rhodesia Herald,* Oct. 16, 1908, 11; *Rhodesia Herald,* Nov. 15, 1908. See also "Darkest England Helpers," *The Darkest England Gazette,* Nov. 11, 1893, 7.

Chapter 5

Father and Son in 1908
"My dear General"—"My dear Chief"

> God-willing, I am off to South Africa on Saturday. I can neither go forward nor backward with Rhodesia. When I want to proceed with the undertaking some obstacle ever blocks my way, and when I want to give it up and know it no more, I am equally withheld...
>
> —William Booth to W. T. Stead, in August 1908.

> What an unbelieving Turk you are! Do you not see, and can you not understand, that your path and mine are both marked out for us by One who is wiser than both of us put together?... The meaning of this seems to me plain enough, namely, that you have a work to do there, but the time has not yet come for action...
>
> —W. T. Stead, to William Booth in reply.[1]

Military jargon and Victorian formality could outweigh father-son expressions of affection by William Booth and his eldest son and Chief of Staff, William Bramwell Booth. Due to William's failing sight, a surrogate, usually Colonel Theodore Kitching, wrote most of his letters, telegrams, and cables to Bramwell. The first of William and Catherine Booth's eight children, Bramwell was born in 1856 while his father was an evangelist in the

---

1. Begbie, *Life of William Booth*, II, 407–8. Who, other than Stead, would ever have dared to address Booth as an "unbelieving Turk"?

Methodist New Connexion. Bramwell came of age while his parents were opening their urban home mission in London's East End after 1865. By 1878, when the Booths renamed their mission "a salvation army," twenty-two-year-old Bramwell was second in command with the title of "Chief of the Staff." In 1890, after his mother's death, Bramwell became his father's link with the five Booth children who had assumed leading roles in the Army. Known by some critics as the "Booth dynasty," when William's extensive international travels began in the late 1880s they led the Army in the U.K., U.S., Canada, Australasia, India, France, Switzerland, Sweden, and Belgium. Bramwell's siblings chafed under what most of them came to see as their older brother's tyranny.

William and Bramwell Booth motoring, circa 1907. William Booth utilized motor cars on preaching tours in Britain between 1904 and 1910. (By permission, The Salvation Army International Heritage Centre.)

In 1912, when William died, only two of Bramwell's four active sisters, Eva and Lucy, were still in "the work," a euphemism Salvationists use to describe the Army's service. From William's death in 1912 Bramwell would serve as the Army's second General. Salvation Army leaders deposed him in 1929 as he was dying, bringing an end to sixty-four years of Booth family rule. The Army was Bramwell's life. With little formal education—what he knew he learned at home largely from his mother—it was at the office he mastered legal and business procedures, often from well-qualified subordinates, and served as an astute manager of his father's international movement. He also mastered enough theology to make him an effective evangelist and apologist for the Army's Wesleyan doctrines. His wife, Florence, and all of their children were Army officers. Few doubted that one of them would succeed to the Generalship. But in 1929 a High Council of the Army's international leaders decided to end dynastic rule and chose the Army's third General by ballot from outside the family. This replaced a method of succession in which the General gave to the Army's solicitor an envelope in which he enclosed the name of his successor. It would be opened by the solicitor after his death.

This chapter deals with correspondence between William and Bramwell while William was in South Africa and Rhodesia for three months in 1908. Bramwell was serving as the Army's chief operating officer at the London headquarters. In the letters and cables we see their formal relationship and their familial relation as father and son. We can also find their shared passion to develop a Rhodesian Land Colony with the aid of the British South Africa Company and its Rhodesian governors, the British government, the four South African governments of Cape Colony, Natal, Transvaal, and the Orange Free State, and of private individuals with whom they shared their ideas.[2]

The Booths' letters provide evidence of the tortured courtship they conducted with the BSAC in London and its South Africa headquarters. Painful negotiations with the BSAC in Cape Town, Salisbury and London, as well as attempts to get funding from the British Liberal government, absorbed the Booths for over two years. It sets the scene for the Army's relations with white settler governments in the post-BSAC era as well as its relations with other churches in Rhodesia and world-wide in the late twentieth century.

William Booth was an elderly patriarch with the composure of a prophet when he embarked at Southampton for the Cape in early August 1908 on the R.M.S. Walmer Castle of the Castle Line. He had visited South Africa in 1891, the year he dispatched the Army's "Pioneer Column" to Mashonaland, and in 1895. His 1908 visit marked the 25th anniversary of the Army's first landing at the Cape from the same ship. Before leaving London by train on August 7, William sent an illegible note, likely in the hand of a man who was losing his sight, to "My dear Bramwell," about a personnel affair that troubled them. He signed the note "Your affectionate

2. I am grateful to the Salvation Army Archives in Johannesburg, South Africa, for these letters between William and Bramwell Booth, August 4 to October 7, 1908. Commissioner Dr Paul du Plessis brought this important cache of letters to my attention.

father, William Booth." He hoped that Bramwell's "rest of mind" was not disturbed by the matter. Hand-written and typed letters, almost all written by his personal secretary Theodore Kitching, were almost always formally addressed to "My dear Chief." Bramwell always addressed his father as "My dear General."

William expressed frustration over the BSAC's intentions toward the Salvation Army in Southern Africa. He wanted the company to give him land on which to settle unemployed English workers, but he told subordinates that he would not humble himself to ask BSAC administrator, Dr. Leander Starr Jameson, for support. Jameson had annoyed Booth with his lack of action on the General's land scheme. Booth wrote that he would not raise expectations on his tour in Southern Africa if the BSAC would not cooperate. He would "leave them to their fate."[3] His correspondence indicates that his goal for the trip was to get land for a colony despite a claim that he was going there to meet Salvationists. He was gloomy about his prospects. Was he trying to lower expectations due to the lack of BSAC support, or was he in one of his dyspeptic moods?

William wrote two notes to Bramwell from the Walmer Castle in Madeira. Emigration statistics sent by Colonel Taylor from Toronto were unsatisfactory. The Army had sent 40,000 English emigrants to the Dominion under an arrangement with the Canadian government but migrants were not repaying their loans. Booth's scheme for moving England's unemployed to overseas colonies relied on the Army's ability to repay those who invested in the scheme. To do this he relied on migrants to repay the cost of passage that the Army provided. About 250,000 English emigrants would travel to Canada under the Army's auspices in the early twentieth century. Booth wanted accurate figures to present during his African tour. He wanted to tout Canada as the best example of the Army's efficiency in running overseas land colonies and he needed evidence.[4]

A second note told Bramwell, who was in Berlin at the time, that they had not parted "in the right fashion." Feeling his age, William likely wanted his heir to know that they should have spent a day or two discussing "more prominent things which concern the present and future." William said that he was "all of a heap with what I want to cable." But in spite of this anxiety, the old man was enjoying the passage on a smooth sea with beautiful weather and excellent service. His sight was bothering him and he was missing a

---

3. William Booth to "My dear Chief," 7 August 1908.
4. Ibid.

tooth spring, but his health was "fair."[5] There were only fifty to sixty passengers in First Class instead of the 280 that the ship could accommodate.

He was hearing complaints about South Africa's commercial affairs and "things generally," but a Copper Mine Director headed to Rhodesia on business advised him that Rhodesia "was a Country that was likely to come to the front in the near future."[6] A "nice young fellow" headed for Rhodesia was impressed with its ideal climate, like "Celifornia" [sic]. And he met a man named "Troupe" who intended to transfer people to Rhodesia on "business principles," as Booth intended to do on philanthropic lines. Troupe informed him that when the BSAC transferred land it retained all mineral rights. William filed that information for the future.[7]

On August 15 Bramwell sent William an eight-page "South African Campaign: Official Letter No. 1." On his father's concern about Canadian migrant repayments Bramwell responded that publicity on the matter was dangerous. To claim that the Army was not getting its money back had a bad effect on emigrants who did not want to pay. They were claiming that the Army was making money and did not need the payments.

Dr. Jameson was "shooting in Scotland" and other BSAC officials were away, likely on holiday since it was August. Should William go to Rhodesia? The Army's Southern Africa commander hoped so. He believed that if the General saw Rhodesia he would be aware of difficulties settlers would have to overcome to make his emigration scheme succeed.[8] Bramwell reported on his Berlin trip and signed off, "very affectionately, Bramwell." On August 22 Bramwell wrote "Official Letter No. 4" to William at East London, Cape Colony. Since "London is empty" of BSAC and government officials Bramwell reported only "trifling movement" in Rhodesian matters.

Probably after consulting Commissioner David C. Lamb, the International Social Secretary and Director of its Migration Program, Bramwell proposed to William that the Army help British Poor Law Guardians save money spent on a "certain class of people." Lamb was negotiating with Poor Law Guardians on how to cut costs and at the same time assist the Army in sending their unemployed clients to Canada. They could do this while they were seeking land for a colony in Rhodesian land. The Booths and Lamb were promising that they would move people to Rhodesia who were not yet "paupers," but who could not pay their own passage. For the rest of the

---

5. A tooth spring was a device to help secure dentures in place.

6. William Booth to "My dear Bramwell," 10–11 August 1908, from the R.M.S. Walmer Castle.

7. William Booth note from the Walmer Castle, 11 August, 1908.

8. Bramwell Booth to "My dear General," 15 August 1908.

transport cost the Army would set up a Limited Liability Company and sell shares to the public with "a conditional guarantee of success." The Poor Law Guardians would "cheaply" get rid of "some of their burdens" and the Army would have migrants for Rhodesia. Bramwell, again with Lamb's advice, proposed to send a "better class of men" to the Army's Hadleigh Farm in Essex. To ease London's economic distress he would raise £20,000 to send "genuine working people of the lower strata" to Hadleigh to prepare for emigration. Hadleigh would also provide food for the poor and support the Army's London workshops. He anticipated that English wages would drop if the price of English exports were to compete with those of Germany and Japan and new Slavic countries. He was going to Sevenoaks for "furlough" (army jargon for vacation), but would work "to carry out what I conceive to be your wishes."

On a matter of an Australian Salvation Army officer's resignation, Bramwell revealed a misogynist hue that would have displeased his mother, Catherine Booth, who had died in 1890. Colonel Gilmour had "tendered his resignation." His wife was an invalid and he had been unwell since he came to London, so one of his sons offered him a position in a "cinamatograph" business. Bramwell surmised that Gilmour's wife had unduly swayed him; "one of the prices we have to pay for giving women so prominent a position that her opportunity to influence the wrong way is more important."[9] In the Army husband and wife held equal rank, but in nearly every case men had a superior office to women.

William dictated his first letter from the Cape's welcome terra firma on August 25. When his ship docked at 6:30 a.m., Territorial Commander Richards and Colonel Rauch briefed him on his itinerary. He was upset that there was no cable from England and he was grumpy that Dr. Jameson was not coming from London. However he was delighted with his 9:30 a.m. reception by the mayor, a band, the press, photographers, and a good crowd on the wharf. A member of the legislature drove him to his "respectable apartment" at the Castle Line's Mount Nelson Hotel. Everyone was "of intensist [sic] curiosity about Rhodesia" and expected that he had brought "a pocket full of money" and was going to Rhodesia to make a settlement. He concluded that "if we had a Company ready formed and had 250,000 shares to dispose of, they would all have been sold during my stay here." In that case Bramwell would have to deal with "the unemployed in the Cape and other colonies." South Africans were letting the General know that they

---

9. "South African Campaign 1908, Official Letter No. 4." Bramwell Booth to "My dear General," 22 August 1908.

wanted their own unemployed to move to Rhodesia, not what they saw as riff-raff from London. The Cape's Governor invited Booth to lunch.

In the evening there was a Civic Reception at the Town Hall with 2,000 "respectable people," including over a hundred Members of Parliament. Booth found "only one thing wanting to make it perfect and that was a collection" of money. He would give several civic lectures for ticket-buying audiences during his stay. He met Prime Minister John X. Merriman, whom he had heard was an "infidel," so he spoke to him about "godliness" and "what the power of God can accomplish." Most people expected that Merriman's Cape government would not survive another election due to opposition from farmers over taxes and the difficulty of getting white men to settle in the colony. Competition with cheap African labor drove white workers away. Booth met the executive of Cape Town's Church Council before he left for Johannesburg.[10]

Bramwell responded to what he termed William's "meagre" telegram. The weather at Sevenoaks was bad and Bramwell was testy on account of problems with brothers-in-law who were Army leaders in Sweden and India. William had given Emanuel Booth-Hellborg, husband of his daughter Lucy, a long furlough in 1907 due to illness. Now Hellberg's coal business was suffering from a lack of capital. Bramwell asked if William wanted him to advise Hellborg. When Hellborg died in June 1909 Lucy Booth commanded the Army in Denmark.

In William's correspondence Frederick Tucker was seldom referred to as Booth-Tucker, the name he took after marrying Emma Booth who had died in a train crash in the U.S. in 1903. In 1906 Tucker had married Mary Reid, daughter of a former British Acting Governor of Bombay. His problems also concerned finance. They began with a loom-making business at the Army's land settlement in India that was losing money. He wanted to turn the business into a private company with outside capital, but Bramwell saw it as "speculation" in that it involved sales and employees. In a second Tucker matter, William had approved the sale of the Army's Bombay building as long as a certain price was obtained. It sold for less than William hoped for, but Bramwell thought Tucker had done well. Tucker wanted to move the headquarters to Simla, the cool Himalayan summer capital of the British Raj. There were also staff problems in India.[11] Tucker later became disaffected with Bramwell. In 1929 he sided with those who deposed his brother-in-law as General. William, a distant father, and Bramwell, the

---

10. William Booth dictated to "My dear Chief," 25 August 1908, from Cape Town.
11. Bramwell Booth to "My dear General," 28 August 1908, from Sevenoaks.

Chief of the Staff, both found it hard to play the diverse roles of father, mother, brother, and boss to the family.

From Johannesburg, in a forty-six-page hand-written letter to Bramwell, William indicated that he had found the narrow-gauge rail journey from Cape Town tiring even though the DeBeers Company had loaned him a private coach. Stops at Pearl, "Atwater-Tworcester," and "Trufersdorf," brought presentations by local officials. He was greeted at the Johannesburg station by the Mayor, after which Abe Bailey, a legislator and entrepreneur, drove him to his home, "Friedeuheuer." Booth's first lecture was attended by lawyers, doctors, "magnates" and ministers, including the Archdeacon. He spoke about "The Secret," apparently a common lecture topic. In the afternoon the Mayor led a "conversazione" with refreshments for 150 invited "gentlemen." At night he spoke to a meeting of Salvationists. After Sunday meetings he went to Pretoria on Monday afternoon.

Regarding a Rhodesia visit, Abe Bailey, who had returned from Rhodesia the day before Booth arrived, cabled Dr. Jameson in London: "If the proposal [to give the Salvation Army land and a grant] has been dropped it is a good chance to resurrect it," and "this is probably the last chance of securing the General's influence." William had cabled Bramwell the day before to tell him that a trip to Rhodesia would only extend his absence from England by a week. Bailey said that he was willing to buy £200,000 worth of debentures in the scheme. Bramwell had told William that the British government would likely communicate with "the Governor General of South Africa," but there was "no such office."[12] Bramwell apparently meant Lord Selborne, the British High Commissioner. A call to Selborne's office at Pretoria found that the British government would likely have contacted the BSAC's "Administrator General of Rhodesia" about Booth's Rhodesia trip. Booth was upset that Selborne had not met him in Pretoria. Bailey assured Booth that Selborne had no influence with the British government.

Bailey tried to reach Jameson who was still in Scotland. He told Kitching that by going to Rhodesia Booth would show the British government, the BSAC and the public that he was convinced of the soundness of his scheme. He would prove that his scheme was the best one "for Rhodesia, for South Africa, for the empire, and for humanity." Then the public would force action. Bailey would do all in his power to help. He offered to cable Colonial Under-Secretary Winston Churchill and Prime Minister Asquith to underline his conviction that "the thing must go through." William wrote that Bailey would give £10,000 at £2,500 per year over four years; and if needed he would "spring up to £25,000 or even £30,000" rather than see the

---

12. The office of Governor General in South Africa was inaugurated in 1910.

scheme fail.[13] Booth found that there was great enthusiasm for the scheme in South Africa, but understood that the British government paid little attention to the area in the aftermath of the ugly Boer War.

Leander Starr Jameson. Cartoon by 'Spy' from *Vanity Fair*, 9 April 1896.

Abe Bailey. Cartoon by 'Spy' from *Vanity Fair*, 9 September 1908.

Lord Selborne apologized for not presiding at Booth's "conversazione" in Johannesburg on account of a prior engagement. Kitching went to Pretoria with Booth's letter asking for Selborne's views on the Rhodesian scheme and learned that Selborne had heard nothing from the British government, though unnamed BSAC Directors told him that they were sorry that the company had been unable to raise the capital Booth needed. William told Bramwell that Selborne believed that BSAC Directors would put the thing through. Selborne did not know that the British government was also weighing collaboration in the scheme. He underscored Bailey's view that Booth should go to Rhodesia, at least as far as Bulawayo in Matabeleland, to make the BSAC and government see the scheme's value. He wanted Booth to look at the Marandellas District as the place for the enterprise. The Army could tutor English colonists in African agricultural and climatic

13. William Booth to "My dear Chief," August 29–31, 1908, 1–25, from Johannesburg. The Booths found Churchill supportive of their aims.

conditions. Selborne did not believe that the Transvaal government's idea to employ "Poor Whites" would work, but he thought they might succeed if they worked on the idea in connection with the Salvation Army.[14]

Booth's lectures at Johannesburg's Empire Theatre went well with packed audiences in the morning, afternoon and evening. They turned away 6,000 in the evening and called the Fire Brigade to clear the street. For the lecture the next morning people were paying 10 to 15 shillings for standing room.

Abe Bailey held British High Commissioner Selborne in contempt and again said that he would cable London to urge the Liberal government to join the BSAC in support of Booth's plan. Bailey told Kitching that he had been helping the Army for fifteen years, not as "a religious Salvationist" but the General "may always count on me to be a Cheque-Book Salvationist."

William told Bramwell that he was feeling "that we shall get something by my having come here. Perhaps it is going to be the 'African surprise' you were talking of just before I came away. Let us hope so!" Kitching inspected the Army's 30-acre farm near Johannesburg where Salvationists worked with over twenty criminals. Commissioner Richards, the Army's Southern Africa Commander, almost made the farm pay its way with prize-winning pigs and fowls. Booth hoped to put Richards in charge of his Rhodesian settlement scheme if he received the capital he needed to start it. He was impressed with Abe Bailey and his business acumen, but saw his natural shyness as a cause of his fear "of my attacking him about his soul."

As for the Rhodesian scheme's prospects, William Booth divided his possible funding sources into four parts. First he needed the British government of Liberal Prime Minister H. H. Asquith, who had succeeded Sir Henry Campbell-Bannerman in April 1908, to give him what he had requested. Second, he needed £100,000 from the BSAC and £50,000 from Abe Bailey. Third, the rest would come in smaller bits. He hoped the Transvaal would give him £50,000 from the £700,000 it had set aside for "Poor Whites," farmers who were hurt by the war and other problems. Maybe the Cape Colony would help. Abe Bailey waited to hear from Dr. Jameson, the BSAC administrator who would take over as Prime Minister of the Cape Colony in 1909, before he wired Winston Churchill, Britain's thirty-one-year old Colonial Office Under-Secretary. To make all of these sources of funding come together Booth agreed that "I shall have to go to Rhodesia. . . . It is very desirable that I should clear the way with the Rhodesian people

---

14. William Booth to "My dear Chief," August 29–31, 1908, 26–32, from Johannesburg.

and make them friendly to it." He signed off in his own hand, "affectionately, William Booth."[15]

William wrote to Bramwell on September 3 from Government House, Bloemfontein, where he was staying with Sir Hamilton Gould-Adams, Governor of the Orange River Colony. Booth described his host as an "Irishman," "frank, homely, and thoughtful; a Soldier, anxious for the prosperity of the Colony." Gould-Adams thought that Booth's land settlement scheme was workable, but Booth was not impressed with Gould-Adams' knowledge of the people or country. The Governor estimated the income of a mutual friend, John Newberry, at £30,000 per annum. Booth "smiled at this." And Gould-Adams declared that nothing in Rhodesia was worth having, a contradiction of what Selborne and others had said about the Marandallas district. Booth gave his lecture at a night meeting; the Governor presided. No more than 1,100 were present and the collection was only £107, but "things are far from prosperous."[16]

William wrote a second letter to Bramwell on September 3 that he posted from Kroonstad after a reception by the Mayor, Church Council, and Temperance Societies, that drew 600–700 out of a population of 2,000 whites. Three things in South Africa had surprised him. First, an "absorbing interest felt in my Rhodesian Proposal." Second, that he should do something for poor South African whites, "many of whom are practically starving," instead of bringing poor Englishmen to settle Rhodesia. Third, concerns of the "Dutch element" that the scheme "was a Political dodge to catch votes against what they consider to be their interests at the Polls." He enclosed an article from the *Bloemfontein Friend* to show that "British and rational Dutch" are coming to terms with each other. The Dutch Reformed Church was also looking at a settlement scheme, but Booth argued that they would fail and when that happened there would be an opening for his Rhodesia plan. William asked Bramwell to say nothing in England about their Scheme being useful to keep a British hold on Southern Africa. Negotiations were beginning that would lead to a South African union in 1909. He felt that "the British have got hold and the sensible Dutch people are willing to be British, want to be British, and want a United Nation." Many oppose "the wild Passion for keeping up the Dutch Language; [but] they feel that the British Tongue is going to prevail." Not an unusual view given that the people with whom Booth had been talking were nearly all British.

The rest of his letter deals with Eva Booth's personnel problems in America, how best to use Canadian migration statistics, the Army's attempt

---

15. William Booth to "My dear Chief," August 29 -31, 1908, 33–47.
16. William Booth to "My dear Chief," September 3, 1908, from Bloemfontein.

to develop its work in Russia, division of Germany into two Salvation Army territories, and personnel and building issues Bramwell had written about from Berlin. He also discussed how to go about soliciting donations from philanthropists Lord Ashton, John Newberry, and Sir John Whitney. And he noted the Army's shabby treatment of Tilden Smith, a BSAC Director who had reported in 1906 that the BSAC's opposition to assisting the Army's Rhodesia Scheme had vanished, but does not identify the nature of the treatment. In conclusion, he referred to St. Helena, a subject that Richards, the Army's South Africa leader had discussed with him. Booth saw it as a splendid place to segregate "criminals of the earth, especially English-speaking ones, but that cannot be." He signed off, "Yours affectionately, WB."[17]

From Sevenoaks Bramwell wrote on the 4 September "Official Letter No. 7," a response to William's letters from Johannesburg regarding Rhodesia. Bramwell is concerned about his father's health and the wear and tear of a Rhodesia trip. He assumes that a one week trip is so short that he would "wish you had given yourself a day or two longer to look at the country in view of the labor and expense of the journey." He reminds him of his itinerary in Germany and London when he returns home, and in Sweden and Norway in 1909. But the heart of the letter deals with two intriguing British matters.

First, F. A. Mackenzie, a journalist, had written a book that Bramwell regarded as "too much of a testimonial" to his own role in a fund-raising effort. The Army had paid for the work, but had expected that Mackenzie would return the cheque. In Bramwell's view the Appeal letter that Mackenzie wrote did not beg enough, and it failed to take advantage of the General's personal appeal, including his trip to Southern Africa. They also disagreed on the title of the book. Mackenzie liked Bramwell's title, "Waste," but thought that a second idea, "Man-Waste," smelled of Socialism or pacifism. In 1929 Mackenzie would write *The Clash of the Cymbals: The Secret History of the Revolt in the Salvation Army*, which took the side of the Salvation Army leaders who deposed Bramwell.

Labor Party leaders were accusing the Army of "sweating" practices for not paying men in urban workshops for their work. Bramwell suspected John Manson, writer of *The Salvation Army and the Public*, a 1906 critique of the Army, of stirring up the trouble. Bramwell was disappointed that "Ramsay McDonald, Keir Hardie, Shackleton, and Henderson" would "lend themselves to this sort of thing." He did not list Frank Smith, the first Salvation Army Social commissioner, now a labor leader and member of London's County Council. It was Smith who would write Bramwell's defence in

---

17. William Booth to "My dear Chief," 3 September 1908, from Kroonstad.

1929, *The Betrayal of Bramwell Booth*, the year Smith won a seat in Parliament at age seventy-five. After sending Army spokesmen to labor meetings, Bramwell decided that the Army did not have anyone clever enough, and besides most "of our fellows do not understand controversy." He proposed that the Army create a "Defence Department . . . even though we may not give it a name." Bramwell had discussed the Army's Canadian emigration program with Sir John Whitney. The Ontario government grant of £1,000 would cover another year of expenses, but the [Canadian] Labor Party . . . opposed emigration from England. He signed his letter, "Yours affectionately, Bramwell."

September 4, 1908 William received his first letter from Bulawayo, Rhodesia, the southern capital that by this time had attracted a larger white population than Salisbury. J. S. Loosley, a son-in-law of Anglican missionary J. S. Moffat, anticipated Booth's trip to Rhodesia and sent him the *Rhodesian Agricultural Journal*. As Secretary of the Rhodesian Agricultural Union that represented white farmers, Loosley offered assistance and advice. He had been in Rhodesia for seventeen years and managed a farm for William Cooper and Nephews of "Berkhamsted," England. Since Rhodesia needed population, Booth's immigrants should be welcomed, although he predicted that most Rhodesian farmers were "against your schemes." They feared "competition with inexperienced but supported men who might eventually become an incubus." Loosley advised "close settlement on small areas" worked by settlers and their children and focused on dairy cattle.[18]

Posted from Pietermaritzburg on the 5th, William wrote to "My dear Chief" his "Latest and Last." William had "decided to see Rhodesia whatever happens." He would count on Bailey and the Orange Free State Governor to influence the British government while they were in London. For now, "I am made up to see Rhodesia. I don't see that it can possibly do any harm. I need not plant my tree. . . . I can simply go and see what I think of it and give my opinion."[19] Later on the 5th William sent bad news to Bramwell in a cable.

> The Chartered [BSAC] are not able to give any money to the Scheme. It is no use my describing the mortification that this is calculated to cause me, although they may say that this is in harmony with what they told us through Hawksley immediately after the failure of their loan. Still Jamieson gave me to believe that they would do something, and you say that he had an interview with the Officials at the Colonial Office. I fully expected

---

18. J. S. Loosley to General Booth, 4 Sept., 1908, from Library Buildings, Bulawayo.
19. William Booth to "My dear Chief," 5 Sept., 1908, from Pietermaritzburg.

that on their hearing of my appeal to the Government, which was on condition that the Chartered would do their share, that they would either have said "We can do our share or do nothing, whatever the Government says or does." Instead of that they allow me to come to Africa, say something in the Papers, which I was compelled to do by the expectation reigning everywhere, and to appeal to Mr. Abe Bailey, and now at the last moment they turn round and say they can do nothing. Still let me just review the present situation.

Here is an example of William Booth's mind at work in his assessment of South Africa prior to going to Rhodesia:

1. All the best people in South Africa so far as I can learn are interested in the Scheme and wish it success, and a great many think that if I asked, which I have no intention of doing, the people to do something in the way of subscribing to it, the money would soon be raised. Commissioner Richards had a letter this morning from a Member of the Legislative Assembly somewhere offering £100 per year for ten years on the condition that we put 40,000 people into the Country during that time, and says that there are a great many other people who would do the same. I only mention this to show the interest that is felt in the Scheme.

2. From all I can learn from People who have lived in the Country and understand the working of the thing, Rhodesia is an admirable place, if not the best place in the world for making the experiment.

3. The method proposed commends itself to all who have done any kind of farming in the Country. A gentleman has been telling me this morning that he himself brought out six families 28 years ago, made them work, gave them land, ultimately settling them on it and all six have prospered. The gentleman with whom I was staying interposed that one of them at least had 6,000 acres of his own.

4. With regard to finance, Kitching will tell you what Mr. Bailey told him. He would go up to £30,000, and I think he would be squeezable for £50,000. I cannot draw back now from going to Rhodesia and reporting on what the Country is like.

5. You are evidently in a corner with regard to somewhere to send those Emigrants who are looking to you. You are prepared I suppose to continue the loan system. Is there any absolute obstacle to your speculating that sum of money for Rhodesia which you would for Canada, and consequently might we not join in the Advance required for the preliminary experiment?

6. I think we have talent in this Country which with an

admixture of Officers from England either by means of exchange or otherwise, who could carry out the experiment satisfactorily.

7. Now seeing that we have expended so much effort, said so much, talked so long, and felt so deeply, are we to give the thing up? Or shall we seek to finance the Scheme in some different way?

8. Mr. Abe Bailey openly confirmed to Kitching what was stated in the English Papers with respect to his having an Agent in Rhodesia selecting the best farms, and buying them in the most economical fashion he can by buying them cheaply because as he toldCed Kitching there was no land which could not be bought for two shillings per acre, and the bulk of it could be bought for one shilling, and if he had anything that was suitable to us, he would let us have it at the same price that it had cost him.

9. The Rhodes Trustees are a great deal better off already and will be paying a Dividend shortly seeing that the news is there is an improvement all round in the Diamond Market. The Rhodesian Shares have also advanced in value.

10. Now would any financial scheme be possible of the following description: Say for instance Bailey and others who would doubtless be willing to associate themselves with him [for] £50,000, the Rhodes and Chartered £50,000, The Salvation Army, and from the payments of the Colonists that had money £50,000, that would make in all £200,000, and then cut our coat according to the cloth.

Then there is another source of Income. It is quite certain I think that if we will accept a certain number of poor white farmers from the different [South African] Colonies that a reasonable amount of money will be provided for them. The Transvaal alone has £700,000 laid aside on purpose to settle these people on the land, and they feel awfully uncertain whether they can do so with any success. A large number of their leading people deny the possibility. I feel sure that they would be pleased to collaborate with us, but it would not be wise to say anything about this, because the bulk of those who are intensely in sympathy with our idea want "Britishers," or anyway Scandinavians, or Germans, or somebody who would not have the bitter feelings in their minds now entertained by the extreme Hollanders. In this case we should have all the money we required, and as much as we should have done on the original plan.

William then turned rhapsodic:

11. I think if you were here and heard of the success which meets the most ordinary efforts in dealing with the land; I think

if you were here feeling the luxury of the Sunshine [sic], and the freshness of the atmosphere, and saw the possibilities of what could be done with the land, supposing you treated it in a friendly manner, and occasionally supplying the irrigation which appears to be so possible, you would feel that it was not a speculation but calculation; that if the thing once got afloat the people would volunteer in every direction, people who had the money and the courage needed to make the thing a success.

Were I twenty five years younger I should certainly go into the thing with no other encouragement than the gift of the land and the Railway facilities that are offered us by the Chartered, and the £50,000 I feel quite certain that by the sale of the land I could make such arrangements in the way of roads, bridges and other things as would lead to the success of the Scheme, but I don't ask you to do that.

12. I had a bad night after Kroonstad. I slept in the car, and the occasional disturbances inseparable from a Railway Station made sleep almost impossible. However I got a little extra rest the next day. We had two wayside Meetings, one at Bethlehem and the other at Harrismith, both with Civic Receptions and great crowds of people, many of whom had come 50, 80 and even 100 miles to be present the few minutes the Meeting lasted. Both were interesting Gatherings.

13. One incident to show the intense interest that is felt in all directions with regard to my visit will interest you. The Mayor and the other Civic Authorities of Lady-brand drew up an Address of Welcome and desired that it should be presented to me at the nearest place I called, and that was Bloemfontein, which was no less than 184 miles distant.

14. Ladysmith. We arrived half an hour before the Meeting. There was a great crowd of people in spite of the fact that it was dark. The Mayor took me in his carriage to the Town Hall where the Meeting was held. All the seats were occupied at 2/- and 1/-. The ordinary prices being 2/6 & 1/-, but in this case the Commissioner reduced the higher price to 2/-. I was more than a little weary with the journey, and with the close sultry condition of the hall made my share of the work a difficulty. I stood up to it however and made a good speech, and I find that everybody were [sic] delighted. I have not heard what the proceeds were, but the collection was £9, which was not bad considering the depressed state of things. I suppose there will be £30 in door money.

He was billeted with Mr. Sparks, a "modest and diffident person" who was a leading businessman in Ladysmith. Sparks provided Booth with "very interesting information" on race relations in the Colony. Ladysmith had a population of about 2,200 whites and about an equal number of Natives and Indians. Booth "was surprised to hear of the hold the Indians, who are nearly all Mohamedans, have got of the Country." While the White population was just over 100,000, there were 110,000 Indians. Although there is no evidence that Booth had personal conversation with Indians or "Natives," he believed that "Indians are much superior in every respect to the Natives, and they not only supply a large amount of the labor on the Farms and in the Towns, but are gradually becoming Masters of the Country, stealing and acquiring the business, selling at the very lowest prices, and altogether becoming a very serious question to the Colony." He heard that the government managed the approximately 1,000,000 Natives "very badly." And the establishment "don't know what to do with" the large number of poor whites; ". . . a very serious problem."

The Prime Minister had sent William a telegram asking to see him to discuss matters about which Booth had experience. William fancied that it concerned whether the Salvation Army would take charge of juvenile offenders. He signed his letter to Bramwell, "Yours affectionately, W. B. Muchlove."[20]

On the subject of "Natives," William must have received his information from white British businessmen with whom he billeted during his trip. He gave no evidence that he spoke with Africans or that they attended his meetings apart from a Salvation Army service in Durban. As with his views on the Boers, those with whom he associated skewed his views on "natives." He wrote in his next letter to Bramwell that he was less concerned about whether the Dutch or British would prevail, since in a few years the question would not be

> what Nation of Whites shall have mastery, but whether the Whites will have any mastery at all. Not whether it shall be Dutch land or British Land, but whether it shall be a white man's land. The repeated growth in intelligence of the African and Indian combined will soon give them so great a preponderance that they will capture the Agriculture and trade generally.

His British informants had a high view of Indian intelligence but a low view of their business acumen and practices and religion.

---

20. William Booth to "My dear Chief," 5 Sept. 1908, from a train en route to Pietermaritzburg, Natal.

William argued that to keep the "mineral production" and "mastery of the Country in general" from falling into the hands of non-whites, the "white man" must "add to his numbers such as will join him." This was what Booth's emigration plan would achieve. As for the "dangerous colored element," he held that they must be converted "into Righteousness and Truth, and Honesty, and Industry." He wanted to press his sentiments "upon the attention of our [British] Government, if you can say we have a Government at all."[21]

At Durban Booth held the only "Zulu" meeting mentioned in his letters. He was exuberant: in some respects it excelled "anything of the kind I ever had, even in Japan." By his count at least 4,000 to 5,000 people jammed into the Great Market, with another 2,000 outside, "all black;" in fact some whites were turned away. There were 120 seekers at the "Penitent Form crying for Mercy" after his preaching. "Oh what an opportunity there is here if we only had an Apostle, a man who would be a flame of fire. If I am spared I shall want to come back again to the Natives only." He commended Brigadier J. Allister Smith who was "capable" and had "a real love for the Zulu" in spite of a disagreement they had thirteen years earlier, when Booth considered Smith "impertinent" in something Smith did about "trousers."

William had visited the Army's Fairview Farm that morning, six miles from Durban, where forty men were turning "a Wilderness into a Garden" and were "nearly self-supporting," the latter being the most significant measure of success for Booth. The Army had paid £100 per acre for the 35 acres, indicating that land can become quite valuable. He concluded his letter with a commendation of three men he wanted to keep an eye on for Salvation Army leadership—Smith, Cunningham, and King.

Also at Durban, just before he went to Rhodesia, Booth met Mr. Orpen, a former "Minister of Agriculture" for Rhodesia, who agreed with Abe Bailey that the "Mandarillas [sic] District is excellent," but he preferred "Melsetta." Bailey informed Booth that his train to Rhodesia would have extra engines to get him back to Cape Town in time for an additional week before he returned to London. Booth received invitations from the "Administrator of Salisbury" and "Mayor of Bulawayo" that indicated he would receive a friendly welcome. Abe Bailey, who had arranged for Booth's travel in South Africa, was setting up his trip to Kimberly and had telegraphed Rhodesia about his itinerary there.[22]

On September 8 William received a cable from Bramwell that indicated that he "had seen Dr. Jamieson again. It now seemed likely that money

---

21. William Booth to "My dear Chief," 5 Sept. 1908.
22. An incomplete letter from William to Bramwell, 3–8.

from the BSAC would be forthcoming after all." But when William asked Bramwell to repeat the cable in another code he found that Bramwell meant "the money would not be available." William was "exceedingly mortified."[23]

William arrived in East London on the 8th and stayed with Colonel Crewe, Lord Crewe's cousin and husband of Mr. Orpen's daughter, whom Booth had met in Durban. Colonel Crewe gave William a low down on South Africa's social, political, and financial elite. Booth had a "lofty impression" of Lord Crewe as a "thoughtful, dignified, and reliable person," but the Colonel revealed that Lord Crewe had "gambled" on the stock market an inheritance of £40,000 a year from his uncle, whose name he had inherited, and £150,000 from his second wife, Lord Roseberry's daughter. "So much for Lord Crewe."

William, born into poverty, may have been too eager to bow to wealth and social standing. As for Mr. Hawkesley, whom William had heard "got £100,000 out of the Chartered" when it went bankrupt, Colonel Crewe said, "Oh! He has got more than that."[24] Crewe's highest praise went to Dr. Jameson, "a thoroughly trustworthy individual." Abe Bailey is rich, with a fortune close to £6,000,000, but Crewe questioned the success of his farming experiments. His Colesberg farm, the biggest in the world with 80,000 sheep, 800 horses, Crewe considered to be "a failure so far as profit is concerned." Booth thought he was mistaken. Crewe cautioned that "you cannot get anything out of Bailey unless you push him at the time he makes his proposals." Crewe thought De Beers would be up and running again in a year, but until then he did not have any hope for Booth's Rhodesia Scheme. Nevertheless, "he thinks there is no question about its success if we can get money to turn around."

The Sergeant Major of the Kroonstad Salvation Army Corps visited Booth while he was with the Crewes. His parents had been converted at meetings Booth held in Penzance, Cornwall, forty-six years earlier when William Booth was still an itinerant revivalist moving from one Wesleyan church to another. The Sergeant Major had made a "little fortune" in repairing railroad tracks and bridges that were damaged during the Boer War. Members of the Corps Band worked for him "until better times" returned. He was interested in helping with the Rhodesia scheme as were his men.[25] Meanwhile Booth had heard nothing from Kitching who was visiting Abe Bailey at his Troyeville home in Johannesburg that would become the Army's

---

23. William Booth to "My dear Chief," 9 Sept. 1908, from Durban. (IHQ had codebooks for communications with the territories, both to save on the cost of telegrams and cables, and to maintain confidentiality.)

24. Bourchier Hawksley was the BSAC's solicitor.

25. W.B. to "My dear Chief," 14 Sept. 1908, from East London.

officer training college in 1924. In 1929 Bailey made a large contribution for the Salvation Army Training College at Denmark Hill, London, which was named for William Booth.

On September 15 William left for King William's Town, sensing that he had made an impression on the Crewes, as they had impressed him. Mr. Whittaker, with whom he billeted in a "decent house," was a Member of the Legislative Assembly. He had a "melancholy" view of the future of whites in Africa. Like most of the British in South Africa he disliked the unification plan which ensured that the Dutch would dominate the British. William claimed that he took what Britishers said with a grain of salt, but he also found it strange that Transvaalers would govern after Britain had spent so much money and blood fighting them in the Boer War.

That afternoon William had a "Native Meeting" of Xhosa and Fingos in the Big Market House. He was annoyed that white Missionaries sat at his right so that the natives could see them. Yet he felt he gave a "powerful Address" and there was "good Penitent Form business" with sixty or seventy adults and about twenty children seeking salvation. A night meeting was spoiled by an entrance fee of 1/-. The "stupid Captain" had ignored his instructions that there was to be no entrance fee that shrank the crowd. Nevertheless he again felt that he made a "powerful address" and £20 income was not bad for a small depressed town. He was pleased with a new Salvation Army "college" at Tashoxa, four miles from King William's Town, that cost £1,000, but it was "built and designed by an Englishman!" It burned down shortly after Booth's visit. At 3:00 his train arrived at Alice. There was a nice reception, but "no colored people came." The Mayor's daughter gave him £7–16/- for the Army's work.

Next came Lovedale, a mission complex in the village of Alice in the Ciskei, founded in 1841 by Dr. Stewart of the Glasgow Missionary Society of the Free Church of Scotland. The mission was "an utter disappointment" in that it was not "self-supporting." Lovedale supplemented the few thousand pounds that it received in school fees and the sale of products with £14,000 to £15,000 in grants and gifts from the parent Society and other sources. Booth advocated Hudson Taylor's self-support idea, whereby a mission station at home or overseas lived on income it raised in the area it served.

That night, when Booth addressed 600–700 students and a hundred towns-folk and officials he reacted to the academic atmosphere as a "cold blooded, stiff affair," in an "Institution for the repression or annihilation of all natural enthusiasm, without supplying any Divine Spirit to take its place. This sort of thing will never convert the teeming millions of this Continent. The aggravation is that you can feel the latent ambition to do a great deal of the same sort of thing amongst our own people." Like the African, Booth enjoyed hearty singing and emotional sermons to which a congregation responded with shouting. His greatest fear was that his Army would ossify into a formal sect without energy and growth.

William had begun the day at 8:30 a.m. and finished at 10:00 p.m., after which he had a "long talk over supper" with Lovedale's President, the Rev. James Henderson. He wrote to Bramwell that Henderson was an "intelligent, earnest, and well-meaning lover of the Native," but he was altogether mistaken in his view of Africa's future when he prophesied that "'Africa for the Africans' seems to be as certain an issue for the mixed various Native populations as anything well can be, and perhaps he is preparing them for it to an extent of which he has no idea. More of that when we meet."[26]

The General had pondered who in the Salvation Army could take charge of his Rhodesian Scheme. He proposed Commissioner Richards to Bramwell as the man "if it goes through." To assist him Booth was impressed with Major [John] Cunningham who was already in South Africa and knew the lie of the land. On September 11 Booth went through mail that Bramwell had sent from London. In Germany "bad feeling" toward England had caused Bramwell to propose an International Friendly Society. William approved and suggested that "[W. T.] Stead would be pleased to help." William was concerned that Bramwell not carry "all these affairs" with him on his "furlough" (vacation). As for carpets [apparently at his home]: "they are so liable to turn up and trip me." He preferred bare floors. Bramwell had edited an article "about the sea" William had written; his father termed it "a very poor affair." On sending a "better class of men" to the Hadleigh Farm in Essex, he agreed with Bramwell. London was experiencing "distress" and there were riots in Glasgow. He found South African newspapers to be up on world affairs. He thought he might cancel his trip to the States. He would like to spend Christmas in India, depending on his health.[27] He wrote about a proposed "Campaign" in Switzerland and his welcome home ceremonies in London.[28]

William had picked up a great deal of intelligence on the rich and well born from hosts like Crewe in East London who gave him the lowdown on contributors to his projects. To Booth, Crewe, who had been Colonial Secretary of the Cape, was "thoroughly reliable," "thoroughly British," and

---

26. William Booth to "My dear Chief," 14 Sept. 1908, from East London. See Isichei, *A History of Christianity in Africa*, 124, on Lovedale. Also see her sparse comments on the Salvation Army in Africa, 202 and 266. For more on Booth's trip see J. Allister Smith, *Zulu Crusade*, 111–14. Tuck, *Salvation Safari*, provides general information, but nothing on Booth's 1908 visit.

27. William Booth to "My dear Chief," 11 Sept. 1908, from East London.

28. William Booth to "My dear Chief," 14 Sept. 1908, from East London.

"anxious for the prosperity of the Country." Crewe advised that "moderate people" and "Dutch people especially," saw the old British colonial regime as mainly working for "De Beers people, and Capitalists generally." Thus Crewe did not view Booth's scheme to bring more British into the country as succeeding. After conferring and praying, Booth decided to go to Rhodesia. Crewe told him that African finance was controlled by "Rothschild (with large holdings in De Beers), Werner, Beit & Co., De Beers, the Chartered, and the Rhodes." For Booth this was "an awkward crowd to be mixed up with, but God knows our motives. I am still loth [sic] to let the thing go. It would be an awful wrench, but I see no alternative."[29] Booth also learned from South African Salvation Army officers, mainly whites, many of whom sympathized with the natives' predicament due to their close association with them. Booth was able to learn from all sorts of folk and the details of conversations did not escape him.

Abe Bailey telegraphed on September 15 to assure Booth that he and Colonel Kitching had met and arrangements were in good order for his Rhodesia trip. The Rhodesia Administrator had agreed to take care of Booth's party "free of charge."[30] After Alice, Booth stopped briefly at Adelaide Station on September 17 and spoke with a brilliant acetylene gas light over his head that "flared and roared all the time I was speaking while myriads of mosquitoes, gnats, and moths whizzed and stung us all through the Meeting." The Mayor, Councilors, and "others of what might be styled the Upper Class" met his train. Of the 1,500 population, 700 attended. After he spoke for fifteen minutes they continued their trip, but a telegram notified them that they would stop for a similar welcome at Bradford. At 11 p.m. the train stopped for the night at Cookhouse where they slept till nine in the morning. At about 4 p.m. on Friday the 18th they arrived at Grahamstown where he had been in 1891. Mr. Fitchat, M.L.A., presided at the Meeting "in the most wooden fashion I have ever known" and served as Booth's host. To an audience of "well dressed, intelligent and kindly people," Booth made a "good speech" to which they responded with "a decent collection." On the 19th, after seven hours of travel through "hills and valleys clothed in the most luxurious of bush I have ever seen in any of my travels," the train reached Port Elizabeth. In all but a few spots where a "solitary Dutchman" cultivated the land, acres that "would maintain cattle or sheep or goats fat and flourishing [were] left to the production of unprofitable growths." The Sunday night meeting on the 20th at the Port Elizabeth Town Hall was

---

29. William Booth to "My dear Chief," 12 Sept. 1908, from East London.
30. Abe Bailey to General Booth, 15 Sept. 1908, from Arundel.

"down right good" with thirty-four "out" for salvation. The next day he held three Meetings in the Feather Market.[31]

On September 18 William had responded to Bramwell's letters Nos. 5 & 6 dated August 28, and a handwritten letter. On health, William expressed concern for Bramwell's "bad throat," which William attributed to "the strain to which you put yourself in connection with your Public Work, especially when you do two or three days at a stretch. . . . The idea of your being incapacitated even for a season makes me shiver. He responded to several matters: an issue he labelled "Kris," the Hellborgs, good news of "the British Field," Dartford, his own good health, "sad news" of Dr. Kidd, Miss Wells' will, Cassel, Treen, Miss Emery, John Cory and Miss Fowler.

On India, William had written to his son-in-law "Tucker" a "long and gossipy letter" as Bramwell had suggested, in order to keep in "touch with him [while] not professing to deal with his business." But William told Bramwell, his intermediary in contacts with the family, that when it came to Tucker's business proposal, "we will not have any such company [making looms]. We cannot have outside money like that without having outside people, and that we will not have." He had ordered that "we would not sell that Bombay Property for less than a certain amount. My decision ought to have been carried out."[32]

The same day he dictated a letter to Bramwell regarding Rhodesia. William found Bramwell's comment about Rhodesia in "Official letter No 5" dated August 28 "very interesting." Bramwell, whose letter we do not have, had written about Lord Selborne, "Governor General of South Africa," an office that William had told him did not exist. Selborne, as "High Commissioner," had commended the Rhodesia scheme and proposed the Marendellas District as "the district of the World." But William had telegraphed and written to say "all that I have to say on the Subject. Really I am getting heartily sick of it, at least I am tonight."[33]

On September 19 Bramwell wrote to "My dear General" his 12th South African Campaign 1908 letter discussing Army business. Commissioner Howard would visit the US and Canada where Eva Booth was in command. The Army had concerns about Russia. Colonel Bates would do an audit on financial problems in India, settle the Bombay property sale, and spend Christmas with Tucker in Simla. Bramwell reported a "considerable increase in the unrest" in India where the government had allowed "the

31. William Booth to "My dear Chief," 18 Sept. 1908, from Grahamstown.

32. "Yours affectionately WB," to "My dear Chief," 18 Sept. 1908, dictated at Grahamstown.

33. "Yours affectionately WB," to "My dear Chief," 18 Sept. 1908, dictated at Grahamstown.

Native press to continue the attacks and criticism of the British Government which are still going on." Bramwell would demote an officer named Horn to Brigadier and give him another appointment after consultation with Commissioners Howard, Higgins, and Kitching. As for labor union accusations that the Army had engaged in "sweating," the newspapers "have not done badly for us, but there are many reports of great bitterness amongst certain classes of the people, and the Labor [unions] have undoubtedly succeeded in making a very widespread impression that somehow we are acting unjustly and unfairly toward the poor people whom we employ." Yet "radical and liberal papers condemn, or at any rate, very feebly support, the attitude of the Labor Party." Bramwell had sent William a copy of Punch that had made a "great impression favorable to us." A. M. Nicol, the Army's Foreign Secretary, had "worked like a slave" on this problem.[34]

From Port Elizabeth on September 20 William wrote a "Private" letter in Kitching's hand. He was being entertained by Mr. McIntosh, M.L.A. He had conversed with him and "Mr. Brown, also a Member of the Legislative Assembly," about the "Native" question, the "one subject of concern in the country." McIntosh had told Booth that Abe Bailey "broke his wife's heart with his immoralities;" she had "died in England with a broken heart." This must "influence our public recognition of him." Bailey had sent a telegram in response to William's question about Dr. Jameson's return to South Africa. Jameson was leaving on the 19th. He would have left earlier if it had not been for "important Rhodesian business." From that William surmised that a "further development has taken place."[35]

William followed with a "private" note on Abe Bailey and "the use to which I think we might put him." Commissioner Isaac Unsworth, the Army's new South Africa commander, might meet him at London's Waterloo Station to tell him that you will be glad to meet him. Unsworth should "get into friendly relations with him as soon as possible." Bramwell should

---

34. "Ever yours Bramwell," to "My dear General," 19 Sept. 1908, from London. "Sweating": The Salvation Army was accused by some in the labor movement of having people in its workshops for the unemployed work long hours for below minimum wages, undercutting other workers. Nicol himself, after leaving the Army, admitted that there had in fact been "sweating." Of the "notorious Harbury Street carpenter's shop," he wrote: "It was alleged that sweating was practised there–I know it was. . . . [A]n arrangement was come to by which both the men and the Army will, I think, eventually be the better." He also averred that "I do not think that the evil associated with this is as serious as has been described. Until the State can devise something better than the casual ward for these out-of-works, it is sheer folly for anyone to assail this rough-and-ready method of affording temporary aid." Nicol, *General Booth and The Salvation Army*, 202, 375.

35. "Private," "Yours ever WB,"—"Continuation from the General," 20 Sept. 1908, from Port Elizabeth.

meet him for an unrushed discussion. He is shy, but Kitching says he is "a genial hearty individual." Bailey had "expressed his admiration for The General" and is "determined to help The S. A. with its work—though how far he may have contemplated doing anything for . . . our South African schemes I do not know." William suggested that Florence, Bramwell's wife, and some women's social officers might "show him something of that side of things." Bailey had told Kitching that he wanted to see "all that he can of us" while he was in England. William wanted to avoid "further humiliation in my anxiety for the scheme." Let's "bring it to a settlement—either to be or not to be." The "advantages and disadvantages are so great—or seem so—that if it can only be brought to a conclusion I should be content."[36]

On September 21 William wrote about a conversation Colonel Kitching had had with Commissioner Richards. Booth had hinted to Richards that he might be the person to head up his Rhodesia project. Richards indicated that he would be willing "if he was properly instructed as to what we should . . . require of him." But after writing to his wife, Richards said that they hoped to "never again be asked to do a Social appointment of any sort whatever. The last one was so full of disappointments and difficulties and unhappiness he could never stand another." William had thought that Richards was more "at home at farms and pigs and goats . . . than at the ordinary duties of a Territorial Commander." But Richards told Kitching that he had joined the Army "for soul saving and the platform . . . rather than for the Social." In the Army social programs were seen as lesser work than soul saving. William was afraid that "this development destroys one of your possible alternatives for the London Men's Social [City Colony]—which is unfortunate."[37]

In yet another letter that day William mentioned Richards' promotion to Commissioner in connection with his "Masonic business." He surmised that "his relationship with [the Masons] is known of by officers and others pretty widely and that it has let him down proportionately with many of them. But whether this in itself is sufficient to prevent us from making a Commissioner of him I am not at all clear." Army regulations forbade Masonic or any other secret society membership. William left it to Bramwell to decide and asked him to use the word DRESDEN in a cable to tell him to go ahead with the promotion; LEIPZIG would tell him not

---

36. "Private," "Yours ever WB" to "My dear Chief," 20 Sept. 1908, from Port Elizabeth.

37. "Yours ever WB," to "My Dear Chief," 21 Sept. 1908, from Port Elizabeth.

make the promotion. Bramwell responded with an ambiguous note: "the Masonic business which I led Poyotte seems to close the door to promotion at present."[38]

In a third note that day William briefed Bramwell on "present ideas" on Rhodesia.

> If the Army chose not to go public to get people to buy shares or to ask the government for land, would it stir up the public? After all, nobody cares about the unemployed. The Chartered Company and Rhodes Trustees do not care, Bailey does not care, the Rhodesian people do not care. And fear about its implications would largely disappear if the Army said nothing about its pity for England's poverty-stricken people; they only care about the home country when they can "get something out of it."

William asked, what if the Army experimented privately with emigration of two classes: "Those who are wanted and can be paid for as workmen; and those who have the means to pay for their own settlement?" If successful the Army could carry out the original scheme with confidence. If not the Army could continue on a small scale with a "private Salvation Army thing" or abandon it. £100,000 would do the job. £150,000 or £250,000 would be better, but in that case the Army would have to take out so many unemployed people that it would be open to criticism on the ground that public money had been furnished for this purpose. Where could the Army get £100,000? Bailey had promised £30,000 that might be £50,000. And Rhodes and the Chartered Company could each contribute £5,000 or £10,000 a year for 5 years. "There you have the £100,000 or more, or the £150,000."

William was sensing a problem in depending on public funds. Bramwell had cabled to say that the government was willing to "keep the matter open until my return." William had no idea what that meant and had "no further information to give them." He would have to go to Rhodesia with a question: "Shall I proclaim the impression made upon me, if it is a good one . . . before ascertaining for certain whether anything can be done to carry out my scheme in it?" Bramwell knew that William's "notion was that something should have been settled and that while I was on the ground I should plant a tree or turn a sod—or said or done something that would have been equivalent to saying 'This thing is going to be done!'" William asked Bramwell not to worry that it would break his heart to give up the Rhodesia scheme—"so far as my present feelings are concerned. It won't."[39]

38. "WB," to "My Dear Chief," 21 Sept. 1908, from Port Elizabeth. Richards was later promoted.

39. "Yours ever, William Booth," to "My Dear Chief," 21 Sept. 1908, from Port

On September 22 Abe Bailey wired Colonel Kitching that a "special engine and a De Beers car" would be available to General Booth for his Rhodesian trip.

On the September 24 and 25 William wrote to Bramwell en route to Kimberley to catch his train for Rhodesia. His South African "Campaign" had pleased him beyond expectations. He would return to London on October 31 and then go to Berlin for Repentance Day. But he wanted an exact calendar of his future travels. The Labor Party charge that the Army was "Sweating" workers was "a perplexity." South Africans had heard of it but had "a supercilious smile as though they attached no importance to it." Although it was important in England, South Africa had "no white Working Men; it is the colored men who constitute that Class." William had not heard news of a Trafalgar Square protest meeting, but was sorry that Bramwell's idea for answering the charges did not succeed. "It was hardly likely that we should have anybody who could meet their babble." Bramwell proposed to retain a reporter, F. A. MacKenzie, to deal with the press on the matter, mainly the "Amalgamated Press" to which MacKenzie belonged. The Lancashire strike and "the poverty of the coming Winter" would give Labor more fodder for "vituperation" than the Army's plea for help for "seventy poor creatures at Hanbury Street [an East End] shelter for poor women." Bramwell should go ahead with his idea to set up a Defense Department.[40]

Following his previous reference to Rhodesia as a "trying anxiety" and "bewildering perplexity," a voice seemed to say to William, "we must deal with it" unless problems are impossible. Abe Bailey had told him about the BSAC's problems. Bailey had bought £200,000 worth of debentures to help save the company. William questioned Bailey's confidence but thought the Imperial Government might take over the Company and the debentures would be safe. William hoped that a government take-over would put the Army in a better position to carry out its scheme. An "agreement" had assumed that the government would furnish money directly or as a loan. If it was a loan the government would see "that it is honestly used for the purpose for which it is acquired." If it were a gift Booth would agree to use it to transfer the unemployed to their settlement and arrange to be repaid by them. The loan repayments would be used to help other people migrate. If the government took over the BSAC, the Army must come to an understanding with the M.P. John Burns, the only cabinet member who might

---

Elizabeth.

40. "Yours affectionately, WB," to "My dear Chief," 24 & 25 Sept., 1908, dictated en route to Kimberley.

be a problem.[41] Since repayment of loans to emigrants to Canada had gone well, the Army assumed that émigrés to southern Africa would repay what the Army spent on them. William commended Bramwell for "securing a repetition of their offer" from BSAC's Dr. Jameson. Abe Bailey and Tilden Smith had assessed the Chartered's Directors, apart from Dr. Jameson, as "a lot of—fools," and even Jameson would do little "unless there is somebody with a goad behind him all the time, except it comes to grouse shooting and golfing."

William added to his previous idea that the Army might get by without government aid or a private sale of shares. If the Army could "be clean rid of dealing with the unemployed, that is people without money; and then I should think a much smaller amount would enable us to make the experiment, seeing that it would be possible to get a few hundred Settlers (Families) who would have money of their own." He was willing, even anxious, to go in a non-philanthropic direction. But he reasoned that such emigrants "would not be as likely to be amenable to law and directions as those who were without, or who had only a little." On the whole he concluded that "our original plan of settling people of different grades of financial ability would be best."

Kitching heard from a former school-fellow at Ackworth, now employed by De Beers as an engineer. He had worked for the Rhodesia government for seven or eight years and spoke of the country in a "rapturous manner." He left because his new wife "could not stand the solitude." His concern about the Army's scheme was the lack of markets, but William recalled that "people who landed on the Boston Rock in the Mayflower had no Markets," only "trackless forests, and savage Indians, and wild beasts, and stormy seasons, and all manner of difficulties to contend with, and yet see what has followed." He noted in his questionable history that America's Pilgrims had a seaboard settlement and strong religious principles. He hoped that the Army's settlers might also have special advantages, including a forty or fifty hour journey, a railway car, heat, and uncertainty of success. He would keep his opinion to himself until he returned to London, although "I have said something about this elsewhere."[42]

Kimberley's Mayor Sagar, Councilors, Clergy, and leading citizens greeted Booth at the Station. He had held meetings at Uitenhage and Cradock along the way and hoped that his health would hold up till he returned from Umtali to Capetown, about 150 hours. Given that he faced a "heavy

---

41. Formerly an Independent Labour MP and now Liberal, Burns was President of the Local Government Board 1905–14 in the Liberal administration.

42. "Yours affectionately, WB," to "My dear Chief," 24 & 25 Sept., 1908, dictated en route to Kimberley.

Campaign" after his return to South Africa and then London, he expected it "will be one of the greatest strains that I ever went through in my life." If he could "climb unassisted the side of the 'Carisbrooke Castle,' I think I shall have much cause for gratitude, and have a claim for a little forbearance, if not a little rest when I get back to [his home at] Hadley Wood." He stayed at De Beers Sanatorium, a large hotel surrounded by gardens, used by De Beers "Magnates" when they inspected their mines, and by friends and "distinguished visitors." Sagar, a "Jew," emphasized the "strong position of the Diamond Syndicate," in which William fancied that Jews had a "strong pull." He had heard of Lord Rothschild's investments, but Sagar said the principal owners were the Joels, whom Booth knew as "Successors of the Barnatos."[43]

On September 26 William handled Army business. He signed a Power of Attorney for Tucker in India and worked on an Appeal [for funds] letter. Catching up on his newspaper reading he noted a Liberal government MP's defeat in Newcastle by the "Liquor Traffic," and mentioned a great improvement in the Diamond Market that "ought to make it possible for the Rhodes Trustees to do something in the way of assisting our Scheme." Labor "Riots in Manchester" were a "sign of troubles to come;" a £50,000 loan would soon be "swallowed up in soup and that . . . very largely by the loafing section of the Community." He had a "Good Meeting" on the 25th, although "stiff and cold," and would have a "Conversazione" that afternoon. He was "getting heartily tired" of "this sort of Campaigning" and needed "new kinds of Lectures" or else he would abandon it. He was less comfortable with social lectures than with revival preaching.

Concerning Rhodesia, William received a cable from Bramwell: "After careful consideration—Cannot recommend—Smaller—Price per—Head—Very much—Increased—Colonists—With—Capital—A limited number—Chartered—Have had no business Relations with—Government—Have ascertained—Nothing will be done without—Parliament—Lovechief." Such, apparently, was their code. William took the tone to be "anything but cheering." But he assumed that Bramwell had not understood the question he had asked and responded: "I told Kitching that you would not." William was convinced that securing £250,000 was impossible. The Liberal government would not make the loan "unless they have made up their minds to defy the Socialists (Labor Party)."

Since Bramwell had said that the BSAC and Rhodes Trustees were moneyless, William felt that "the whole thing is a practical slump and actually at an end, and the terrible journey that is before me seems like a piece

---

43. "Yours affectionately, WB," to "My dear Chief," 24 & 25 Sept., 1908, dictated en route to Kimberley.

of cruel madness." He had sufficient evidence that "this is not God's plan, and therefore must be abandoned." And they had no promise of "the necessary and suitable quantity of land." Bramwell would see Bailey, but William would "not care very much if I were not to be the butt of all manner of enquiries from Press and Platform between now and then."[44]

On the train on September 26 to Mafeking where he would pick up the Rhodesia Railways line William's unsteady hand wrote that in Kimberley he had failed to get information on the practicality of the scheme. No one seemed to know anything reliable about Rhodesia and his time there would be too short to form a judgment about the land. His aides would gather information, but he needed "a sensible man" to judge reports given to him by biased people. He had asked Bailey to tell him if there was "suitable land," his own or anyone else's worth inspecting. He had heard that the BSAC had disposed of all the land that was worth anything. Bailey only advised him to ask for advice from the BSAC Administrator in Salisbury. At this point William favored having £150,000 before commencing operations. After his party gathered information, if he was certain that the scheme was feasible, he would see if financing could be secured.

Booth had learned that South Africans wanted to save De Beers' reputation and believed that the mines would be working in a few months. At present 1,500 or 2,000 fewer (white) hands were employed than had been and they worked five rather than six days a week. Yet diamond output was strong and there was a large inventory. De Beers' aim in the work slowdown was to keep the price up and keep the number of diamonds on the market from growing. Thus the status of poor whites was that they feared being driven out or becoming a perpetual burden. A large investment would provide for them to be placed on the land. But should it be a large or a small scheme?[45]

On September 26 a glitch caused Kitching to wire the BSAC Administrator in Salisbury that Kimberley's railway people had no knowledge of travel arrangements for Booth's party to travel from Vryburg to Salisbury. Ten days earlier Booth's Director of Land Settlement had written to Captain Masterman in Salisbury to make the train arrangements for his party of eight to travel in Rhodesia. Booth would arrive at Marandellas, about forty-five miles south-east of Salisbury, on Wednesday the 30th at 11:30. Since his party would be guests of the Administration, "His Honour" had asked Masterman to provide transport. Booth would leave Marandellas for

---

44. "Yours affectionately, WB," to "My dear Chief," 25 Sept., 1908.
45. "Yours," to "My Dear Chief," 26 Sept., 1908, train: Kimberley to Mafeking.

Salisbury on Thursday afternoon or Friday morning. Since Marandellas was past Salisbury they would pass the capital and then return by the same rail route.

Colonel Kitching asked the BSAC Administrator to wire immediately to "instruct all parties concerned." The Administrator wired Kitching that the Kimberley traffic master had been told to arrange for the "general's saloons" to proceed. He had been informed on Monday that arrangements had been made. He regretted inconvenience to "general Booth" and trusted that everything was now satisfactory and they could proceed to Marandellas on Monday."[46]

On September 27 Kitching wrote to "My Dear General" on what he had discovered about Rhodesian land. He had met C. D. Wise, head of the British South Africa Company Laws and Estates Department. Wise listed lands suitable to the Army's purpose in the Hartley, Lomagundi and Mazoe Districts, contiguous to each other. They discussed the health situation in Hartley. Wise assured Kitching that although at one time the District was "unhealthy, it is now much improved." The district's medical men assured him that it was almost clear of malaria. In a short time it would be free from it, and "as healthy as any of the most healthy parts of the country." The altitude ranged from 3,250 to 3,850 feet at the top of the watershed. All three districts were suitable for agriculture and cattle. Tsetse Fly problems were in a small area of Hartley east of the railway and not at all on the west. Rainfall averaged 32 to 34 inches a year, "fairly well spread over the year." He would supply copies of Official Meteorological Reports.

Kitching told Wise that he was surprised that they had invited Booth to Marandellas, since it was unsuitable and the Fareus area land had been given out. Wise said that when Sir William Milton told him of Booth's visit he had immediately asked, "Whatever does the General want to go to Marandellas for? That is not the place for him! Cannot we get him to stop and look at the Hartley District instead?" After conferring they concluded that Booth had a day to spare and wanted to spend it in a district renowned as a health resort. He wanted to see all that he could from the Railway and chose Marandellas as a stopping place due to his train schedule.

Kitching tried to get Wise to admit "the inconsistency of this line of argument with the statements he made to Comm. R[ichards] and myself yesterday." Instead he claimed that "he had not the Facts in his view when speaking yesterday." Kitching asked why Wise took Comm. B[?] and Col. Jacobs to Marandellas. Wise said that he told them that he was about to

---

46. Colonel Kitching to Administrator, Salisbury, no date, Stationmaster, Kimberley. Administrator to Col. Kitching, 26 Sept. 1908, Warrentown, sent 7:55 p.m., arrived 8:30 p.m.

leave for an inspection tour of Marandellas and they had asked to join him. He agreed, but warned that they would gain little by doing so since the land was unsuitable for the General's scheme. Furthermore Salisbury knew nothing about the Chartered Company's recent renewal of its offer of land. The last telegram from London had arrived on May 3 and said that "negotiations with the S. A. having broken down all reservations on lands might now be withdrawn."[47]

Concerning Marandellas William wrote an angry letter to Bramwell on the return trip from Salisbury to Cape Town on October 3. He recalled that he had agreed to visit Rhodesia in a hurry because of pressure from Bailey. William thought, "in my simplicity," that BSAC people would help him inspect the land and "make my visit useful." Kitching gave Bailey the dates of the visit and was assured that travel and land inspection arrangements would be made. Bailey or the BSAC would cover expenses. They had also asked Bailey if he knew which districts they ought to inspect; he referred them to the Administrator. They had told the BSAC Administrator of their visit, supposing he would recommend districts they should inspect. They told him that Salvation Army officers Hellberg and Jacobs had "strongly recommended" Marandellas. Major Cunningham, in his advance visit to arrange details, had also made plain this interest. When they reached Salisbury, Wise told them that he was going with them, but not a word about the unsuitability of land they were going to visit.

William recalled that he had a hunch that the BSAC had disposed of some of the farms Commissioner Hellberg had visited. He asked Commissioner Richards and Colonel Kitching to go over the list with Wise, who, to their surprise, announced that "the bulk of the lands had been disposed of and those remaining would be of no use to us." William was "dumbfounded," but "since there was no way of getting back to Salisbury," he decided to stay at the Marandellas Hotel that night as had been arranged, and visit farms and a BSAC Settlement that had experimented with tobacco and citrus fruits.

Later General Booth felt that a better plan would have been to go directly to Salisbury to see the Administrator. Wise claimed that he had told Hellborg [?] and Jacobs that "the District was in no way suitable for agriculture," only for ranching and growing tobacco and citrus crops, and that farms he showed them were "under offer to Farmers in the Orange River Colony." He knew of nothing "suitable for our purpose" anywhere in the country. Hartley was "unhealthy" and all of the farms within thirty miles of the Railway had been sold. Land beyond that could not be inspected due

---

47. T. H. Kitching to "My Dear General," 2 October, 1908, from Salisbury.

to a lack of horses and conveyances. William saw that "we should have sent Majors Cunningham and King, and Mr Kingwell around straight away as they could have had a look round and joined us on our way back."

Thursday night they returned to Salisbury. Booth immediately met BSAC Administrator Sir William Milton, who said that he had not been consulted and that he supposed Booth had wanted to go to Marandellas. Booth read from Milton's manner that "he either felt no interest or had no faith in the Undertaking, or that there was somebody about him, or above him, who were opposed to the Success of the Scheme." Booth saw the BSAC's "pusillanimity and ... vacillation all along" as a result of a belief of Wise and other Officials that they could bring in Settlers without the Army's assistance. Wise and his assistant Morris, who owned 10,000 acres with his father on top of his salary, maintained that a farmer could not survive without 3,000 acres; "with 1,000 acres a man must starve." On the return from Marandellas Richards and Kitching insisted that they knew that tracts of land that were suitable were available. Wise insisted that Land Syndicates had bought all large tracts, and that there was nothing in the 40,000 acre category. Milton was surprised that Wise had said so much to Booth. Booth had sent Kitching to meet Milton to submit a list of lands the Army had looked at. Milton had acknowledged "that the List was to be depended upon" and he "would back it," especially Districts listed as "No 1."

Booth and his advisers decided that Sir William Milton's main advisors, perhaps excepting Mr Wise, had no antipathy for the Scheme and would like to see it tried. Kitching especially felt this with regard to Marshall Hole, the Chief Secretary, and "a superior and well educated person." Booth's party passed through the Hartley District on their way back to South Africa. They watched through the windows and made inquiries at stops from those who came to greet them. They agreed that "the District presents a marvelous opportunity for the experiment, and the idea of four million acres all intact greatly modifies the Marendellas disappointment." Milton and Wise asked Booth to send his experts to inspect the land in the Hartley District for two or three weeks with the BSAC's assistance. Kitching wrote to Milton "to say that the thing now appears more likely than it did at the first blush," and that the offer must hold until Booth met Dr. Jamieson, which he would do on Wednesday, and "have time to arrive at a decision."[48]

On October 7 William wrote to Bramwell from Cape Town, the last day of his six-week tour of South Africa and Rhodesia. Bramwell had sent official letters 11, 12, and 13, and enclosures for William's consideration. William

---

48. "Yours affectionately WB," to "My dear Chief," 3 Oct. 1908, en route from Salisbury to Cape Town.

was about to leave for Groote Schuur, Dr. Jameson's residence. Jameson would send a motor car for him. Booth believed that Jameson wanted him to see the late Cecil John Rhodes' residence. He was ready to give Jameson his "line" which was that he could not comment on Rhodesia, since he had only seen it from the railway car due to the bungled arrangements.

But Booth had studied the ground plans and decided that if the districts the BSAC offered were healthy, and if he could assume that there would be "sufficient financial assistance," the scheme could be a success. William and Bramwell differed on his view that the scheme could begin on a small scale and grow. William thought that the large amount of land and money they were asking for had caused difficulty with those who knew that settlers had succeeded with smaller amounts. He argued that the Salvation Army could start with £50,000 and be astonishingly successful. William thought that if the BSAC would provide 4,000,000 contiguous acres of the Army's choosing from 12,000,000 to 13,000,000 acres that the BSAC had "bracketed together," then it would be "folly to let it slip," and if it did it would not be his fault. If they went ahead with Rhodesia, they would need to brief Cunningham or Richards in England on "what we want," and "hear what they propose." Booth would begin with one settlement and use its products to extend the work as the Army was able.

In other business, William was convinced that he and Bramwell must improve their cable transmissions to avoid confusion. He told Bramwell that he felt well enough to take on a Switzerland "campaign," since "I believe in whipping the willing horse, and pushing the thing that is already on the move." He was to write an introduction to a new Staff Review publication. He commented on MacKenzie's Social Report whose "dashing romantic and running style" accorded with what Salvationists like and with what was successful in the case of "The Abandoned Child." He referred to a Lloyd-George "scandal," possibly involving the wife of his election agent. The Liberals had won the election of 1906 and formed a new government which was passing new social legislation, such as the Old-Age Pension Bill in 1908. William was pleased that Lloyd-George had denied the accusation, but "the beastly falsity will be there and leave a nasty impression, and do him harm in the future. How ready the human heart is to take up anything that will lower a man in the estimation of the public."

On "sweating" charges against the Salvation Army being made by labor unions and the Labor Party, Bramwell sent a pamphlet for William to read. William attacked "the lying, jealous, God-hating crowd who have so senselessly attacked us," and hoped to "turn the tables on the Labor Party—both Socialistic and Trade Unionist wings—by associating them with the speeches of Trafalgar Square [protest rally]." He said "the same applies to the Mansonian [John Manson's book had attacked the Army] parties."[49] An official Salvation Army historian wrote that Manson had a negative effect on Member of Parliament John Burns' attitude toward Booth.[50] The General claimed that although he was "not agitated on the subject," when he returned to London he would "certainly say something very strong if I am spared until Monday night next."

On Commissioner David Lamb's Emigration plan to send the unemployed as settlers to Canada, Booth saw no potential problem with "health or markets or native labor or any of the difficulties that must necessarily face us here" in Rhodesia. He hoped that Ontario's Prime Minister Whitney would help. He wondered about other likely countries and areas for emigration of Britain's unemployed, even a passing thought of the American state of Texas that would interest Mr. Brattenbridge who had travelled with Booth to South Africa on the "Walmer Castle."[51]

General Booth had heard no one in his six weeks in South Africa express a desire to return to England. The climate, most of the year, is "enchanting," "moderate," or "endurable." And "Rhodesia is the best of the lot." He was sorry to hear of the death of Commissioner Howard's son in India, a "brave, beautiful, valuable boy. I wondered at the time whether it was wise to risk so valuable a life in India—so young and so promising." Kitching had gone to Pretoria to see Lord Selbourne at Government House and had become ill, likely with diarrhea, so William was without his trusted aid; he was now dictating his letters to Major Deverell.[52]

William recalled his Rhodesia discussion with "Jamieson"[53] at Groote Schuur for Bramwell, "one of the most beautiful places conceivable" with a view that "equals anything within my recollection." On "the Marandellas incident," Mr. Stevens had briefed Jamieson, who saw "Wise as a fool" and said that they were getting rid of him as soon as possible. They had paid him a "large sum of money." Booth noted that such a sum, along with his own expenses, "might have made up all that I asked for," and Jamieson "did not deny it." Jamieson called Sir William Milton, "a good man in the Office, but an ass out of it." He promised to send Stevens to instruct him to do every-

49. Manson, *The Salvation Army and the Public*.

50. Wiggins, *The History of The Salvation Army*, vol. V.

51. Dictated to Major Deverell who apparently forgot to get William's signature on the letter to "The Chief of the Staff," 7 Oct. 1908, from Cape Town.

52. Dictated to Major Deverell, "With all affectionate remembrances to Flo, whom I hope is safely home, and the children, and all concerned. Believe me. Your loving Father. WB, to The Chief of the Staff." Cape Town, 7 October 1908.

53. Those to whom Booth dictated spelt the name both as "Jameson" and as "Jamieson."

thing he could to get information regarding suitable land, and would write Marshall Hole to the same effect. Jamieson said that neither the BSAC nor the Rhodes Trustees would have any money until they had received support for a railway they were constructing.

Dr Jamieson explained the complex financial situation of De Beers, Rhodes and the BSAC. William told Bramwell that Jamieson told him that "with the payment of the first Dividend of De Beers then Rhodes would do £10,000 a year for five years, and as to the Chartered [BSAC], if the Government would give them the guarantee of the money they ask for so as to enable them to borrow at three instead of five percent for their Railway, the Chartered would do the same." Booth asked Jamieson if the Government gave the Salvation Army the £100,000 he had requested, would the BSAC and Rhodes Trustees give him £5,000 a year for ten years. Jamieson was "rather smitten with the idea," but he returned to the railway financing problem "and as good as said that if they could not get the guarantee for the Railway they would go to smash." So Booth came away with what he saw as a promise of land, but no money. Booth told Jamieson that Bailey might get some rich men interested in Rhodesia to join him in giving £50,000, but nothing of Bailey's personal promise to give £10,000.

Booth again pondered two ideas. If the Army failed to get £150,000 to £250,000 from the BSAC, Rhodes trustees, or the British government, to send the unemployed to Rhodesia, then the Army would ask those who could pay their own way to do so and begin a settlement that cost "£150 [thousand?]." Or they could raise £100,000 and do it without the unemployed. Booth thought that "In either case you make the experiment and if it is successful you will get plenty more, and if not you work steadily on, but I will say no more, and I don't know that you will understand this."[54] In the event, it was not possible to proceed with either of these plans.

---

54. "Yours affectionately, WB," to "My dear Chief," 7 Oct. 1908, from Cape Town.

Chapter 6

The Salvation Army and the Rhodesian State, 1908–65

> It seems likely that the Army's work in Africa fell between two stools: it was a Western mission, but it lacked educational and medical programs that larger missions had. It came with an evangelical message, contrasting "spirit-filled officers" with "educated pastors" but lacked the freedom from European control and an adaptation to the African world which, together with the practice of healing through faith, form the strength of independent churches.
>
> —John Coutts[1]

To better control the African population, particularly in the wake of the First Chimurenga of 1896–97, the British South Africa Company created "Native Reserves" comparable to "reservations" the American government created for its indigenous population after its Civil War in the 1860s. Two key differences should be kept in mind. In the United States reservations were based on treaty obligations, however poorly kept, with native tribes. And, unlike Rhodesia, the American natives, by the 1860s, made up a minority of the population. This does not diminish the scandal of the theft of native lands and the debasing of native customs as "pagan" that must be replaced by cultures of allegedly "Christian" Western civilizations in both Africa and North America.

---

1. Coutts, "Half a Century in Nigeria," *Salvation Army Yearbook, 1970*, 19–22.

BSAC Rhodesians created the first African native reserves in Matabeleland, the area around Bulawayo. In 1894, after the defeat of Ndebele King Lobengula, the BSAC sent Ndebele-speaking natives to Gwayi and Shangani Native Reserves. Mashonaland's Native Reserves for Shona-speakers followed the First Chimurenga (1896–97). White settler occupation of land outside the reserves meant taking the most fertile agricultural lands, seizing cattle, "expropriation of wildlife hunting rights, and the creation of exclusive forest reserves," according to historian Sam Moyo. What was left, almost always the least arable, was set aside for the Native Reserves. Professor Moyo found that "while the indigenous population was sparse at the turn of the century, with densities below three persons per square kilometre, as population grew and land alienation ensued, black people's access to fertile and arable lands declined rapidly, and so did the natural resources."

By 1980, the year of African independence (majority rule), land use experts argued that "over 66 percent of the [African] communal lands had excess populations of more than double their assessed carrying capacities."[2] In addition, white settlers had also used the Native Reserves' people as sources of labor for white agricultural, mining and industrial enterprises. This was particularly the case in the 1930–70 period, during which rapid growth of the Rhodesian economy's demand for development capital occurred. By the end of the colonial era in 1980, whites, only 4 percent of the Zimbabwe population, occupied most of the commercially viable land, according to C. Rossiter.[3]

But before the British South Africa Company had begun to gather Africans onto Native Settlements in order to remove them from Rhodesia's prime real estate, its administrators had offered Christian missions some of the best land it had expropriated from the Shona around Fort Salisbury. In Matabeleland the BSAC had taken land to give to the Jesuits in 1890.

In summary, in 1892 the BSAC had given the Salvation Army a Mazoe Valley farm on land occupied by the Shona people of the Hwata dynasty. The BSAC also gave the Army a couple of urban plots in Salisbury. On each addition to its property the Army eventually established a church, a state-financed primary school, and when possible, a clinic. When there was a

---

2. The 1924 Mazoe Native Commissioner's Report on the Chiweshe Native Reserve (an infertile plateau to which people were deported from the fertile Mazoe Valley to make room for European settlement) described it as over-populated, overstocked and suffering deforestation. (Report in Zimbabwe National Archives.) The population of Chiweshe was then around 5,000; by 1970 it was over 50,000.

3. Moyo, *The Land Question in Zimbabwe*, 129–32, 106; see Whitlow, "Environmental Constraints and Population Pressures in the Tribal Areas of Zimbabwe"; see Rossiter, *The Bureaucratic Struggle for Control of U.S. Foreign Aid*.

village school on the land the state paid most of the Salvation Army officer-primary teacher's salary. This arrangement continued until a white-settler Rhodesian Republic under Prime Minister Ian Smith ended the practice in 1971 by placing primary education under the control of local councils.

Major Charles Clack, the Salvation Army commander in Salisbury in 1908, initiated a social scheme for urban white settlers as a result of General Booth's Rhodesia visit. Clack established a "city colony" in Salisbury, the first stage of Booth's social reform plan that aimed to train the urban unemployed in workshops prior to moving them "back to the land." But Clack's program began and ended in the city, in spite of his pleas to the British South Africa Company (BSAC) to provide the Army with a settlement farm like those Rhodes had given to the Army in the Cape Colony, Natal, and the Transvaal, in South Africa. That did not happen in Rhodesia. In fairness, the BSAC may have felt the Army's Mazoe farm, already given by Rhodes, might serve this purpose.

Therefore, instead of the Army's three-stage, back to the land program, Clack adapted Booth's plan to accommodate a modified reform program acceptable to Salisbury's city government and business leaders. He would first help unemployed white settlers find jobs in the city. If he failed in that he would send them on their way, "out of the country," passing transient workers on to other places to seek either employment or a handout, generally termed "outdoor" charity. By May 1909 Clack managed to get Salisbury's city government to agree to finance the Army's aid to "wayfarers." This plan kept them from going door to door begging from Salisbury citizens who would refer them to the Army. Clack also asked merchants to help him find work for those who encountered misfortune "through no fault of their own." In abolishing "indiscriminate charity," by finding work for those on the public dole, Clack received the applause of the *Rhodesia Herald*'s editor.[4]

After 1909 the Salvation Army in Rhodesia also developed a strategy to evangelize, teach, and heal Africans. Like other church missions the Army built its native policy on financial support the BSAC government offered in the form of land grants and financial stipends for schools and clinics. BSAC policy was rooted in a paternalistic attitude of whites who held Africans and their culture in contempt and thus strove to Westernize and Christianize them.

In 1905 Staff-Captain Robert Sandall had written in the Army's missionary journal *All the World* that schools would make a difference for a native population south of the Zambesi River, which he estimated at 10 million.

4. "Unemployed," *Rhodesia Herald*, May 28, 1909; "The Unemployed," *Rhodesia Herald*, Sept. 24, 1909, 3.

Sandall saw himself as a progressive educator. He held that "there appears to be in the native mind no inherent incapacity to comprehend the truths of Christian teaching, or to adopt Christian morals as a standard." He believed that African culture was based on "debasing habits and customs" that led to "childishness," but this could be overcome through what he regarded as the Africans' "universal desire for education." This would be the missionary's best key to altering African culture. Nevertheless with William Booth he urged missionaries to remember that "school is but a means to an end." Education was not the African's total salvation.

Soul-saving evangelism must be the principal goal, a position held by all Salvation Army missionaries. But on the basis of Sandall's philosophy the Army gradually opened schools that the Rhodesian state regulated and supported with financial grants.[5] These institutions, mainly village primary schools for rural Africans, operated separately from the Army-run urban social services for white settlers that began in 1908, also with state support and regulation.

This led the Salvation Army to a question that likely occurred to all Christian missions in Rhodesia, although the issue became a particular goad to missions that, like the Army, were financially challenged. Could the Army's missionary officers run churches, social agencies, schools, and hospitals solely with gifts from supporters back home, or from donations by local white-run businesses and British charitable trusts, or from the meagre offerings and fees it charged its African members? Or must the Army rely heavily on government grants and the regulations that accompanied them? The answer became increasingly obvious between 1908 and 1965.

While at first the Salvation Army begged the state for grants of money and land for which it was grateful, over time it found itself increasingly at the mercy of a BSAC–Rhodesian government run by white settlers. Would financial support from the Rhodesian state and from other external secular sources cause the Army to modify its approach to social services and even its evangelistic ministry? Yes. Since the state had the power to open or close mission-run schools and hospitals if they did not satisfy state examiners, the Army had to bow to the state's oversight. The Army's corps (church) depended on income derived from the village, state-supported, primary school to support its officer's salary since he or she was expected to be the primary school's teacher-administrator. It was the corps officer's stipend for teaching that made it possible for the Army to have a corps in the village.

Did the Army's international headquarters in London plead for the principle of separation of church and state? Did the General direct the

---

5. Sandall, "Native Work in Africa," *All the World*, Oct. 1905, 541–54.

Army's leaders in Rhodesia to relinquish the state's largess and control if it interfered with their evangelical missionary agenda? Did the state's educational standards for teachers make it difficult for the Army to recruit and train African and expatriate (foreign) officers so that they would qualify to teach at the village school? Seldom did the Army resist state regulations, and when it did it was nearly always to no avail. Were the Army's leaders in London and Salisbury frustrated by state regulation? Yes. But they found no way to avoid it without cutting off the financial aid which allowed them to continue to operate their village corps.

Much of the concern of Salvation Army leaders in Salisbury and London between 1908 and 1965 revolved around the extent to which the Army's religious mission was affected by its reliance on money that only the BSAC or settler-run Rhodesian state could supply. The colonial state was prone to confine its support to African education and health, although it offered additional social services to whites. Globally many Salvationists saw social programs in general, even when William Booth promoted them, as diversions from the Army's main task of being a Christian, soul-saving mission.

Local Salvationists holding an open-air meeting in a village, 1930s.

Salvation Army congress meeting near Howard Institute in the late 1930s.

In the twenty years after General William Booth visited Rhodesia in 1908 the Salvation Army opened 167 corps (churches) and ninety-one outposts. Two of the 167 corps, one in Salisbury and one in Bulawayo, had only white European soldiers (members).[6] This meant that roughly 98 percent of Rhodesia's Salvationists were Shona or Ndbele speaking Africans. An Army missionary officer, Leonard A. Kirby, claimed that in 1925 "6,000 people [attended] the Howard Congress [annual summer camp meeting]."[7] Not all of them were members of the Army, but all were African. The Army's historian in Zimbabwe, Major Misheck Nyandoro, says that by 1931 the Army had 4,458 soldiers in Rhodesia (all senior and junior members above the age of 8), 1,214 recruits, and 137 officers. The Army ranked at least seventh among Rhodesia's churches in membership. It may have been at the top in its percentage of African members.

How comparable are statistics provided by various denominations? It depends on who they count as "members." If for example, Anglicans, Roman Catholics, and Methodists counted all baptized members (including infants) their figures would be greater than the Salvation Army count of members over the age of 8. And there is always the issue of whether nonactive or deceased members are removed from church rolls. If numbers provided by E. W. Smith are fair approximations of reality, they indicate that

---

6. Nyandoro, *Flame of Sacred Love*, 204, provides Salvation Army membership statistics for 1931.

7. Kirby, "Early Days in Rhodesia," 5.

by 1927 the mission churches ranked in the following general order: Anglicans had 21,898 members; Roman Catholics, 20,657; Wesleyan Methodists, 9,763; Dutch Reformed, 9,438; American Methodist Episcopal, 8,176; Seventh Day Adventist, 2,650; London Missionary Society, 2,273; American Board Mission, 2,100; Brethren in Christ, 1,206; and Swedish Church Mission, 507.[8] While Smith leaves the Salvation Army out of his count, perhaps because he did not regard the Army as a church, its 4,458 members would have placed it behind the American Methodists in sixth place. If the Army's junior members and children who were "dedicated" (the Army's replacement for infant baptism) were counted, it could have ranked much higher—assuming that Anglicans, Catholics, and Methodists were counting baptized children. Thus it is apparent that by 1931 the Salvation Army was succeeding statistically in its work among Africans, with the financial support of the Rhodesian state.[9]

Although the Rhodesian government made its first grants-in-aid for African education in 1901, by 1904 there were still only three African schools in Rhodesia. Not until 1927, four years after the British South Africa Company transferred government control to white settlers, did the state appoint the first Director of African Education, assisted by three school inspectors. Prior to this there was one department for both white and African schools. In 1947 the government began to pay all approved teachers' salaries in addition to paying capitation amounts for the number of students. The African Education Department produced syllabi for teachers to follow in all classes and it prescribed books for both pupils and teachers. African children began primary school at age 7 when they started to learn English as a second language.

In 1918 the Salvation Army's Staff Captain James Barker opened a school in Bulawayo and listed himself as Superintendent. His wife and children were staff, along with Moses Sebotsiso, who had been educated at a London Missionary Society school. Unfortunately, the School Inspector's report claimed that most of the seventy-seven pupils at the school were "kitchen boys" who "cannot come each night at the same hour." Thus, when Barker called roll at 6:30 only 60 percent of the pupils were present. School Inspector Lenfestey held that since the Army "could not guarantee" attendance the school could not be graded as a Second Class Native School; it did not meet the two-hours of class time requirement. A 1926 inspection at the Bulawayo Railway Reserve Evening School, another Army attempt to

8. Zvobgo, *History of Christian Missions*, 335, cites Smith, *The Way of the White Fields in Rhodesia*, 53, 56–57, 62–66, 69–71.

9. Commissioner A. R. Blowers, "Rhodesian Territory Memorandum," Overseas Dept., International Headquarters, London" (Feb. 1942) 14.

educate Africans, found only eleven of twenty-four on the roll were present. The Second Class Native Mission School had only fifteen of the forty-four on the roll present. A Day School had only twenty-four of fifty-five.

Inspector A. R. MacKenzie was "disappointed." He warned the Army that to keep the Class II status the Native Mission School would need better trained teachers and "more effective supervision." The Director of Education wrote to Adjutant A. M. Anderson that "It is clear that the standard reached in these three schools is considerably below what the Department is intitled [sic] to expect of second class schools; and some part at least appears to be due to the lack of effective supervision." If they did not improve they would be "placed in the 3rd class of Native Schools," which meant that grants "will suffer diminution accordingly." And he would not approve the grant for the Bulawayo Night School for 1926 unless the small paraffin lamp was improved upon.

But in 1928 when African Schools Inspector H. C. Finkle reported on the 600 Matabeleland district schools, he evaluated Salvation Army schools as "very good." Other missions with schools were: Methodists, the biggest; Seventh Day Adventists, next; "Catholica"; Anglicans; then Salvation Army; Church of Sweden; Matopo Mission (Brethren in Christ); Presbyterian, "very small"; and African Methodist Episcopal, "a breakaway church" with four or five schools. First Class Schools were usually those with a Teachers' Training College. Second Class Schools taught students up to Standard Six and had Industrial Work. Third Class Schools were the old Primary School in a Village (Kraal). Fourth Class Schools were Community Schools and Night Schools. Christian missions ran virtually all African schools until the late 1960s.

Under the new white settler Rhodesian government that took over from the BSAC, the capitation system in 1927 provided 5 shillings for the student average daily attendance. There was often only one teacher with eighty to ninety students in twelve to fourteen groups. Order D set teacher qualification standards. A school year began January 5 and ran through September (just before the rains came) for 180 days. In 1928 the government separated African and European Schools. In 1929 the syllabus increased the hours from two to four and weeded out lower-grade teachers who did not meet standards. The Salvation Army realized that it was important to entice students since "without the school the mission wouldn't operate. It was the school that kept the mission going and the church going." But this also meant meeting higher teacher training standards and lengthening the school day.

Reports for Salvation Army Schools in Mashonaland in 1922, by contrast to the School Inspectors' reports for the Army's Bulawayo schools, were on the whole excellent. When the Army first opened a school at Mazoe (Pearson Farm) in 1922, with Captain Leonard Kirby as Superintendent and Ensign Kunzvi Shava as native teacher, the school was an adjunct to the corps (church) program at Pearson Farm. Inspector A. R. MacKenzie found the building "very satisfactory," and the discipline "excellent." Both the academic work in English, arithmetic, and writing, and the Industrial work were "very good." Classes went to Grade V (Native School Code). There were thirty-five boarders with additional students coming from the area. MacKenzie's report in 1923 found the First Class Mission School (Native School Code) to be down to twenty-two boarding pupils, with only fifteen present, but the inspection had come three months early. He found the work to be below the 1922 standard.

Back in 1923, when the British South Africa Company had given the Salvation Army a grant of 105 acres in the Chiweshe Native Reserve north of Salisbury, the Army moved its Mazoe School to the new location along with its training school for Salvation Army officers. As it had done at Pearson Farm (Mazoe), the Army named the new location for an English Salvationist, T. Henry Howard, who had no connections to Rhodesia. "Trouble" at Pearson Farm in the Mazoe Valley had led Captains Kirby and Kunzvi Shava to move to Chiweshe at the invitation of a BSAC Native Commissioner at Concession. At Pearson the Army had been surrounded by white farmers who resented the presence of forty African boarders, thirty African Salvation Army cadets in training, and five staff members on 2,000 acres that they coveted for themselves. Also, another sect had drawn away some of the Army's converts.

When the Salvation Army moved to Chiweshe (Howard) in 1923 it already had five corps in the area. Soon there were eleven. Like Mazoe, Chiweshe was part of the area north of Salisbury in which the Army was the predominant mission.[10] Major James Barker and Captain Kirby chose a site that was closest to the Army's largest corps in Chiweshe, at Nyachuru. There was a good supply of water and the area was covered with forest. Howard became the Army's primary educational center, with a "Practicing School" (a model village school where student teachers could practice in a classroom), a Central Primary School with a boarding section, and schools for training teachers and nurses (after 1939). The Army promised that the place of religion at Howard would be "at all times unobtrusive, but significant."[11]

10. In rural areas most missionary organizations largely opted to operate on the principle of "comity," dividing up a territory into spheres of influence so that they were not in direct competition with one another for proselytes or for school pupils.

11. "Copy of Notes of Interview with Major L. Kirby, Sr., Concerning Beginnings of Howard Institute," at the Salvation Army Archives, London; Captain Caughey

Homecraft class and women Cadets at Howard Institute, late 1930s.

School prefects at Howard Institute, late 1930s.

Under government regulations, all teachers belonged to the Unified Teaching Service, regardless of their religious denomination. They enjoyed

Gauntlett, "Howard," at the Salvation Army Archives, London.

the same terms of service, leave and pension, and were subjected to the same discipline. Teachers had to sign an agreement with the mission for which they worked in which they promised to comply with mission policy. Government grants assisted the travel costs of school managers, generally Divisional Commanders in the Army's case, involved in making school inspections.

Open-air lesson at a village school, 1930s.

The government and the mission expected parents to erect a primary school building in the village, initially made of poles and mud with a grass roof. When they added a second year of schooling, parents made bricks and built a permanent structure, still with a grass roof. When they added a third year class, they placed the school under an iron roof. The Committee of Parents then organized for fund-raising and continued work on buildings. Major Ronald Cox, a Salvation Army school manager in 1966, complained that at times the Parents' Committee had caused trouble for teachers and managers by interfering in "matters of policy and discipline," without having experience in handling money. This led to "heated 'ndabas'," (discussions). But, Cox saw that it was the urgency of their children's need for education that caused them "to make very real sacrifices to give their youngsters a chance of going to school."[12]

Principal reasons for the parents' concern that their children receive a good education were that they depended on them to assist with their own

12. Cox, "Village Schools in Rhodesia," *All the World*, January–March 1966, 4–6; Kendrick, "Missionary Education," *All the World*, July–September 1960, 78.

work and they expected them to care for them in their old age. There was no government pension for the aged. At the time this was not unlike Western countries in the years prior to the development of pension systems. Third World countries lack retirement systems to the present. Few employers provide pensions for African workers and there are no state provisions for disability caused by work-place accidents. Thus a well-educated child provided all of the security that was available to dependent parents.

In 1928 the Rhodesian government, under the control of white settlers rather than the BSAC, provided grants to hospitals. That year a Salvation Army nurse, Adjutant Agatha Battersby, who had prior experience running a dispensary, opened the fifteen-bed Howard Hospital. Howard students were the first to occupy the beds.[13] The connection between the first offer of state funds for hospitals and the Army's opening of Howard Hospital is obvious. In 1939 the Howard Institute added a Nurses Training School, with government support, to train assistant nurses who received a government certificate.

As late as 1967 the Salvation Army still did not provide social services for Africans like those it provided for whites in Salisbury or Bulawayo.[14] But it had an important role in the African educational system in the pre-1965 period until the Ian Smith government took over the operation of schools from the missions.

In the 1930s and 1940s internal Salvation Army memoranda reveal that the Army had become dependent on the Rhodesian government for grants. Army leaders were frustrated with the resulting state control over some of the Army's internal mission policies. For example, in 1931, when the Army's London headquarters separated its Rhodesia command from the South Africa territory, leaders in London advised the new Rhodesia commander on how to deal with government rules and grants. The Rhodesian government, since taking over from the BSAC in 1923, had set a new standard for educational qualifications of teachers at kraal (local African) schools, raising the grade to Standard IV, the eighth year of school.

Since "government grants-in-aid were generous," Salvation Army leaders concluded that they had no choice but to use the same standard for educating its officers (ministers) as the state had set for teachers. This would allow the officer-teacher to draw the stipend for teaching at the state-supported village school located at the same site as the Army's corps (church).

---

13. Zvobgo, *A History of Christian Missions*, 288, 301; Nyandoro, *A Flame of Sacred Love*, 90–93.

14. Salisbury, "Howard Hospital," at the Salvation Army Archives, London; F. J. Adlam's Remarks, Minutes of the Annual General Meeting Held At Howard Institute (29 May 1967) 1.

Army officers, who had been running village schools as well as the Army's village corps, could only qualify for a government stipend if they met the new educational standard. Neither the Army's poor African soldiers, nor its mission funds, were sufficient to provide an officer's salary without the state stipend that came from his/her work as a teacher.[15]

In 1942, Commissioner A. R. Blowers, the Salvation Army's International Secretary for Africa, wrote an internal memorandum at Army's London headquarters expressing his frustration that a secular state was, in effect, dictating the Army's training policy for its officers (ministers). First, Blowers argued that three-fourths of the Army's teachers in Rhodesia were not even Salvationists and therefore did not wear the Army uniform. Yet they were pastors at the Army's corps. This was necessary because the Army did not have enough officers who met the state's educational standard for teachers after the state increased the qualification to Standard V.

So the Salvation Army's dependence on the state's grant and teacher education standard were forcing it to employ non-Salvationists as pastors of its corps as well as non-Salvationist teachers at its primary schools. If it failed to meet the state standard the Army would have to forfeit grants on which it was financially dependent. As a result, at 75 percent of the Army's corps, a non-Salvationist teacher was the pastor. Blowers' problem was that a rural African congregation could not afford to pay the less-educated Army officer to function solely as a pastor, and the Army felt that it could not afford to educate African officers, most of whom came from families of rural peasants, to a Standard V level. Thus to acquire an education stipend the Army had to compromise evangelism and bow at the altar of state regulation. The Army's only alternative was to raise educational standards for its officers-in-training (cadets) to the level the state required for teachers who were studying at the Army's teacher training program at Howard Institute. The Army was susceptible to the tyranny of state regulation due to both the inadequacy of its educational standards for officers and its reliance on state funding.

Blowers also worried that better students, who were drawn to teacher training because of better compensation and social status in the community, were of higher quality than cadets the Army was training to become officers (pastors). Since both future teachers and officers were enrolled on the same campus at Howard Institute, this distinction became blatantly obvious to both groups. The situation had a "psychological effect" on cadets who, according to Blowers, "rarely exceed Standard 5."

15. "Brief for Lt. Col. Archibald Moffat before Becoming 1st Territorial Commander in 1931, prepared by the International Headquarters Overseas Department," Salvation Army Archives, London.

Howard Institute, near the village of Glendale, was the Salvation Army's premier educational center, as well as the site of its best hospital. To operate Howard Institute the Army relied on government grants. For two years, 1939–40, government grants amounted to £2,824. Student fees brought in £1,335. The additional cost to Army funds was £3,349.[16]

At the same time the Army lacked enough officer-teachers to staff village primary schools, it also had a leadership problem. Salvation Army Divisional Commanders supervised both village corps and village schools in their district. For their work as School Inspectors and School Managers they received state stipends that helped cover their Salvation Army salaries (the Army calls the salary an "allowance"). This meant that Divisional Commanders had to have adequate educational credentials to meet state standards for School Inspectors. It also meant that they were taken away from supervision of evangelistic work in corps on a regular basis, although having both the school and the corps at the same site may have meant few additional trips. But the Salvation Army once again had a problem meeting leadership demands when it came to educational qualifications. Colonel Joseph Smith, the Salvation Army's Rhodesia commander in 1943, complained that "no other Church or Missionary Society" in Rhodesia "has such a poor type academically as some of our Divisional Staff." Down to the 1960s the Army drew its Divisional Commanders from white missionaries who were largely from the under-educated rural and urban working classes of England, North America, and Australia/New Zealand, where the Army required no prior college training of its cadets when they applied to enter its officer training schools. Thus both the Army's corps officers in villages and its headquarters supervisors suffered when compared to African pastors and missionary leaders of other denominations. More important for the Army's skimpy financial resources, most officers fell short of the educational standards that the Rhodesian state required of school supervisors.[17]

Beginning in the 1930s with such officers as Thomas Lewis, George Tabor, Kingsley Mortimer and Philip Rive, and increasingly after World War II, university-educated Salvation Army missionaries arrived in Rhodesia from Britain, Europe, North America, Australia and New Zealand.[18] This was not due to higher admission standards at the Army's training schools in those areas, but more likely due to Salvationists' rise into the middle class or educated working-classes in Western countries. It may also have been

16. Blowers, "Memorandum," 2–5.

17. Colonel Joseph Smith, Territorial Commander, "Annual Report to the Chief of the Staff, Rhodesia Territory, 1943," Salvation Army Archives, London.

18. Hill, "Howard: The Years That Have Gone," *All the World* 7.20, July-September 1973, 219–22.

assisted by recruitment of officers from other denominations as had been done throughout the Army's history. While the Army's training schools extended their program from one year to two in 1960, the Army worldwide still did not expect its cadets to have any prior college education. In spite of a few academic courses in bible, doctrine, history, literature, and psychology, the Army did not intend that its officer training program should mimic a liberal arts college. Much of the course work was in practical administrative chores such as bookkeeping, raising of funds to support their work, or public speaking and preaching preparation.

Nonetheless, an increasing number of Salvationists after World War II attended college before or after their officer training program. Fortunately for the Army in Rhodesia, by the 1950s many of the Army's best-educated officers were becoming missionaries. This was particularly true of single women, the Army's chief resource for officer recruitment since the 1870s. In the 1950s women made up over half of the Army's officers, single and married, including its missionaries. And most of the women missionaries taught and administered at the Army's leading mission schools. A smaller number were physicians or nurses at its hospitals.

In the 1950s, as the colonial era began to end with a "scramble out of Africa" by European countries, including Britain, educated Salvationist missionaries also began to see Africa anew. Major Richard Williams witnessed the damage that Europeans had done to Africa's "delicate tapestry of a finely balanced social order." He compared African customs to those in early books of the bible that were "foreign to our Christian [European?] thinking." Under the influence of new anthropological insights, Williams perceived that "primitive" Africa, "untouched by civilization, observed standards of truth, honesty and morality far more closely than its European counterpart." Williams distinguished his thinking from that of pioneer missionaries in Rhodesia who had attacked lobola (bride price) and polygamy, customs that he argued were best understood in terms of African "social necessities that gave rise to the custom." However, he claimed that the Africans' static view of religion did not help them resist "social evils of drink, gambling and vice of all kinds, rampant in towns and [native] locations." He recognized, as did only a few earlier missionaries, that these same habits flourished in the "Christian" West, and that evil persons had taken their evil habits from the West to Africa.

When Williams made the case for a new anthropological study of African culture he did not deny the importance of the Salvation Army's evangelical mission. In fact, he saw the Christian message as the only antidote for preventing Western "civilization" from turning Africans "into an unenlightened, discontented, grasping and half-baked rabble without moral sanctions, a menace to themselves and possibly to the world." He was pleased that the Army was sending Rhodesia "consecrated officers with teaching qualifications and University degrees" to meet the state's new requirements for missionaries with proper credentials.[19] Soon the Southern Rhodesia Director of Native Education would tell a public gathering at Howard Institute that the Army's largest boarding school "was second to none in its academic results." The Army had come a long way since it began in the school business in Bulawayo in 1918.

By 1953, religious organizations were responsible for 98 percent of all elementary education in Rhodesia and the Salvation Army was sixth in the number of students with 14,600, behind the Dutch Reformed, Roman Catholic, Anglican, Methodist (U.K.), and Methodist Episcopal (U.S.) churches.[20] In 1955 Prime Minister Garfield Todd proposed a five-year Plan to spend £12.5 million on education. Two years later the Salvation Army opened its first secondary school, housed at Howard Institute in the Chiweshe Reserve. In 1959 the Army transferred the school to the Pearson Farm, to the site of the late-nineteenth-century mission buildings that the Salvationists left in the area in 1923. The school's new name was Mazoe Secondary School.

By 1960 there were 2,665 African schools in Rhodesia with 388,000 pupils. Yet only 60 percent of African school-age children were in school. Only six out of every hundred Africans who began school in the lowest class completed Standard VI, the eighth year of schooling. Less than 1 percent of those who began school reached Form 4 of Secondary School. That year 90 percent of all African education was still being done by missions, but the Rhodesian government's interest in taking control of African schools was increasing.

Kathleen Kendrick, an English Salvationist officer-teacher at Howard, observed that tensions had increased by 1960 over "white domination" and African resentment against whites, even missionaries, for the lack of opportunity they were providing for Africans in leadership positions. Kendrick was hopeful, nonetheless, that "in spite of the danger of equating western education with Christianity, there lies to our hand here the possibility of raising the intelligent leadership of the future."[21]

The Salvation Army opened a few advanced education programs in the 1930s to 1950s. In 1933 Captain Thomas Lewis started a Teacher Training

19. Williams, "At Work in a Changing World," *The Officers' Review*, Jan. 1948, 28–33; and "Rhodesian Dawn," *The Salvation Army Yearbook, 1950*, 14.

20. For statistics see Holbrook, "Salvationist Survey, XIV—Rhodesia," *The Officer*, Jan. 1953, 35, 38; and Kendrick, "Missionary Education," *All the World*, July-Sept. 1960. 79.

21. Kendrick, "Missionary Education," 78–81.

Program at Howard Institute, whose alumni staffed the Army's primary schools as teachers and often as pastors. In 1939 Adjutant Isabel Sloman began a Nurses Training Centre at Howard Hospital. However the Salvation Army failed to accept Africans into leadership ranks at its headquarters, although between 1950 and 1965 it was sending well qualified teachers, medical missionaries, and administrators from Europe, North America, Australia, and New Zealand to Rhodesia to meet higher standards the Rhodesian government was setting. A similar pattern occurred in nearly every Third World country, but in spite of the interest of missionaries in developing African leaders, the Army's leaders in London and the Third World placed little emphasis on educating Africans for advanced administrative, teaching, and medical work. In 1959, 29 percent (104) of the Army's active officers in Rhodesia were overseas (expatriate) missionaries, whereas 98 percent of its soldiers were African. After almost seventy years in Rhodesia the Army's leadership was still all white.[22]

Many Salvation Army missionaries, especially teachers at its African schools and medical missionaries at its hospitals, including a few at its London headquarters, realized that it had done less than any mission to develop African leaders. The Army was, in fact, a mirror image of the white settler government that had done little to expand the franchise or advance the educational and leadership opportunities of Africans in the Rhodesian state. The Army's argument was that its African officers were less talented than those in other Christian missions, and thus could not be placed in positions that required administrative skills. But this belied its counter-claim that the Army's secondary schools, where many African Salvationists received their education, were outstanding. And it also ignored the fact, noted by its pre-World War II leaders, that its white missionaries were seldom of a quality that could be compared with leaders of other churches.

Why were graduates of Howard, Mazoe, Usher, and Bradley, the four Salvation Army secondary schools opened in the 1950s and 1960s, not rising to the top in the Army's officer ranks? Why, when the Army's General, Wilfred Kitching, visited Salisbury in 1959, did the Rhodesian Salvation Army fail to introduce him to any African business or political leader? Why did he meet the nearly all-white Christian Council of Southern Rhodesia (CCSR), but not councils of African ministers? Misheck Nyandoro observed that of the ten Salvation Army voting members at the SRCC, only two were African: Sr. Captain Joseph Nhari and Sr. Captain J. Chinake.

---

22. "Rhodesia," *Salvation Army Yearbook, 1960,* 156–58.

Of the ten who served on committees, only one was an African, Captain Misheck Nyandoro.[23]

One may conclude that the Salvation Army had accommodated itself to the white Rhodesian culture's view of the inferiority of Africans, while it was trying to meet the Rhodesian settler state's demands that it comply with its regulations. In the 1950s this was not exceptional for European colonies with a minority white population struggling to maintain control. Was the failure to advance Africans in the Salvation Army due to the Army's difficulty in recruiting young educated and talented African Salvationists into its officer-corps? Could African youth have been embarrassed by their affiliation with the Army, a mission to and of the poor? Could this have caused most of them to find employment outside the Army? A more significant factor, already noted, would have been that educated young Africans needed to look for well-paying work, commensurate with their educational qualifications, both for reason of personal ambition and because of family expectations upon them. Those who had sacrificed to pay their school fees looked for some return on this investment, including the willingness of the successful students to support the studies of their siblings and other family members, and their parents in old-age. Salvation Army officer allowances were inadequate for these purposes.

While there were African and missionary voices in the Salvation Army that called for the promotion of Africans to administrative posts, they were not heard. Missionaries who served at schools and hospitals in rural areas, and who had close ties to their African students and patients, bemoaned the Army's failure to develop African leaders. But with few exceptions, the administrators at the Army's headquarters in Salisbury took no decisive action to redirect the Army's leadership development toward Africans.

Major Nyandoro recounts that in 1950 the Salvation Army sent Bernard Mangizi Makone to its International Training College in London, an honor previously restricted to white Rhodesians. Makone took this honor to mean that the Army recognized his leadership potential. But after he returned to Rhodesia from London the Army did not place him in an appointment that he deemed appropriate to his training. He soon resigned from the Army and began his own church, the "Soldiers of God," to whose ranks he recruited disenchanted African Salvationists.[24]

Not until 1963, as tensions built in the African community, did an African Salvation Army officer, Major Joseph Nhari, become a divisional commander, a mid-level administrator, as leader of the Central Mashonaland

23. Nyandoro, *Flame of Sacred Love*, 115.
24. Ibid., 41–42.

Division around Salisbury. In that post the Army kept him under the close supervision of missionary officers who worked in the same headquarters building. Army leaders kept Salisbury's only white corps, Salisbury Citadel (later Harare City) Corps, out of Nhari's command, although it was located in his district. This corps reported directly to the expatriate territorial commander.

By 1965, a "European" school manager in each Salvation Army division supervised up to thirty village schools with a total staff of over 120 African teachers. To open a school the Army had to provide evidence that it was needed and that the parents would build a building and provide equipment. The new school had to be at least three miles from another village school. The school manager hired a staff, properly balanced between trained and untrained teachers who had met the state education standards. In one Salvation Army division (district) there could be over 5,000 children in schools for whom the schools manager had to provide textbooks, pencils, and rulers. The school year commenced in January, the middle of the rainy season, a difficult time for children to pick up their supplies from a central location and carry them back to their school.

Parents paid school fees to cover the cost of supplies and books, plus a small amount for school equipment. Head teachers (called Principals in the U.S.) brought this money to the Salvation Army headquarters where it was checked against each school's enrolment. The amount collected at a school varied from £25 for a new school with one grade to £600 for a large school that ran through Standard VI. The sacrifice of peasant farmers, whose income may well have been only £3 per month, indicated the parents' great desire to educate their children and the effort they made to raise the fees.

A school manager visited each village school at least once a year for about five hours. The manager visited every classroom to see the teacher teach, check his or her preparation book, look through pupils' books, and check progress in penmanship, arithmetic and physical education. The manager inspected the physical facilities: latrines, buildings, and gardens where students practiced crop rotation. Maize, groundnuts, and rapoko were the usual plants. The inspection concluded with a check of the equipment inventory and the dates of ploughing, planting, and cultivating the gardens. The day ended with a meeting with parents.

In this open meeting Major Ronald Cox observed that the manager "must curb his western impatience for nothing will ever be settled except first the problem be thoroughly aired." A white schools manager likely saw this village discussion session as a lesson for African adults in formal western democratic exchange. But Africans no doubt saw it, as Cox implies in his description of the time consuming exchange, as a lesson for the manager in the long-held African system of reciprocal village governance in which all parties participated in decision-making. We shall see that in 1981, some African Salvationists demanded a more open exchange of views and the inclusion of more Africans in Salvation Army local and international governance.

In 1966 Cox complained that while 85 percent of the school-age African children were able to start primary school, there was a "bottleneck" that kept them from moving on to Standard IV, and another bottleneck that kept them from making it all the way to Standard VI. The "bottlenecks" were due to the lack of money from the state, parents, and mission funds to provide teachers and facilities for the village schools. Although Cox claimed that the system's goal was "to give a good standard [education] so that the African child is led on to compete on the same level as white youngsters . . . maintenance of standards is costly." This lack of government support for African education, even though it was "the largest single item in the national budget," meant that by 1966, as the liberation war was breaking out in Rhodesia, only half of the African children were able to attend Standard IV after they had completed Standard III. Of those that did make it to Standard IV, only a third were able to make it through to pass Standard VI.

Cox concluded that it had been only since 1950 that "real pressure for education has been coming from the African people themselves." Before that it was Christian missions and the Rhodesian Education Department that were the sources of pressure to produce change.[25] He did not pursue the question of why it was that Africans in Rhodesia had not sought educational opportunities prior to 1950. Or was he wrong in his reading of the situation?

25. Cox, "Village Schools," 6, 8.

Chapter 7

Colonial, Conciliar, and Communist Forces Collide, 1950s and 1960s

> Americans must count religion in order to see or show its value. ... To them big churches are successful churches. ... To win the greatest number of converts with the least expense is their constant endeavor. ... Americans are essentially children of this world; that they serve as teachers of religion ... is an anomaly.
> —Kanzo Uchimura, first generation Japanese Christian converted through an American mission.[1]

So far I have spotlighted evidence that the Salvation Army's relationship to the white Rhodesian state and to other churches in the Christian Council of Rhodesia was that of a weak mission dependent on a strong colonial state's paternal largess, and the generosity of business tycoons and philanthropic trusts. Larger, well-heeled missions—Church of England, Roman Catholic, Dutch Reformed, and British and American Methodists—had educated leaders who cultivated personal contacts in the government and business community. The Salvation Army's leaders came mainly from outside the Rhodesian and European class systems and played a weaker hand. That the Army's leaders, with limited status and education, did as well as they did in commanding state and business support for their work indicates a political aptitude born of nature, not nurture.

---

1. "Can Americans Teach Japanese in Religion?" *Japan Christian Intelligencer* 1 (1926) 357–61; quoted in Andrew F. Walls, "The American Dimension in the History of the Missionary Movement," in Carpenter and Shenk, eds., *Earthen Vessels: American Evangelicals and Foreign Missions, 1880–1980*, 1–2.

In spite of this deficit, between 1923 and 1965 the Salvation Army developed an extensive African primary school system in villages, a system that was regulated and supported by the Rhodesian state. By the time British colonial rule ended in 1965 with Prime Minister Ian Smith's Rhodesia Front government unilaterally declaring independence (UDI) from Britain, the Army had 226 primary schools, mostly in remote villages, and four secondary schools at Howard, Mazoe, Usher, and Bradley, two of which had teacher training programs. The Army ran an impressive hospital at Howard Institute and four clinics.[2]

The Army's urban social services still focused on the homeless poor and aged within the white settler community. The Army's rationale for this race-based tilt was that most of its private funding came from the white Rhodesian community. (Oxfam and Beit Trusts awarded grants to supplement Salvation Army funds for hospitals and schools, channeled through and audited by the Army's London headquarters.) The Army's homes for the homeless in Bulawayo and Salisbury accommodated white men. Not until 1973 did the Army begin the construction of Bumhudzo ("a place of rest") Eventide Home and Hospital Complex for Africans in Harare (the post-independence name for Salisbury). This change came after considerable pressure from Africans, including members of the Salvation Army Student Fellowship, a group of Salvationist students and professionals that had begun to meet in the 1950s.[3] In 1969, a late date in the imperial calendar, the *Salvation Army Year Book* gave the number of its expatriate (overseas) "missionary" officers as seventy-seven. African officers made up 75 percent of the officer corps, but they still made up only a small fraction of those in administrative positions.[4]

This was the general condition of the Salvation Army in Rhodesia as an African independence movement gathered strength in the early 1960s. Such movements had established themselves in nearly every European colony soon after the Second World War ended in 1945. In 1951 Winston Churchill's Conservatives returned to British leadership and the elderly Prime Minister almost immediately sought an alliance with the United States to thwart what both governments saw as a Soviet "communist" threat to Britain's colonial empire. During the 1950s the British Commonwealth was increasingly made up of former colonies in Third World nations of Africa, Asia, and Latin America. Through its new commonwealth system Britain maintained the shadow of its old Empire without focusing sovereignty in London.

Historians have debated whether Churchill's decision to ally Britain and its Commonwealth with the United States rather than join a European

2. "Rhodesia," *The Salvation Army Year Book, 1965*, 185.
3. Nyandoro, *Flame of Sacred Fire*, 130–34.
4. "Rhodesia," *The Salvation Army Year Book, 1970*, 156–58.

union was to Britain's advantage. This debate parallels the situation in the Salvation Army in the period from 1950 to 1981 where a similar informal alliance, albeit behind the scenes, was struck by the Army's British and North American leaders.

In this era of Salvation Army internal intrigue our emphasis will be on the collusion and tensions that occurred between the Army's Anglo-American leadership that was a mirror-image of the tension and collaboration between the British and American governments in the post-World War II era of colonialism's decline. British historian John Charmley has described the U.S.-U.K. post-war situation as one of American advancement at Britain's expense and portrayed American diplomacy as hostile to Britain's interests. But in general historians have rejected the idea that Britain would have been better off if it had established a counter-balance to American post-war aims by joining a European coalition. They do not see how such an arrangement would have been advantageous to Britain.[5]

But so far as the Salvation Army is concerned an argument can be made that the influence of its American leaders who held the organization's purse was detrimental to the international integrity of the Army as a global entity. This was primarily due to the American Cold War phobia, which posited a "domino theory" that saw the world exclusively through the prism of conflict with the Soviet Union and its Eastern European and East Asian allies and an unspecified fear of "communism" as an evil force within America's borders. As an element of this Cold War struggle many Americans particularly feared communist influence in international organizations, especially the United Nations and World Council of Churches. Ultimately this phobia took the United States into a lengthy war in Vietnam that turned even its European allies against it.

However, without American dollars Third World Salvationists would have lacked basic funding that permitted the Salvation Army to grow in its membership and services, including its social, educational, and religious programs in Rhodesia until 1980 when the nation became the African-led state of Zimbabwe. African Salvationists were aware that they were at the mercy of American largess. This issue of American influence in the former British colony in the post-Second World War era will be our focus in the remainder of this book.

The historical investigation focuses on this question: to what extent did the international and Rhodesian Salvation Army side with the Ian Smith regime in its struggle against African nationalism because of North American

---

5. Hargreaves, *Decolonization in Africa*, 147–49, 157–65; Charmley, *Churchill's Grand Alliance*.

Salvation Army leaders' Cold War obsessions? The Army's leader in Rhodesia at the climax of the independence war in 1978–80 was an American, Colonel Richard Atwell. His American compatriots, the Army's leaders in Washington, New York, Chicago, San Francisco and Atlanta, were his allies in a struggle to support the anti-Communist Ian Smith regime, to oppose the communist Patriotic Front leaders and their supporters in the Soviet-Chinese block of nations, and against the World Council of Churches in Geneva which threw its support behind the war to remove a white racist regime in Salisbury.

From 1923 a white settler government had ruled Rhodesia, taking over from the British South Africa Company. A majority of white Rhodesians had chosen "Responsible Government" as preferable to a union with South Africa by a margin of 8,774 to 5,989 voters. This 1923 vote ended colonial rule under a company (the BSAC) chartered by Britain and began an era of white settler rule that lasted until 1980.[6]

After World War II, independence movements were evolving in nearly every African colony of the European states. In Southern Rhodesia the independence movement had begun with the organization of the African National Congress (ANC) in 1944. At first a welfare agency, the ANC evolved into a political forum by the mid-1950s. Joshua Nkomo had become its first president in 1948, the year the African Voice Association organized a General Strike in Southern Rhodesia. It was a rather mild form of black militancy that came to birth. White rule was declining elsewhere in central Africa, triggered by strikes, riots, and boycotts in the 1950s, but Britain's Conservative Party governments paid little heed. In 1953 Britain tried to dilute white racism by creating a Federation of three of its southern African colonies: Southern Rhodesia, Northern Rhodesia, and Nyasaland. However the strength of the nationalist movements in Northern Rhodesia and Nyasaland in the late 1950s caused Britain to give those countries their independence and majority rule as the nations of Zambia and Malawi in 1960.

Southern Rhodesia (now simply Rhodesia again) remained under white minority rule.[7] Following a white referendum in 1964 that tallied a 10 to 1 vote in favor of independence from Britain, Ian Smith's Rhodesian Front government party unilaterally declared Rhodesia's independence (UDI) from British rule in 1965.

After 1964 Christian missions, founded by European, South African and North American churches, felt compelled to take a stand, collectively and as individual denominations, on the legitimacy of Prime Minister

---

6. Lapping, *End of Empire*, 456.

7. I am indebted to T. O. Ranger for this sequence of nationalist events. Also see Pakenham, *Scramble for Africa*, 678.

Smith's white minority regime. Smith challenged Britain's attempts to bring about majority African rule by peaceful means. The Salvation Army, never before at odds with white colonial governments, but with a 98 percent African membership, now had to decide where it stood in relation to minority rule by 274,000 whites in a country with 6.1 million black Africans. Primarily at meetings with other missions the Army was forced to face the issue of apartheid (racial separation) and express its views in a public forum. Roman Catholics, Anglicans, and Methodists (British and American), with smaller ratios of African to white members than that of the Army, attacked Ian Smith's intransigence on the issue of majority rule. But white Salvationist officers or soldiers seldom criticized Smith's policies that had increasingly mirrored South Africa's system of racial separation. The Army even found it difficult to take a stand against Smith's decision to take over the churches' village primary schools.

Ian Douglas Smith as a Federation of Rhodesia and Nyasaland MP, in the late 1950s.

Why did the Salvation Army not side with its African members in Rhodesia? At least three issues made the Army hesitate to stand with its African soldiers and officers in this situation. First, it had for a long time depended on white government funding for its schools and hospitals, and secondarily for its corps. Second, the conservative political attitudes of the Army's international leaders, particularly Americans, caused it to fear change, particularly when the independence movement was being financially supported by Asian and Eastern European communist nations. Third, the Army's Rhodesian leaders were all white, as were only about 2 percent of its members. Leaders and members had integrated into the urban white Rhodesian community. This caused them to stand against any revolution that would result in African majority rule. And fourth, the Army in Rhodesia was dependent on financial support for their corps, schools and hospitals from the Army's most politically conservative leadership, the ranking officers in the United States, a hand that they did not want to bite.

Kenneth Skelton, Anglican Bishop of Matabeleland after 1962, observed that the Southern Rhodesia Christian Council (SRCC), the conciliar body that had evolved out of a Southern Rhodesia Missionary Conference in the 1920s, had once taken the lead in African rights issues. But over time the SRCC began to suspect that Africans lacked education or administrative skill, and that the manner in which the Council's Western missionaries discussed issues stifled the African majority voice. In July 1964 a new Christian Council of Rhodesia (CCR) formed and became the authorized conciliar link with the Geneva-based World Council of Churches. Bishop Skelton, the first SRCC president, observed that evangelical churches, a group that included the Salvation Army, "kept aloof" from the CCR.[8] Although the Army joined the CCR, it soon had difficulties with what many white Rhodesians viewed as the CCR's pro-African nationalist stance.

At its meeting at Gwelo on November 4, 1964, the new Christian Council of Rhodesia (CCR) made its first political statement. It expressed grave concern at Prime Minister Ian Smith's "excessive emphasis on the need for immediate independence for this country and [we] are convinced that this emphasis will not lead to unity but to increased bitterness." The CCR argued that more important than independence from Britain was "establishing better relationships between the [white and black] inhabitants of this country . . . ." This resolution became the basis for the CCR's rejection of the Rhodesian Unilateral Declaration of Independence (UDI) by Smith's minority white regime in 1965. Following UDI the CCR President Kenneth Skelton and Methodist Synod Chairman A. M. Ndhlela went to Britain and

---

8. Skelton, *Bishop in Smith's Rhodesia*, 93.

the United States to gain public support for resistance to Rhodesian independence from Britain.[9]

After the announcement of the Unilateral Declaration of Independence on November 11, 1965, the Christian Council of Rhodesia was at first confused as to how it should react. African ministers pushed the CCR to issue a Pastoral Letter at a CCR meeting in July 1966 but there was "too much disagreement to proceed with such a letter," according to Skelton. The Minutes indicated that there was "no common ground."[10] As a compromise, the Salvation Army's territorial commander, Commissioner Ernest Fewster, who had come to Southern Rhodesia from England in 1961, "proposed that members faithfully report back to their Churches the many concerns of the Council and the different points of view expressed by members." The motion was carried, but "not unanimously."[11] Fewster was known for his moderate conservatism and a lack of willingness to take a stand on difficult issues.

The Christian Council of Rhodesia finally took a stand on the Smith government's "separate development" apartheid policy on February 14, 1967. The Council resolved that: "legal and physical separation of our people into racial groups would be an offence against Christian ideals of the brotherhood of all men under the Fatherhood of God." A racial separation policy "would frustrate any co-operative efforts to bring about a just and peaceful solution to the country's problems." The CCR called for a Heads of Denominations forum that would include Protestants and Roman Catholics. The Salvation Army was a member of the Heads of Denominations forum. On June 30, 1967, the CCR urged churches to reject the government's new racially-based Registration fees.[12]

In 1969 the breach widened between the Smith government and the Christian Council of Rhodesia. The CCR unanimously rejected Smith's 1969 Constitution and a Land Tenure Act that claimed that segregation of races supported "Christian ideals." The CCR responded that the new Constitution would entrench "racial discrimination" and announced that churches "would continue their non-racial ministry without regard to the Land Tenure Act" that aimed at separating white and African land and requiring

---

9. Hallencreutz, "A Council in Crossfire: ZCC 1964–1980," 60–61.

10. Skelton, *Bishop in Smith's Rhodesia*, 101.

11. Hallencreutz, "A Council in Crossfire: ZCC 1964–1980," 61, quotes Skelton, *Bishop in Smith's Rhodesia*, 101. Skelton does not cite Fewster by name.

12. CCR Annual Meeting, 14 Feb. 14, 1967; Hallencreutz, "A Council in Crossfire: ZCC 1964–1980," 61–62; Skelton, *Bishop in Smith's Rhodesia*, 101.

registration of churches as "African" or "European." CCR members refused to register their churches.[13]

On 20 June 1969, White Rhodesians voted overwhelmingly in favor of the new constitution. Conservative Catholics and Anglicans split with their bishops who opposed the Smith government's constitution. When churches refused to comply with the new racial provisions, the government altered the Act to exclude churches from the requirement to register. In 1971 the CCR again affirmed that the Land Tenure Act that forced Africans out of their ancestral lands was for them a matter of social justice and human rights.[14] Bishop Skelton claimed that although the CCR resolutions did not affect the government or the white electorate, they did "comfort" the African people.[15]

Relations between church and state deteriorated further when the CCR announced that after 1971 it would not accept a law that forced them to turn over their schools to the government. A Salvation Army response claimed that the Army "spends more money in Rhodesia pro rata, and provides more qualified teachers, than anywhere else in the world." This government decree meant that by 1971 the Army would have to separate its corps (churches) from its state supported schools, since they were served by state-supported pastor-teachers. Its pastors (officers) would have to live from income provided by members (soldiers) and overseas missionary funds. Reliance on state funds had increasingly forced the Army to accept state policy. Now a white minority government, held to be illegal by Britain and much of the international community, was calling a new tune to which the Army and other churches had to decide whether or not they would dance.

In December 1966 the Rhodesian legislature approved Ian Smith's restrictive rules for denominations engaged in primary education for Africans. As of January 1967 churches could no longer establish primary schools in rural areas. In January 1968 only local African Councils could establish primary schools. Expansion of existing schools could only occur if Local Councils approved. After January 1970 churches could no longer open upper primary schools on Tribal Trust Lands or in African Purchase Areas. If churches failed to make up the five percent of the teachers' pay that the government would no longer support, then the entire grant would be withheld. Some churches saw these actions as indications that the Smith government wanted them to completely relinquish their role in African education.

---

13. Skelton, *Bishop in Smith's Rhodesia*, 109.

14. CCR Council Meeting, 8 Sept., 1971; Hallencreutz, "A Council in Crossfire: ZCC 1964–1980," 67–68.

15. Skelton, *Bishop in Smith's Rhodesia*, 102.

On 25 November 1969 the Heads of Denominations responded to the Smith government in a public statement. They had found it impossible to make up the 5 percent for teachers' salaries. Nevertheless, they were willing to work with the government to support the development of African primary education. They asserted that primary school parents were already paying all they could afford for building and maintaining schools, for fees to cover administrative costs and for supplying school equipment. They accused the government of imposing an additional financial burden on African parents that white Rhodesians did not have to bear.

The choice for the churches was either to turn their schools over to Local Councils or to close them. But the government was unprepared to take over African schools and Local Councils were not entirely accepted by most Africans in the Tribal Trust Lands. The churches asked the government to delay implementing its ruling. The government refused, but agreed that churches could turn over the schools to Local Councils only if parents agreed to the transfer. The Heads of Denominations rejected this odd reasoning. The government claimed that its reason for taking the 5 percent from African primary schools was to improve secondary education.

In 1971 the government implemented a law by which there would be three classes of primary schools in Tribal Trust Lands: 1) schools retained by missions; 2) schools temporarily sponsored or formed by Local Committees; and 3) schools taken by Local Councils. At the time the Salvation Army had about 30,000 students in its schools. After it handed over schools to Local Councils it retained forty-five schools. Thirty-one of these were primary schools, 10 were day schools, and four were secondary schools. This ended a long partnership between Rhodesian governments and Christian missions. Henceforth Salvation Army officers would be pastors and professional educators would run the Army's schools. Thus no government funds would any longer support the Army's evangelistic soul-saving enterprises in its corps.[16]

16. Nyandoro, *Flame of Sacred Love*, 99–102.

Chapter 8

Paying the Piper, Calling the Tune
A Salvation Army Power Shift, 1970–78

> It will be readily understood that in 1946 we had to grapple with a sudden world-wide flood of post-war problems . . . [examples given] to point and underline the fact that the Army in the U.S.A. literally salved [sic] our missionary work and an important part of our European organization, by generous and unremitting financial aid at this time.
> —General Albert Orsborn[1]

> IHQ needs to remember where its funding comes from.
> —Former Officer, USA East[2]

By 1970 the Second Chimurenga had begun as an African-led independence war for majority rule. In the next two decades the Salvation Army's international leaders faced conflicting demands, inside and outside the Army. Internally they had a deep concern for the cohesion of their diverse international social and evangelical mission at a time when African members (soldiers and officers) in Rhodesia were turning away from Western colonial domination. In fact, Africans, Asians, and Latin Americans were turning toward anti-imperial, Marxist and liberationist political and theological views that were antithetical to views held by most Army leaders in

---

1. Albert Orsborn, *The House of My Pilgrimage*, 181–82.

2. Contribution to on-line discussion: http://fsaof.blogspot.co.nz/2012/01/positional-clashing-of-cymbles.html.

North America who had long assumed Christian, capitalist, and democratic systems to be the natural fountainhead through which God's grace flowed. A third force was Salvation Army missionaries in the Third World who were troubled that the white minority-run state, to which they had been attached for eighty years, was increasingly adopting the political, social, and cultural policies of South Africa's apartheid regime.

African Salvationists and missionaries also saw long-term conciliar affiliations with other Protestant and Orthodox churches in the Christian Council of Rhodesia (CCR) and in the World Council of Churches (WCC) in Geneva, Switzerland, disintegrating over political differences. The disputes had to do with returning to Africans land that the British South Africa Company and subsequent colonial governments had taken illegally, and a need to give Africans universal franchise and majority democratic rule. The obvious fact was that most of the Salvation Army's African soldiers, particularly those living in Rhodesia's rural areas, supported a "liberation war" that would ultimately produce African independence and majority rule in 1980.

In the 1970s the Chimurenga in Rhodesia was increasingly grabbing the attention of global political and church leaders. In the remainder of this work I will focus on global and Rhodesian church-state relations. As the international Salvation Army and its leaders in Rhodesia chose to stand on the side of the Ian Smith regime in Salisbury during the war, possibly out of long-term loyalties to a white settler government that had funded its churches, schools and hospitals, its African membership and many of its missionary officers increasingly protested this stand. The same conflicts were occurring in other Rhodesian churches.

Outside Rhodesia, by the 1970s the British and American governments were being asked to take a stand in favor of African independence movements and against intrusions into Third World countries by the Soviet block of nations. In addition conciliar associations of churches in Rhodesia and in the World Council of Churches were raising their voices for the "liberation" of African Christians living under white minority rule. And there were African liberation forces operating as guerrillas in rural districts where most Africans and most Salvationists lived. The liberation forces claimed to be "Marxist" in their political orientation, but they might be as accurately described as nationalists seeking independence from white European minority rule with assistance from any country or organization, political or religious, that supported this aim. That support came primarily from communist states rather than from states that embraced democratic-capitalist dogmas.

Salvation Army leaders were ill prepared to stand against an array of external political forces in London and Washington, or African front-line States and Third World leaders in Asia and Latin America. They were bewildered by the African sympathies of the conciliar forces in Rhodesia, in Geneva, and in the powerful Roman Catholic Church. They were also unprepared for the nationalist aspirations that erupted from its long-quiescent African members. And most Salvation Army leaders outside North America were unwilling to tie themselves to the Socialist phobias of the Army's American leaders. Thus the Army was hamstrung both by its close relations with the despised Rhodesian state and by its own political conservatism, the latter being quite different from the nineteenth-century liberal traditions of William Booth's struggle against the alliance of the established Church of England and Tory governments. The American leaders' conservatism, shared to a lesser degree by many Salvationists in other nations, was also in conflict with the rising liberal attitudes advocating racial desegregation, women's rights, civil rights, and anti-war movements during the 1960s and 1970s.

The Salvation Army's General in the 1960s, Frederick Coutts, was a socialist, ecumenist, and pacifist. As such he stood against racial apartheid in Southern Africa and colonial rule in general. A man in touch with his time, Coutts was an intellectual and able administrator who held office from 1963 to 1969. He had written numerous books and articles on theology, particularly the Army's signal doctrine of holiness. He was virtually the only General since William and Bramwell Booth to have addressed at some length the Army's social reform policy.[3] For reasons that are not altogether clear he drew the ire of some of the Army's North American officers. They opposed his 1963 election as General and accused him of unspecified liberal theological views. I assume that a tendency in the Army's North American branch to connect fundamentalist theology to conservative politics and capitalist economics was at the heart of the accusations. Ronald Thomlinson, Coutts' official biographer, lists charges that opponents made against Coutts as socialist, modernist, ecumenist, pacifist, liberal, scriptural non-literalist, and opponent of apartheid and racism.[4]

In an interview with General Coutts in 1981 at his retirement home in St. Albans, England, I asked him why two American colonels had opposed his 1963 election as the Salvation Army's General. They had canvassed fellow-officers to pray that the Holy Spirit would lead the High Council of the Army's international leaders to oppose him when they cast their votes. Coutts said that he knew of no view that he held on the atonement, which he took to be their main complaint against him, which Salvationists would regard as unorthodox. I asked him if he had ever met or received a letter from the colonels citing their complaints. He answered that he had not met or had correspondence from them. But he said to me, "Norman, sometimes

---

3. Coutts, *Bread for My Neighbour*, 1978.
4. Thomlinson, *A Very Private General*, 49, 66–87, 115–16, 164–65.

in life there are those who decide to dislike you, and there's nothing in the world that you can do about it." He expressed an interest in why American fundamentalists were so in awe of C. S. Lewis, who did not share their views in a number of areas of theology and personal behavior.[5] I had no answer.

Coutts' successors as General were Erik Wickberg of Sweden, 1969 to 1974; and then Clarence Wiseman, 1974–77, and Arnold Brown, 1977–83, both Canadians. Two of the three can be fairly described as internationalists; Brown's experience was mainly confined to North America and England. Unlike their attitudes towards Coutts, North American leaders apparently saw fellow North Americans, Wiseman and Brown, as moderate in politics and fundamentalist in theology. Thus the Generals in 1974–83 did not draw North American ire as Coutts had.

As we have seen, problems in Rhodesia began long before the 1970s with issues of African voting rights and a right to reclaim land that had been taken from them by the BSAC and given to white settlers and missions. But even during the 1970s these long-debated matters were alien issues for the insular Salvation Army headquarters in Salisbury, London, and New York. The Army's leaders had little knowledge of and expressed no public outrage at the disenfranchisement of Africans, or at the discriminatory distribution of land between Africans and the minority white population.

The Salvation Army liked to view itself as apolitical, and argued that this was a well-established principle in its military code, published as its Orders and Regulations. Anglican Bishop Kenneth Skelton argued that the Army was not alone in this attitude. He stated that evangelical churches in general, the group into which the Army fell, "were very suspicious of the 'political' tendencies of African Christians."[6] Africans had been seen, but seldom heard, between the 1896–97 uprisings and the 1950s, the beginnings of effective nationalist movements in the post-World War II era. Ian Smith and white Rhodesians who followed his political lead saw no reason why Africans would want to govern themselves. Most Salvation Army leaders agreed. They appointed few Africans to administrative posts.[7]

The Army's leadership brought together an alliance of British Commonwealth and American leaders which mirrored the post-World War II Anglo-American political alliance. The Army's International Headquarters was in London, but since the war its wealth was in North America. Its military-styled organizational structure governed in a top-down command system that

---

5. Murdoch interview with General Frederick Coutts, St. Albans, 1981. I also interviewed General Coutts in 1986, not long before his death.

6. Marsden, *Fundamentalism and Culture*, 81, 85–86.

7. The 1965 *Year Book* shows that only one of the Territory's seven Divisional Commanders was African.

recognized an elected General as a singular final authority in all matters of organization and doctrine. They gradually moved toward a system wherein the Army's Anglo-American leaders acted in consensus, working out their differences behind the scenes. Nearly all leaders, including those in Third World commands, were from the West, largely from the British Commonwealth or North America. But few of the American leaders in the 1950s to 1970s, unlike British, Europeans and Australasians, had served beyond U.S. boundaries, apart from brief stints in the London headquarters. Virtually none had served in the Third World. Thus few American leaders had a global perspective from exposure to cultures in a world that bore little resemblance to their own.

When a Salvation Army General retires, a High Council composed of members of the international staff and territorial commanders from over 100 counties, gathers near London to elect a new one.[8] The Army has one General at a time, in whom leaders vest power under a British Act of Parliament. Prior to the election a High Council asks nominees to respond to questions that evolve from hot topics of the day as well as traditional concerns of doctrine and organization. They might ask, what is your position on the Army's doctrines of the inspiration of canonical Scripture? Or how do you view the relationship of the Army's social services to its evangelical soul-winning within the Army's overall mission? What is your view of how the Army should deal with church and state (political) and inter-church ecumenical relations?

In May 1977 the High Council chose Commissioner Arnold Brown, a Canadian, to be the new General. In response to a question, Brown told the leaders that he would not alter the Army's World Council of Churches membership without consulting territorial commanders. He said that the conflict over the Salvation Army's WCC membership, dealt with by General Wiseman at previous meetings of the international leaders, had begun with the World Council's Program to Combat Racism "grant of $85,000 to the Rhodesian Patriotic Front led by Joshua Nkomo" in 1970.[9] Between 1970 and 1979 the WCC's Patriotic Front had allocated $2,055,000 (U.S.) to segments of the African nationalist movement in Rhodesia and made grants to other oppressed groups, such as American Indians. The allocation recipients included the African National Council (ANC) in South Africa in 1975–76; the Zimbabwe African National Union (ZANU) and Zimbabwe African People's Union (ZAPU) in 1970, 1971, 1974, 1976; and the combined Patriotic Front of Robert Mugabe and Joshua Nkomo (ZANU-PF) in 1978 and 1979.[10]

8. "Territorial Commander" is a title the Salvation Army uses to designate leaders in command of the Army in a nation or several nations, or in the case of large countries such as India or the USA, a leader in an area within a nation. It is comparable to the use of the term "archbishop" in episcopal churches.

9. Brown, *The Gate and the Light*, 229.

10. Baldwin Sjollema, *Isolating Apartheid: Western Collaboration with South*

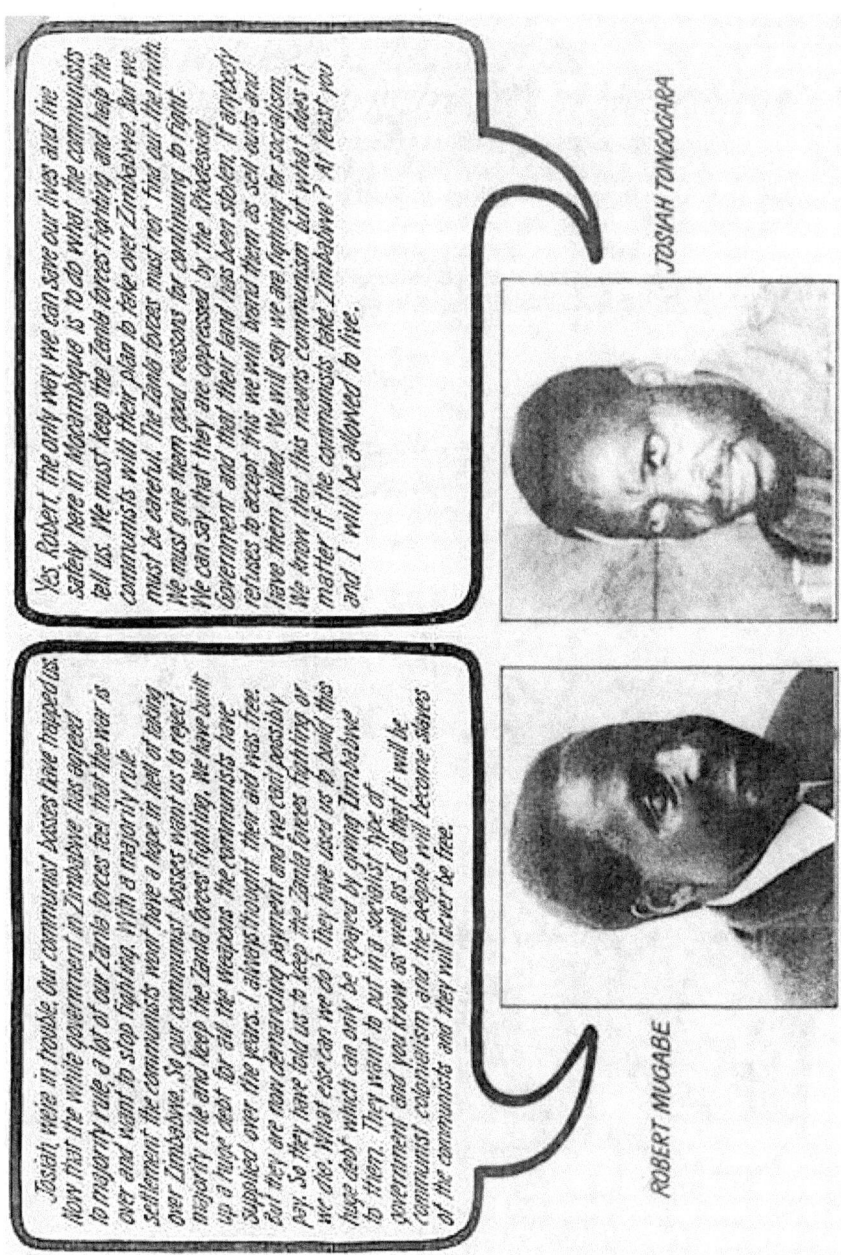

Robert Mugabe and Josiah Tongogara in Rhodesian Government propaganda leaflet produced in the late 1970s.

Joshua Mqabuko Nkomo.

There were North American Salvationists who had argued that biblical "modernism" and political socialism had reigned at the Salvation Army International Headquarters in the 1950s and 1960s. In his 1973 biography of Frederick Coutts, Thomlinson named several members of the international staff in that period who were "socialists." "Socialist" had been a derisive word in the United States since the 1920's "Red Scare." It had become outright divisive in the 1950s "McCarthy era" when American soldiers were fighting "communists" in Korea, and in the 1960s and early 1970s when American political leaders saw the U.S. as holding the line against international communism in Vietnam. The "staunch socialists" named by Thomlinson were close friends at the Army's international headquarters in London: Carvosso Gauntlett, Frederick Coutts, and Bernard Watson. Catherine Baird, Reginald Woods, Benjamin Blackwell, with Coutts, Watson, and Gauntlett were also pacifists. A. G. Cunningham, retired Chief of the Staff, was the first Salvationist on the World Council of Churches Central Committee in 1948. Gauntlett and Coutts had headed the Army's Literary Department that North American fundamentalists suspected of being the locus of liberalism and modernism.[11]

John Coutts, son of General Coutts, traced the Army debate over biblical inerrancy, a central theme of fundamentalists, back to 1905. In that year General Bramwell Booth had written: "the truth of the Bible is established by revelation of Jesus Christ in us and the glorious fulfilment in our hearts and lives of just precisely what it promises."[12] In other words, personal experience is the proof of biblical authority. William Booth had founded the Salvation Army in the 1870–90 era that historian of American fundamentalism, George M. Marsden, describes as being "before the rise of the Social Gospel, [when] holiness-minded evangelists had . . . assumed leadership in American Protestant work among the poor." Between 1900 and 1930 Marsden claims that a "Great Reversal" occurred when "evangelists' interest in social concerns disappeared." In those three decades, "all progressive social concern, whether political or private, became suspect among revivalist evangelicals and was relegated to a very minor role."[13] But, of course, this was not the case in the Salvation Army. So why did the reversal take place in other revivalist-fundamentalist groups but not the Army?

First, the Salvation Army, by the turn of the century, was an international church unlike North American fundamentalist denominations which squabbled over biblical inerrancy and speculative issues of whether a believer who experienced holiness as Christian perfectionism could relapse into sin. Thus the Army, like the Roman Catholic Church, had a global realm in which to debate and a General who exercised final authority. Second, the Army had little or no interest in speculative theological debate—nearly

11. Thomlinson, *A Very Private General*, 66–67, 75. See Coutts, *The History of the Salvation Army*, vol. 6, 168–69. While later a pacifist, Coutts had been an officer in the Royal Air Force towards the end of the World War I.

12. Coutts, *The Salvationists*, 10–11, quotes Bramwell Booth, "The Salvation Army and the Higher Criticism," *The Field Officer* (1905).

13. Marsden, *Fundamentalism and Culture*, 81, 85–86.

none of its officers (clergy) had theological training outside its own Training Colleges and almost none had been to college. The Army's Training College courses had run for a year or less, with little emphasis on systematic theology. They taught a simple gospel to be preached to working-class congregations. William and Catherine Booth had subscribed to Charles G. Finney's suspicion that seminary education muted the message of soul-salvation. And third, by the 1920s and 1930s, in the wake of World War I, the Army was gaining public attention and financial support for its social services, especially in North America. This caused it to want to be known as a church, although it seldom used the word, with broad and tolerant views of religion. So while it maintained a conservative doctrinal stance for its members, it did not encourage theological disputation that would draw attention from "outsiders." Thus the "Great Reversal" did not affect the Salvation Army, at least not in its public persona.

In 1923, Colonel A. G. Cunningham, writing at the Army's London headquarters, squelched the idea of scriptural inerrancy in the Salvation Army's Handbook of Doctrine. This book followed by about a decade the publication of The Fundamentals in the United States, pamphlets that had taken a strong stand for biblical inerrancy. The Bible was God's infallible word not only in its meaning; God dictated every word. Whether that meant words of the original autographs that no longer exist is unclear. Cunningham argued that "the evangelists may make mistakes in dates and in order of events, in reporting the occasion of a word of Jesus," but "the word of God, the revelation of God to the soul in Christ, lives and abides."[14] John Coutts concludes that Cunningham and Bramwell Booth held that "the Bible is inspired, because it is inspiring." Coutts holds that the gulf between "liberal" and "conservative" was much larger in North America than in Britain. Thus the Anglo-American Salvation Army was "deeply divided over its attitude to Scripture."[15] Since the Army drew members from a global sphere it could expect internal dispute to occur, but this dispute was within the officer ranks and was muted by the Army's autocratic rule and military culture.

William Booth was post-millennialist in his apocalyptic views of end times. Like most of his evangelical contemporaries he believed that the great nineteenth-century revivals in the British Empire and in North America, and the spread of the Christian faith by missionaries, would bring about Christ's rule on earth. Nineteenth-century post-millennial holiness

14. Cunningham's formulation was consistent with the views held by William Booth himself as found in *War Cry* articles reprinted in Booth and Cunningham, *The Bible: Its Divine Revelation, Inspiration and Authority*.

15. Coutts, *The Salvationists*, 13–14, quotes from Cunningham's articles in the *Staff Review* (1927).

evangelists like William and his wife Catherine saw the state and other secular agents as God-ordained instruments of progress. They could defeat evil and promote good through such political campaigns as the prohibition of alcohol, the promotion of Sabbath observance and the end of prostitution and the white slave trade. In these public activities the Booths overcame a contrasting Protestant view that in the age of the spirit the aim of Christians should be solely private evangelistic activity of converting sinners and bringing the heathen to salvation. Protestants of Anabaptist and Calvinist-Puritan-Reformed views held that the kingdom of God on earth was almost solely a spiritual affair, not one brought about by human political and social effort or agency.[16] The North American Salvation Army seems to have more readily embraced these pre-millennialist views—at odds with their strong commitment to Salvationist social work as an expression of the gospel.

As we have seen the doctrinal and political divisions that simmered in the Salvation Army manifested themselves in 1963 when some Americans challenged Frederick Coutts' election as General. American officers circulated letters that asked colleagues to pray that the Holy Spirit would cause the High Council to reject Coutts as successor to Wilfred Kitching on account of Coutts' liberal tendencies.[17] But the High Council elected Coutts by the necessary two-thirds margin on the fourth ballot. After Coutts retired in 1969 no other British leader became General until 1999, when the High Council elected John Gowans. During Coutts' Generalship there were no open moves towards secession by the Americans, but divisions became apparent after 1970. In the 1970s a majority of Salvation Army leaders in North America apparently believed that the World Council of Churches (WCC) was promoting violence in Rhodesia through its grants to Zimbabwe's African "freedom fighters"—or "guerrillas"—or "terrorists." Although the Army did not withdraw from the WCC until 1978, relations between the World Council and the Army were increasingly strained from 1969.

The debate had political overtones. One might assume that General Wickberg in London had supported the Rhodesian Territorial Commander Commissioner Adlam's decision to break with the majority of Rhodesian churches on the issue of support for majority rule. The Army's international organizational structure would require support for such a position at the top. If Adlam simply wanted to avoid mixing affairs of church and state, as the Army had generally done for eighty years by taking land and funds for its institutions from a white minority government that denied equality to

---

16. Marsden, *Fundamentalism and Culture*, 88.

17. Major Dr. Jim Watt, a Canadian missionary in Zimbabwe, advises me that letters also circulated in Canada concerning the Frederick Coutts' election as General in 1963.

Africans, that would be a strange excuse. Unlike the Army, the Methodist Church in Britain supported the World Council's financial aid to liberation groups through its Program to Combat Racism.

Leaders of the World Council of Churches (WCC) had developed a Program to Combat Racism at a meeting at Notting Hill, England, in October 1969. The WCC invited three leading Rhodesians to attend the meeting: Garfield Todd, former Prime Minister and Church of Christ missionary from New Zealand; Nathan Shamuyayira, a Rhodesian exile who was Professor of History at the University of Dar es Salaam in Tanzania; and Canaan S. Banana, a Methodist minister and Chairman of the Bulawayo Council of Churches. The Rhodesian government refused to permit Banana to attend. The Notting Hill meeting proposed to send financial aid to international civil rights groups, including Rhodesia's two nationalist groups: the Zimbabwe African People's Union (ZAPU); and the Zimbabwe African National Union (ZANU). The drafters of the Notting Hill proposal intended the fund to be used for humanitarian programs: education, medical supplies, shelter, etc.[18]

Those who opposed the World Council's Program to Combat Racism (PCR) attacked it for abetting violence by atheistic Marxists. Robert Mugabe and Joshua Nkomo, as well as other African leaders, were known to have Marxist leanings. Was it pressure from North American churches that emphasized this concern? Certainly Irish Presbyterians and the Dutch Reformed Church of South Africa were allies of Americans who opposed church interference in liberation wars, particularly when the state opposed communism as southern Africa's apartheid states claimed to do. The fundamentalists' foes in the mainline American protestant denominations and the National Council of Churches in the United States also suffered when large numbers of their communicants opposed donations to the PCR fund. The Salvation Army in the United States was not a member of the National Council of Churches because of its "liberal" policies, whereas the Army in virtually every other country belonged to national councils of churches, as it did in Rhodesia up to 1971.

As a result of the Notting Hill Conference the WCC's Central Committee set up a Special Fund within the Program to Combat Racism in 1971 to give aid to humanitarian and educational services run by the African-led liberation movements in Rhodesia. The WCC intended that the aid would promote social justice in the cause of human rights. Most of the social services the liberation movements provided for their refugees in exile were based in neighboring Zambia, Zaire, and Mozambique.

18. Banana, *Politics of Repression and Resistance*, 306–17.

Was it American Salvation Army leaders, who had opposed what they perceived as the socialist-pacifist politics of Frederick Coutts and a few other British Army leaders, who insisted that the Army's international headquarters in London must not support World Council of Churches' aid to African liberation movements even if it was purely on a basis of voluntary donations to the PCR fund? Did the Vietnam War, reaching its apex at the time of the Notting Hill Conference, influence the Americans' opposition to the African Patriotic Front's Marxist nationalists in Rhodesia? As an international body the Army claimed that it had no political or economic allegiance to any governmental system. But this was hardly true in the post-World War II "Cold War" era when Americans conceived the world as being divided between democracies in the West and "godless" communism in the East.

In 1971 the Salvation Army in Rhodesia broke with the national ecumenical church alliance, the Christian Council of Rhodesia (CCR), over support for African land rights, liberation, and majority rule, and the CCR's support for the World Council of Churches' humanitarian aid to African guerrilla forces. This signaled a possible break between the Army in London and the World Council in Geneva. While that break did not occur until 1978, seven years later, there can be little doubt that deteriorating church-state-conciliar relations in Rhodesia, the international "Cold War" against a backdrop of America's Vietnam catastrophe, and internal Army divisions, triggered the break. What we know for sure is that the break was a direct result of pressure from the Army's conservative leaders in North America on the Army's international leaders in London.

The Salvation Army's evolving political and conciliar attitudes in the 1960s to 1980s reflect an Anglo-American alliance of leaders and the effect that alliance had on Army policies in the Third World. After World War II, Army leaders in America were less and less inclined to permit the Salvation Army's British Generals and their largely British staff in London to make policy without their advice and consent.[19] In other words, American money

19. The Salvation Army has had 20 Generals. In its first century seven out of eight came from the UK where General Booth founded the Army in 1865: William and Bramwell Booth, Edward J. Higgins, Evangeline C. Booth (a British-born, naturalized American citizen), George Carpenter (Australian), Albert W. Orsborn, Wilfred Kitching, and Frederick Coutts. Of the next seven, none came from the UK: Erik Wickberg (Sweden), Clarence Wiseman (Canada), Arnold Brown (Canada), Jarl Wahlström (Finland), Eva Burrows (Australia), Bramwell Tillsley (Canada), and Paul Rader (United States). The next three, John Gowans, John Larsson and Shaw Clifton, were British officers (although Larsson is Swedish-born and with wide international experience). The only American-born General, Paul Rader, had international experience as a missionary in Korea that tempered other Americans' parochialism. Of later Generals, Linda Bond

that financed the Army's international operations overwhelmed financial resources available in war-damaged Europe and swelled the American role in policy-making. Gradually Americans asserted their conservative political and doctrinal views. More than any other issue the Zimbabwe independence war brought this behind-the-scenes struggle to the surface, altering the Army's attitudes on church-state and church-church (conciliar) relations nationally and internationally. And all of this occurred at the same time as a shift was occurring in the Army's membership growth from the Northern to the Southern hemisphere. The result was a clash that brought African Salvationists to the point of protest in spite of their financial dependence on American largess.

---

was Canadian, and the current General André Cox is an internationalist of Swiss-English parentage, born in Zimbabwe, who has served in Africa, Europe and the U.K. Thus five of the eleven Generals since Coutts have been North American.

Chapter 9

Conciliar Movements and The Salvation Army, 1970–78

> For if we are to receive one another as Christ received us, then we must forget our imagined superiorities—our historical superiorities...; our fancied spiritual superiorities.... I may not say to anyone who calls Jesus Lord... your worship is defective.
> —Frederick Coutts[1]

As background for the Salvation Army's local, national and international ecumenical struggles in the 1960s to 1980s, we must first take a look at history, going back to a period before William Booth founded his East London Revival Mission in 1865. Booth had cut himself off from denominational Christianity when he decided not to take a new appointment as a Methodist New Connexion minister in Newcastle, England, in 1861. Pulpits of several Wesleyan societies were closed to the Booths as William and his wife Catherine became itinerant evangelists, depending on Wesleyan sects which still welcomed them to supply them with pulpits and a living.

The Evangelical Alliance, founded in 1845–46 at Liverpool, had triggered a new era of evangelical cooperation in home mission work in cities. Begun as a movement to overlook theological and political differences between protestant denominations, the movement emphasized what it saw as deficiencies in high church Anglicanism (Puseyites and the Oxford

---

1. Frederick Coutts, "Are we great enough to move toward one another as Christ moved toward us?" An address given at a united church service during the Week of Prayer for Christian Unity, and quoted from chapter 7 of Waldron, compiler, *The Salvation Army and the Churches*, 62.

Movement) and Roman Catholicism. In letters "On Christian Union," Edward Bickersteth emphasized Protestantism's simple creed of an "invisible church" composed of "those who truly believe in Jesus and love the brethren."[2] This broad doctrinal statement led evangelical nonconformists to overlook differences between them on such divisive matters as the means of baptism and millennialism, and to focus on their united distrust of the English state church establishment and what they referred to as "popery."

The founding of the Evangelical Alliance led to the organization of a host of lay-led nonconformist extra-denominational groups. When several churches asked Catherine Booth to preach in South London in 1864–65, she asked William to bring their children from Leeds to relocate their home in London where her mother could help with their care. William's itinerant work and his mood were depressed. As he thought about his future he came into contact with a couple of the new extra-denominational groups that had commenced mission work in London's East End slums. Without the support of these groups Booth's East End mission work would probably not have commenced and almost certainly would not have survived.

Booth's first contact in London in 1865 was with *The Revival* (renamed *The Christian* after 1870), England's premier nonsectarian magazine promoting evangelistic work. The editors asked Booth to meet with them to discuss his justification for his wife's preaching in the face of what most evangelicals saw as St. Paul's negative advice on female ministry.[3] They no doubt asked him for his interpretation of 1 Corinthians 11:1–15 and 14:34, 35, which deal with women "speaking" in church. Catherine had dealt with the passage in her 1859 pamphlet defending women's right to "preach." She interpreted the Greek word *lalein* (speak) to mean "imprudent or ignorant talking," not to be confused with women's right to "prophesy" or "preach," which the prophet Joel had foretold.[4] The principal concern of the editors, Richard Cope Morgan and Samuel Chase, seems to have been the public life of Catherine as a woman who was already responsible for six children, and would soon have two more.

---

2. *The Record*, August 7 and 11, 1845, quoted in Lewis, *Lighten Their Darkness*, 97–98. Lewis treats the ecumenical movement in the period before Booth founded a home revival mission in London in 1865 as precursor of the Salvation Army in 1878.

3. Booth, *Female Teaching* (32 pages). Catherine's defense of American revivalist Phoebe Palmer against attacks on her ministry by the Reverend A. A. Rees, *Reasons for Not Co-operating in the Alleged Sunderland Revivals*. Sunderland: Hills, 1859 (24 pages). For access to these two pamphlets I am grateful to Professor Pamela J. Walker of Carleton University. Also see Murdoch, "Female Ministry in the Thought and Work of Catherine Booth"; Parkin, "Pioneer in Female Ministry"; Green, "Settled Views: Catherine Booth and Female Ministry"; and Walker, "Proclaiming Women's Right to Preach."

4. Booth, *Female Teaching*, 11; Murdoch, "Catherine Booth," 353.

Shortly after his meeting with William, Morgan introduced him to the East London Special Services Committee, a group that became a principal support for his work. The Committee asked Booth to preach in its East London tent for a week while the regular evangelist recovered from an illness. Morgan, a member of the Plymouth Brethren and a Calvinist by training, differed from the Booths in theology, but he remained their friend and publicized their work until 1875 when he broke with them over their Wesleyan doctrine of "holiness."

Catherine Booth, who preached primarily in London's West End in order to be her family's breadwinner, made contact with several extra-denominational groups, including the Midnight Movement for Fallen Women, one of many lay-run agencies that combined evangelism and social services. About twenty members of the Christian Community, a group that descended from seventeenth-century Huguenot refugees settled in East London, worked with William, holding open-air meetings in July 1865 at Mile End Waste. The Society of Friends' Open Air Mission, founded in 1853, also supported his work by attending meetings and lending their Whitechapel Burial Ground as the setting for his preaching in the East London Special Services Committee's tent.

The thirty-six-year-old William Booth's main support came from an East London Special Services Committee and an Evangelization Society that supplied his financial support. The East London Special Services Committee had formed in 1861 when evangelist Reginald Radcliffe came to London from Liverpool to ask "representatives and friends of all the agencies carrying on the Lord's work in the East End" to form a coordinating agency. *The Revival's* Morgan and Chase were Committee members. The Committee's work was to pass out religious tracts and bibles, to support home missions, to promote Sunday and "ragged" schools, and to encourage temperance and abstinence. They were not denominational or cleric-led creations. Rather, laymen from various churches were guided by the general goal that had been set by the Evangelical Alliance in 1846. It was the "advancement of Evangelical Protestantism [and] the counteraction of infidelity, Popery, and other forms of superstition, error, and profaneness, especially the desecration of the Lord's Day."[5]

---

5. Kessler, *A Study of the Evangelical Alliance in Great Britain*, 17. For the Booths' connections with the Evangelical Alliance and subsequent lay-led evangelical associations see: William Booth, *Heathen England and What to Do for It*; Railton, *General Booth*, 56; Begbie, *The Life of General William Booth*, vol. 1, 309, 355; Booth-Tucker, *The Life of Catherine Booth*, 279–81, 291; Ervine, *God's Soldier: General William Booth*, vol. 1, 273, 277, 381; Catherine Bramwell Booth, *Catherine Booth*, 266–80; Sandall, *The History of The Salvation Army*, vol. 1, 24–27; Murdoch, *Origins*, chapter 3.

The Evangelization Society, founded in 1864 to send evangelists "to preach the Lord Jesus to the unconverted," provided Booth with generous aid. Thus Booth's work in East London had its roots in a non-sectarian evangelical mentality of the 1840s to 1860s. Extra-denominational voluntary agencies, tied together by "interlocking directorates" of wealthy businessmen, welded believers from competing protestant sects and agencies into an agreed upon, simple creed of faith in Jesus Christ and opposition to heathenism and ritualism. No denomination controlled their operations in working class and slum areas such as that in which the Reverend William Booth planted his home mission in London's East End.[6]

Once William Booth established his mission as a viable sect, he slowly broke his ties to extra-denominational agencies. On April 7, 1869, the Evangelization Society ended its financial support. Thereafter Booth raised his own funds. He became self-sufficient. In 1867 he organized his own Committee of wealthy "gentlemen" to raise money and advise him in management. The names of these well-known men added credibility to his mission. This Committee (renamed a Council) may have lasted till 1878 or later, but it kept no minutes.[7] Booth was still dependent on external funds from subscribers who were often individuals his wife was meeting at her West End services. His East London Mission, renamed the Christian Mission in 1865 and then "a Salvation Army" in 1878 as it grew beyond the East End, continued to rely on contributions from evangelical laypersons of various nonconformist churches, without consideration of creed or sectarian membership.

In 1882 General Booth, now with his General Superintendent (Methodist) title shortened to fit his leadership of a "salvation army," considered accepting an invitation from the Church of England to become its evangelistic wing in the slums. There were three main blocks to such a merger. First, Booth would lose control over his Army. Second, the Church of England would not treat the Army's women officers as equals with men in their calling as preachers, much less in the performance of sacramental rites. And third, it was certain that none of the Army's male officers would be equal to the Church's clergy who were "ordained" in a line of "apostolic succession." This was the ritualism that Catherine Booth abhorred. Thus the Booths again rejected sectarian attachment in favor of continuing in an ecumenical

6. Sandall, *The History of The Salvation Army*, vol. 1, 26, 29, 38–39, 74–76, 80–85, 93–99, 104, 115, 251–52, on the Booths' connection to the East London Special Services Committee and the Evangelization Society, 1865–70. The nature of the "interlocking directorates" is indicated by a comparison of the lists of committee members of the East London Special Services Committee and the Evangelization Society.

7. Horridge, *The Salvation Army: Origins and Early Days*, 25–26.

atmosphere. The Church of England complimented the Salvation Army when it formed a Church Army in 1883.[8]

In 1910 General William Booth, leading a mission that had grown into a distinctive sect with its own doctrines and ecclesiastical hierarchy, made his first move onto the international ecumenical scene by sending Salvation Army representatives to the Edinburgh World Missionary Conference. And in 1916 his eldest son, Bramwell, the Army's new General after his father's death in 1912, sent Colonels Charles Jeffries and A. G. Cunningham to a British Council of the Christian Crusade.

By 1933 the Salvation Army was well acclimated to international ecumenical relations when S. Carvosso Gauntlett, a mentor of Frederick Coutts in the Literary Department, asserted that the Army's internationalism had caused it to stand "among the most ardent supporters of the League of Nations." Salvationists, Gauntlett held, "almost inevitably think internationally," an interest that grew out of a "constant interchange of Officers" between countries.[9] Gauntlett's contention that internationalism was prompted by international experience is interesting in light of the later division in the Army between those who did and those who did not support its membership in the World Council of Churches. Few North American Salvation Army leaders had served overseas prior to the 1960s. Most of those who had no international experience were parochial in their perspective on other cultural, political, economic, and religious traditions.

Brigadier Christine McMillan, an English-born American officer, held that The Salvation Army's social vision in the mid-1960s included work with United Nations nongovernmental organizations that encouraged "social progress and better standards of life in larger freedom."[10] The American officer appointed as the international Salvation Army representative to the UN was usually one who had experience in social services rather than one who worked in evangelistic endeavors, and normally one who had international experience and language capabilities. Similarly, the Army's representatives at the World Council of Churches were almost always individuals with broad international experience culturally and socially.

In 1948 the Salvation Army joined the World Council of Churches (WCC) as a founding member. General Albert Orsborn (1946–54) chose Marcel Allemand of Switzerland, Arend Beekhuis of the Netherlands, George Bowyer of the United Kingdom, A. G. Cunningham of the International Headquarters, and Ernest Pugmire of the United States, to attend

---

8. Murdoch, "The Salvation Army and the Church of England."
9. Gauntlett, "The Salvation Army as a League of Nations," 5.
10. Christine McMillan, "The Salvation Army and the United Nations," 54.

the founding meeting of the WCC.[11] The Army was unique in that it joined the Council as an international body, unlike national churches that make up nearly all of the WCC's members. The Council does not accept the membership of associations or individuals. Therefore the Army's delegates in the Assembly and its representative on the Central Committee spoke for all Salvationists—African, Asian, European, and American, colonialist and anti-colonialist, fundamentalist and liberal.

The World Council of Churches' creed from its first meeting at Amsterdam was similar to that of the 1846 Evangelical Alliance. It required only that members agree to share "a fellowship of churches that accept our Lord Jesus Christ as God and Savior." There was no requirement to observe sacraments: the Army and the Quakers did not. Nor did the WCC statement of faith exclude women from the clergy. Women in 1948 made up more than half of the Army's officers, whereas most mainline denominations excluded women from the clergy until at least the 1950s. In other words, the WCC was tolerant of aberrations from the faith that most denominations believed had been handed down from the apostles. Commissioner A. G. Cunningham, whom conservatives would have perceived as a theological liberal, served as the Army's representative on the first World Council Executive Committee.

Ecumenism flourished after World War II. Western churches, facing a threat from aggressive "atheistic" communism, drew together to defend their colonial mission empires, their national security and religious cultures. The phobias of the era were reflected in the strategic defense alliances formed in the North Atlantic and Southeast Asia Treaty Organization and in the global peace forum of the United Nations. In this defensive posture there is no evidence that Salvation Army leaders in North America found fault when the Army's British General, Albert Orsborn, decided that the Army should join the World Council of Churches. And they apparently agreed with a statement of an English officer, Commissioner Gordon Simpson, concerning the Army's role in the WCC's Second Assembly at Evanston, Illinois in 1954. Simpson said that the Army's participation was a "logical consummation of a progressive policy of participation in interchurch activities."[12]

In fact, from 1948 to 1978 every Salvation Army General stated support for the World Council of Churches, possibly to assuage North American

---

11. Coutts, *Weapons of Goodwill*, 36.

12. RW [Reginald Woods], "The Army and the World Council of Churches—Some Questions Answered," *The Officer* 12, Sept.-Oct. 1961, 324. This is included in Waldron, ed., *The Salvation Army and the Churches*, a compendium of the Salvationist statements. Waldron mistakenly attributes this article to General Kitching, who had written the two introductory pages under the heading, "The Army and the World Council of Churches—Part I."

anxiety about the WCC's faults. Yet the Army in the U.S. never joined the National Council of Churches of Christ in the U.S., while the Army in virtually every other nation, including Britain and Rhodesia, joined ecumenical conciliar bodies. It may be significant that no statements by American Salvationists appeared in the official international *Officer* magazine in this period to affirm the Army's need for an ecumenical affiliation with world Christianity. These are early, but important indications of the American Army's isolation in ecumenical affairs in the post-World War II period.

To accommodate the Army's position that sacraments are unnecessary to validate a Christian's claim to have been saved from sin, a 1958 World Council document went so far as to insert a footnote that confirmed that the WCC accepted the Quaker and Salvation Army belief in "the non-necessity of the outward elements of bread and wine to mediate the living presence of Christ to the believer in the act of communion with Him."[13] Later, Clause 3.2 of the WCC Canberra Declaration of 1991, expressly accommodated the Salvation Army and the Society of Friends with: "on the basis of convergence in faith in baptism, eucharist and ministry to consider, wherever appropriate, forms of eucharistic hospitality; we gladly acknowledge that some who do not observe these rites share in the spiritual experience of life in Christ."[14]

Such statements were an incredible concession for an ecumenical organization to make since it contained a large number of Protestant churches that came close to subscribing to the Roman Catholic belief in baptismal regeneration. Nearly all believed that baptism was a command of Christ. Virtually all embraced an identical position concerning Jesus' and his apostles' command that the Lord's Supper be observed. The Evangelical Alliance of 1846 had made no such concession to the Quakers.

But Salvationist fears in 1958 focused on possibilities that had not, so far as we can tell, occurred to leaders of the World Council of Churches. First, they feared that the Council might become a super church that would rob the Army of its international policy-making rights. At the time certain right-wing elements in North America were spreading the idea that the United Nations hoped to pull all national governments under its control. This was the era of Senator Joseph McCarthy.

Second, some Salvationists feared that the World Council might exclude the Army from membership based on its non-Eucharistic theological position, the worry that had led to the WCC's 1958 and 1991 concessions

13. Woods, "New Delhi Speaks."
14. http://www.oikumene.org/en/resources/documents/wcc-commissions/faith-and-ordercommission/i-unity-the-church-and-its-mission/the-unity-of-the-church-gift-and-calling-the-canberra-statement.html, downloaded 19 August 2009.

mentioned above. It must be said that although the Army did not share Christianity's traditional sacraments, it had several sacerdotal rites of its own, rites that only its officers (clergy) could administer. These included the "swearing-in" of soldiers (members), the dedication of babies, and the "commissioning" of its officers. In 1978 "commissioning" was renamed "ordination," the same word used by the churches for their sacramental ordering of clergy.

And third, there were Salvationists, particularly in North America, who feared that political actions taken by the WCC might place undue strains on the Army's international character, dividing Salvationists in various parts of the world as they had been divided during the twentieth century's two World Wars. An English officer, Reginald Woods, defended the WCC against these concerns.[15] John Coutts has observed that "Hesitations over the Army's membership of the World Council of Churches can be political as well as religious." Coutts notes that in the 1950s General Orsborn withdrew the Army from the WCC's Central Committee for a time, as did General Wickberg (1969–74) "during the controversy over World Council of Churches grants to insurgent organizations in Southern Africa."[16] Coutts does not specify the reason for Orsborn's action.

Salvation Army Generals have sought to assuage fears that the World Council of Churches is a potential danger to the Army's dogma or polity. But the World Council's Program to Combat Racism grants to support liberation movements, begun in 1970, proved to be the provocation no General could defend against. At least, it can be said that the grants were the ultimate excuse used by the Army's General in 1978–81, Arnold Brown, to suspend the Army's membership in the World Council. The grants allowed the Army's North American leaders to insist that its leaders in London withdraw completely from the WCC. This was in spite of the fact that a majority of the Army's leaders in five continents did not approve the decision, at least not in any open forum where debate took place and votes were counted.

15. Woods, "New Delhi Speaks."

16. Coutts, *The Salvationists*, 32. In the case of Orsborn's "withdrawal," it appears possible that the General simply did not think it worthwhile replacing A. J. Cunningham after his retirement from his role on the Central Committee, rather than having some particular reason for taking offence at the WCC. Orsborn was by his own admission a reluctant ecumenicist. His memorandum to the Advisory Council in 1947 concluded with, "I do not wish my period of leadership to be associated with the gravitation of the Salvation Army nearer to church life in faith and order." Having received the Advisory Council's recommendation to join the WCC, Orsborn commented, "It occurs to me to wonder why we should participate in the Assembly . . . but the majority of our leaders think that we should be represented and therefore I have told the Chief to arrange it." Hubert Westcott, Unpublished paper given at 1969 Commissioner's Conference, 1.

The first catalyst for the suspension of the Army's World Council membership in 1978, and then withdrawal in 1981, was the WCC development of grants to liberation forces in Southern Africa, but the precipitating event was the death of two Salvationist women missionary teachers at Usher Institute, a Salvation Army girls' school in southern Rhodesia on June 7, 1978.

Chapter 10

The Program to Combat Racism and the Salvation Army Reaction, 1969–78

> Any form of segregation based on race, color or ethnic origin is contrary to the gospel and is incompatible with the nature of the Church of Christ. The Assembly urges the churches within its membership to renounce all forms of segregation or discrimination and to work for its abolition within their own life and within society.
>
> —Second Assembly of the World Council of Churches at Evanston, Illinois, 1954[1]

> Few contemporary issues have more profoundly marked the life of the World Council of Churches and how people perceive it than the struggle against racism and in particular the involvement in South Africa.
>
> —Konrad Raiser, General Secretary, World Council of Churches[2]

> Christ our Lord did not come to bring peace to the world as a kind of spiritual tranquilizer. He brought to his disciples a vocation and a task—to struggle in the world of violence to establish his peace not only in their own hearts but in society itself.
>
> —Thomas Merton[3]

---

1. Sjollema, *Isolating Apartheid*, 1.
2. Konrad Raiser, forward to Webb, ed., *A Long Struggle*, vii.
3. Merton, quoted in Webb, *A Long Struggle*, xiv.

The Program to Combat Racism and the Salvation Army Reaction

In 1969, the World Council of Churches' second General Secretary, Eugene Carson Blake, convened a meeting at Notting Hill, England, of church leaders and "representatives of radical movements struggling for racial justice and liberation." The consultation particularly looked at racism in southern Africa, the United States and Europe. Three days before the meeting, an assassin's parcel bomb killed the keynote speaker, Eduardo Mondlane of Mozambique's Frelimo independence movement. Oliver Tambo, South African ANC chairman and an Anglican layman, took Mondlane's place. Tambo quoted from a speech by President Kenneth Kaunda of Zambia to the United Nations: "We are determined to avoid violence where this is possible but we cannot and will not do this at the expense of the tremendous suffering, oppression and exploitation of the majority in southern Africa." The Notting Hill meeting ended with a recommendation that: "all else failing, the church and churches support resistance movements, including revolutions, which are aimed at the elimination of political or economic tyranny which makes racism possible."[4]

The Notting Hill group proposed that the WCC executive and central committees establish a Program to Combat Racism to aid groups that were fighting for racial equality in opposition to the last vestiges of colonialism and racism. When the WCC committees met three months later at Canterbury, General Secretary Blake told the members: "We must examine the implications of the general coincidence of whiteness with economic, political and military power. We must decide whether a new program of study and action, with the emphasis on action, should be undertaken."

The Central Committee debated at length, and then voted to establish an Ecumenical Program to Combat Racism with a Special Fund "to support organizations that combat racism, rather than the welfare organizations that alleviate the effects of racism." The Central Committee presented its criteria for the Executive Committee to distribute grants from the Program to Combat Racism (PCR) Special Fund. First among the six areas of racial conflict that PCR would support was Southern Africa, including Zimbabwe's liberation war. Groups fighting racial injustice would use the grants for "humanitarian activities" that did not conflict with the WCC's "general purposes." Grantees would raise "the level of awareness" and help the racially oppressed to organize. The grants would be awarded "without control" over how they were spent to demonstrate the PCR's commitment "to the cause

---

4. Sjollema, *Isolating Apartheid*, 12–13. Sjollema provides an excellent history of the ecumenical movement's anti-racism ideology from 1921–69 in chapter 1 of Webb's *A Long Struggle*.

of economic, social and political justice." This did not mean that the WCC would not monitor the funds through dialogue with recipients.[5]

The Salvation Army was not the PCR's only strident critic. One conservative commentator claimed that the WCC "grants to African terrorists" surpassed any other act it had taken to arouse "bitter controversy." After 1970 the WCC gave over £500,000, including grants to groups engaged in warfare, to show "moral support for the justice of the terrorists' cause and their political objectives." Some WCC members asked how it could be certain that money given for humanitarian aid was not spent on weapons. In 1970 General Secretary Blake allowed that he could make no guarantee. And in 1975 Blake's successor, Philip Potter, stated that the World Council "would not send inspectors to see whether the money had been spent in the way that it was given—and for good reason. There could be no real sense of solidarity with the people if you did not trust them." In September 1970, the WCC made the first grants to several Southern Africa liberation movements.[6] South Africa's Prime Minister John Vorster criticized the WCC as being "communist-infiltrated" and providing the funds that the terrorist organizations would use to buy arms.[7] Such were the complaints at the peak of the Vietnam war and "Cold War" struggles, at the last gasps of colonialism, and during the international struggle in the United Nations, with its increasing Two-Thirds World membership, over the post-colonial issue of racism.

It was in this context that the Salvation Army leaders' most vocal clashes with the World Council of Churches occurred, reflecting the general turbulence of the volatile era from 1969 to 1981.

Internally, the Army's membership was declining in the United Kingdom and the United States, while its growth was occurring in what has been described correctly as "the Two-Thirds World," a crisis that was also facing other Christian denominations. Since the 1950s African Salvationists had joined and even held positions in their own countries in ecumenical councils that addressed African problems that were being ignored by Salvationists in the West. In 1957 an All Africa Church Conference (AACC) in Nigeria was a major moment for African Salvationists and missionaries who sympathized with them, when Africans asked the Army to develop indigenous leadership. When the AACC wrote a constitution in 1963 in Uganda, conference leaders, including a Salvation Army leader Frederick Adlam, observed that the church's role had to adjust to "conditions of rapid social

---

5. Sjollema, *Isolating Apartheid*, 13–14.
6. Smith, *Fraudulent Gospel*, 5. Smith quoted a speech by Potter in Glasgow, May 1975.
7. Sjollema in Webb, *A Long Struggle*, 15.

change" and that Salvationists relished the fellowship of other churches in the ecumenical councils. Africans advised Western churches to ride the tide of African nationalism so as not to be drowned by it. In August 1968, the Salisbury Area Christian Council Chairman John H. Roberts said: "Racism for the Christian must be put in the same category as adultery, theft and covetousness."[8] The fight against racism had become a moral crusade long before the Program to Combat Racism grants. What was new was that the grants turned rhetoric into action.

The Rhodesian churches' debate over the Program to Combat Racism proposals was brisk. A majority of Africans and whites in the 1969 Methodist Synod held that "Christians ought not to support violence in any form," although they agreed that the World Council of Churches was "not supporting the military purposes of the organizations to which it made grants."[9] The first African Methodist General Superintendent, Andrew Ndhlela, argued that WCC funds "should be used for church projects."[10] The Reverend Fred Rea, a white Methodist pastor, was "distressed" that the WCC and the British Council of Churches would support ZANU (Zimbabwe African National Union) and ZAPU (Zimbabwe African Peoples' Union), the two elements of the Patriotic Front. The Reverend Canaan Banana, in the minority at the Synod, argued that most Africans welcomed WCC action as evidence of "international support for their cry for justice."[11] Dr. Herbert Ushewokunze and the Reverend Philemon Mzongwana agreed, and complained about "the silence of many church leaders on issues of injustice in Rhodesia" that "makes nonsense" of their attacks on the Christian Council of Rhodesia and WCC. When did white church leaders "use their pulpits to condemn oppression, injustice and even the violence inherent in our own society?"[12]

A meeting of the Rhodesia Council of Churches in November 1970 endorsed (with four dissenting votes) the action of the WCC in making grants to guerrilla organizations, including ZANU and ZAPU.[13] Following this meeting the Salvation Army withdrew from the RCC.[14]

8. Adlam, "What is Best for the African People Today?" 45; *Rhodesia Herald*, Aug. 30, 1968.

9. Banana, ed., *Century of Methodism in Zimbabwe*, 139–40.

10. *Rhodesia Herald*, Nov. 5, 1970.

11. Banana, *Century of Methodism in Zimbabwe*, 141.

12. *Rhodesia Herald*, Nov. 18, 1970.

13. Peaden, "Aspects of the Church and its Political Involvement in Southern Rhodesia 1959–1972," *Zambezia* (1979) VII (ii) 208, cites the *Rhodesia Herald*, 11 December 1970.

14. Hallencreutz, *Church and State in Zimbabwe*, 106.

If Salvationists had debated, which their Orders and Regulations did not permit, would their views have been similar to those of the Methodists? Since there was no official forum for debate among Salvationists, no one knows how the majority stood on the issue of PCR grants in 1970. Is it likely that they would have followed the lead of other Rhodesian churches that followed South Africa's white churches in objecting to WCC support for attempts to "change the social order in South Africa by the use of force?"

In 1960 the Dutch Reformed Church left the WCC with the blessing of B. J. Vorster's National Party, the architects of apartheid.[15] In 1971 South Africa's Presbyterian Church voted 75 to 57 to suspend financial contributions to the World Council of Churches, but it did not withdraw from membership. Methodists, Anglicans, and the United Church of Christ followed the Presbyterian lead. Since the Army was an international member of the WCC, its South African and Rhodesian branches could not withdraw from WCC membership or withhold funds. But debates in Southern Africa in other churches did foreshadow debates at meetings of the Salvation Army's international leaders, the only forum for debate in the military-structured organization, where all decisions were left in the final analysis to the General, albeit in the context of lobbying from national leaders. Among the national leaders, the Commissioners in North America had the most clout.

In 1970 the Salvation Army's General and collective international leadership did not take a public stand on the World Council of Churches' grants to liberation movements in Southern Africa. But in 1975, forty of the Army's international leaders met with General Clarence Wiseman near London to discuss the Army's World Council relations. Wiseman claimed that he had had "private misgivings" in 1965 when he served as a member of the Council's Central Committee, but the minutes did not reveal what his misgivings were. Nor did he reveal what he thought in 1975 when he visited Rhodesia and spent several days travelling with Colonel Richard Atwell, the American who was the Army's commander in Rhodesia until 1979 and subsequently served at the London headquarters as the International Secretary for Africa. At the time of that visit, villages north of Salisbury, where the Army had many corps, schools and a hospital, were already "restricted" due to active combat in the region.[16]

At their conference, the Salvation Army leaders' first decision was to reject the World Council of Church's "political involvement" in Rhodesia.

---

15. Pityana, "Tumultuous Response: The Voices of the South African Churches," in Webb, *Long Struggle*, 88–92.

16. Wiseman, *Burning in My Bones*, 150, 232.

Second, they objected to the use of the term "eucharistic fellowship" by the Council since the Army as a full member of the WCC did not practice traditional sacraments of baptism and communion. Third, the leaders argued that the World Council's statements did not carry an "essential evangelical emphasis," a common complaint of churches with a revivalist heritage. Fourth, they claimed that they harbored a "profound unrest" over the Council's defense of "violence in the fight against racialism." They warned that it might "become imperative for the Army to part company with the World Council on this last issue."[17]

But in spite of these strong sentiments, the leaders' press release gave no indication of heated discussions in the closed-door debate, unlike the open minutes that were published by democratic denominations like Rhodesia's Methodist synod. The press and Salvation Army soldiers and officers who were not at the conference only knew what the Army's press told them, namely, that the Army's international leaders had agreed "to maintain our political neutrality while always recognizing the necessity to obey God" in "an age of increasing polarization." In spite what they saw as the World Council of Churches' unwelcome "political attitudes and actions," the Army's leaders' conference only "recommended that the Army should continue its [WCC] membership."[18]

But subsequent correspondence between leaders reveals that Richard E. Holz, American territorial commander in the Western states, expressed a minority view. Holz's letter to the American National Commander Paul S. Kaiser asserted that the *New York Times* had reported a statement that World Council of Churches' General Secretary, Philip Potter, had made in Jamaica. Without revealing the content of Potter's statement, Holz claimed that it supported his views about the World Council's political leanings expressed at the 1975 leaders' conference. Holz asserted that "certain senior [Salvation Army] members" at the conference had told him that his "information was not correct, whereupon I produced the World Council of Churches' publications which supported my fears." Holz thanked Kaiser for an article he had sent to him from the *Presbyterian Layman* concerning the World Council's "Christian terror."

---

17. "Conference of Commissioners and Territorial Commanders," *War Cry*, USA, Aug. 31, 1975; and a clipping at the Salvation Army Archives, Alexandria, Virginia, dated 1976.

18. Coutts, *Weapons of Goodwill*, 312-13.

Rev. Philip Potter, General Secretary of the World Council of Churches. (By permission, Nationaal Archief of the Netherlands, fotocollectie Anefo accesnumber 2.24.01.05 nr 925–8110.)

The context of this exchange between two Salvation Army leaders was the Vietnam war era when the United States was polarized into camps supporting and opposing the war, and by inference, were for or against communist advances in Asia. American Salvation Army leaders held conservative views of communist insurgencies. Holz had served in the United States Air Force as a chaplain during World War II.[19] Holz did not reveal what Potter had said that upset him, nor did he give the citation from the *New York Times*. There is no evidence that other leaders, apart from Paul Kaiser, and almost certainly other American Salvation Army leaders, shared Holz's concern. Later evidence would indicate that the Americans were quite alone in their Cold War fears. This is not surprising since almost none of the nations represented by other Salvation Army leaders were supporting the American war effort in Vietnam.

In November 1975 Harry Williams, a surgeon who had served as a medical missionary and later as a Territorial Commander in India, led the Salvation Army delegation to the World Council of Churches' 5th Assembly at Nairobi, Kenya, where the Program to Combat Racism received its final vote of support. Williams was the Army's WCC Central Committee representative from 1975 to 1980. However, he was not on the Executive

19. Letter from Richard E. Holz to Paul S. Kaiser (Jan. 18, 1979), in the author's possession.

Committee that approved PCR grants. He expressed "misgivings over the operation of this fund." In his 1990 biography he said that he "found it hard to vote for resolutions supporting alternative governments whose own pronouncements offered little hope of understanding or support of the Christian Church and its ethos if and when they came to power." He was apparently referring to the Zimbabwe Patriotic Front leaders. He proclaimed that the Salvation Army's "distinctive ministry" was to save individuals from sin, not nations from imperial rule. Yet he pondered how poor the Army would be "were we not involved in this dialogue with the world," and how poor the World Council of Churches would be without the Army's evangelical witness.[20] He did not share the American view that the Army should resign its membership over the Eucharist or over the World Council's alleged support for violence.

Dr. Williams commented at the World Council of Churches Central Committee in 1976 that the Salvation Army believed a Christian's "fundamental call" was to assist each individual to find Jesus Christ as Savior and Lord, and for the Salvationist that calling "takes precedence over involvement with politics." Violence, he claimed, was not the solution to oppression; and "rightful ends" do not justify violence. Furthermore, he held that the Army believed that the Council had a "political bias" that caused it to hold only certain countries guilty of "infringing human rights," while other "prominent countries, just as guilty, are not mentioned."[21]

Since 1961 communist-bloc nations had sent Orthodox Church delegates to the World Council's meetings. Some Western churches, especially in the United States, pointed to what they thought was an imbalance in the WCC. In fact the American delegates alone outnumbered the entire eastern bloc. The real shift in membership had been from North to South, to the Two-thirds World. In 1948, 42 of the 147 WCC members were from the Two-thirds World. By 1968, 103 of the 253 members were from the Two-thirds World; 41 of the 103 came from Africa.[22] The Salvation Army representatives on the World Council Central Committee were all Anglo-Americans yet these Western members represented all Asian, African and South American Salvationists who made up over half of the Army's members. If there was injustice in representation it was in the Salvation Army, where the international leadership was overwhelmingly white.

---

20. Williams quoted in the *War Cry*, London, Jan. 17, 24, 31, 1976; and in Coutts, *Weapons of Goodwill*, 315. Williams, *I Couldn't Call My Life My Own*, 133–35 and chap. 10: "The Church and the Churches."

21. "The World Council of Churches," *The Officer* 27.8, Aug. 1976, 368–69.

22. Sjollema, "The Initial Challenge," in Webb, *Long Struggle*, 11.

The World Council of Churches vehemently defended its Program to Combat Racism grants to liberation movements in the Two-Thirds World. In 1974, Associate General Secretary Alan Brash objected to the accusation that "political ideology," either "leftist" or "rightist," governed the World Council. He blamed the lack of correct information on bad "newspaper reporting." The WCC had sent $1.5 million a year to South Vietnam for refugees, but only its $300,000 gift of school books to North Vietnam had received "great publicity." While $9 million for schools, hospitals, and farms had gone to Africa, only the $1 million of educational material for a "liberation movement becomes notorious." PCR Director Baldwin Sjollema argued that the Council was in fact acting out "Bible study, prayer, and preaching."[23]

Moderates in the Salvation Army were inclined to see the World Council of Churches as a forum that was open to evangelical as well as liturgical expressions of faith and worship, and to those with emphases on both social and individual expressions of salvation. William Burrows, the editor of the Salvation Army's American edition of the *War Cry* wrote in 1974: "it is too glibly stated that evangelicals stress personal conversion as their mission in contrast to the 'ecumenicals' who emphasize a social gospel." In 1975, after the Salvation Army leaders' meeting near London discussed the World Council, Burrows argued that "what is important is that the voices of evangelical Christians are heard in the WCC and its primary aims reinforced." Burrows, from Britain, proclaimed that the Army "is an international movement with doctrines it shares with the mainline churches."[24]

---

23. Brash, "World Council and the Gospel," 13.

24. Burrows, "Outlook: Evangelism and Dialogue," *War Cry*, US, Aug. 31, 1974, 2; Burrows, "Outlook," *War Cry*, US, Nov. 29 1975, 2.

Chapter 11

The 1978 Deaths at Usher Institute

> My conviction and desire point to a path that I have not yet had the courage and patience and gentleness to follow. We Americans with our ideas of efficiency and organization, with our urge to change, improve, produce—we want to streamline the world and get it going in high gear. The British, less consciously, less openly, but with equal intensity, want the world to be British. The African who is host to us both does not, strangely, try to make us African. God help us—for our American drive becomes disruptive, the British correctness becomes paralyzing; our initiative becomes harsh and willful, the British steadiness becomes reactionary, and the work suffers.
>
> I wish I could walk alongside every other man, without wanting him efficient, with only a desire to make along with him a path for Love to travel. With all the intensity of my being, I wish I could leave all the western claims and ways, that I might go to Africa bearing only one brand—the mark of the Lord Jesus.
>
> —From a letter home to Arkansas by Major Margaret Moore, a missionary teacher who retired from the Salvation Army's Usher Institute in 1977.[1]

A year after American Major Margaret Moore left her teaching post at Usher Institute, a Salvation Army secondary girls' boarding school near Bulawayo in southern Rhodesia, violence reached its peak. Ian Smith's government's determination to hold on to power, British attempts to alter its colony by

---

1. Needham, "Arkansas Traveller with a World View," 4–5.

insisting on majority rule, America's division between support for African rule and its cold warriors' virulent anti-communism, the international Christian humanitarianism of the World Council of Churches, and the African urge for liberation, all played a part.

In March 1978 Ian Smith proposed an Internal Settlement in Rhodesia that excluded the Patriotic Front (PF), the nationalist African liberation movement of Robert Mugabe and Joshua Nkomo. Smith supported Methodist Bishop Abel Muzorewa's election as Prime Minister in 1978 as a cover for his minority rule. Muzorewa's government gained support from the Zimbabwe Christian Council and fellow Methodists, and was favored by Colonel Richard Atwell, the Salvation Army leader. The name "Rhodesia-Zimbabwe" evolved out of a compromise in which Smith promised eventual majority rule. But it was soon apparent that Bishop Muzorewa was Smith's puppet as his white Rhodesian Front party claimed key government posts. The United Nations and African Frontline States refused to recognize the Muzorewa government's legitimacy. Neither did the United Kingdom or United States.

The crisis that led the Salvation Army to exit the World Council of Churches in 1978, and nearly led to a schism in its own ranks in Rhodesia-Zimbabwe, occurred because of one of many vicious wartime incidents.[2] The *Bulawayo Chronicle* carried a page one headline: "2 Salvation Army Mission Women Slain." On June 7, 1978, between 7:00 p.m. and 7:30 p.m., African attackers that the white press called "terrorists" opened fire on five white teachers at the Army's Usher Institute near Figtree, a village 57 kilometers southwest of Bulawayo, the principal city of Matabeleland in southern Rhodesia.

The armed intruders gathered five white missionaries and four African teachers from their cottages along the main road that led to the school's administration building. They went from one teacher's home to the next and insisted that each come with them. John Ncube, one of the first African teachers to hear a knock on his door, was boiling water for supper. He was expecting a friend to join him, so when the intruders knocked he was not surprised. When he went to the door, he asked to be allowed to return to his kitchen in order to turn off the gas stove, but the armed intruders ordered him to come immediately. When the attackers knocked at the door of Angela Cotton, a Salvation Army missionary teacher from London, she walked to the back of her house, which apparently caused them to think that she might be calling the Rhodesian Security Forces. They demanded that

---

2. Curiously this incident appears in almost none of the books on the war, either secular or religious.

she come out right away. As they moved down the road from the teachers' cottages toward the administration building, the attackers surrounded the African teachers and kept the white teachers in front of them.

The African secondary teachers at Usher included Joseph Pfende, Rushwaya, Aloisy Ngwenya, Moffat M. Mhlange, Mrs. Tazitsona, and Pathisa Nyathi. Two of them had been drinking that evening and had gone to bed. Apparently the attackers could not arouse them and they were not among those being escorted down the road.

As they passed the administration building, the attackers suddenly heard the sound of a truck. They may have thought that it was Rhodesian Security Forces and suspected that Angela Cotton may have tried to call it. In fact, the sound came from the Usher Institute kombi returning from an errand. But the attackers panicked and their commander ordered his men to fire. Two white teachers lay dying and two more were severely wounded.[3]

The AK47 gunfire killed Diane Thompson, aged twenty-eight, a Salvation Army lieutenant from Shepherd's Bush, England, and her friend, Sharon Swindells, aged twenty-five, a Salvationist from Bangor, Northern Ireland. Thompson had been at Usher for two years and Swindells had been at the school for ten months. Just a week or so earlier the two women had supper with John Ncube and another African teacher. Ncube recalled that Sharon Swindells, who was more outgoing than her friend Diane Thompson, had mentioned how safe she felt in Zimbabwe compared to her home in Northern Ireland. The two injured Salvationists were David Cotton, a thirty-eight-year old Salvation Army captain from Hadleigh, Essex, who had been a missionary for thirteen years and taught math and physics; and Gunvor Berit Paulsson, aged thirty-seven, a Swedish woman major who was Usher's Vice-Principal. Cotton's wife Angela, who taught art, escaped injury.

---

3. Murdoch interview with John Ncube at Bulawayo, Zimbabwe, on Aug. 20, 1998. John Ncube, an African teacher at Usher and an eyewitness to the shootings, provided me with a reliable account of the killings. I also interviewed Pathisa Nyathi, at Bulawayo, on Aug. 20, 1998. Nyathi was not an eyewitness. Another teacher, Moffat M. Mhlange, declined an interview due to the Zimbabwe Official Secrets Act; he teaches at a government school and comes under this regulation. Other African Salvationists and expatriate missionaries gave interviews during my research trips to Zimbabwe and London in 1991 and 1998. The first newspaper report was, "2 Salvation Army Women Slain," *The Chronicle*, Bulawayo, June 9, 1978, 1. I have written to the Zimbabwe police in Bulawayo and to survivors. The police said that the outgoing Rhodesian government destroyed records in 1980. David Cotton, now a teacher in Hadleigh, Essex, and no longer a Salvation Army officer, refused an interview. I was not able to contact Gunvor Palsson in Sweden. Jean Caldwell has died. While I was a Research Associate at the University of Zimbabwe in August 1998 I addressed a graduate seminar. Dr. Paul Gundame, a lecturer in Christian history, and his graduate students offered me excellent leads for my research.

The Principal, Jean Caldwell, a major from England, was in her house. When she became aware of the seriousness of the injuries she ran to the Clinic to ask Sylvia Nevanji, a young African nurse from Gweru, to leave her two children to attend to David Cotton's wounds. Nevanji found Cotton crawling toward the Principal's house. She ran to the house, grabbed a doormat, and went back to find Cotton. She placed him on the doormat and dragged him back to Caldwell's house where she stopped his bleeding and administered first aid. Mrs. Nevanji asked Major Caldwell about the fate of Thompson and Swindells. Caldwell said they were both dead. Mrs. Nevanji ran back to her children in the dark. At the time her husband was a student in London. He heard the news of the killings on television.[4]

The security forces police of the Joint Operations Command (JOC) for the Tangent sector arrived at 11:30. They did a cursory search for the killers, but did not question the eye witnesses, the African teachers, who were back in their cottages at the time. The teachers' first impulse was to run away from the school into adjacent fields, but they realized that these were owned by a white commercial farmer, so they decided to return to their cottages. The report the police gave to the media and Salvation Army leaders was not based on any eyewitness interviews with the African teachers who had seen the killings from their vantage point in the midst of the guerrillas.

The next morning buses arrived to take the 300 children to the Bulawayo YMCA, escorted by Security Forces who made arrangements for the children to go to their homes. Only a few laborers remained at Usher. The Salvation Army closed the school.

In the absence of a thorough police investigation of the evidence that was available at the time, the media, white Rhodesians, Salvation Army leaders, and African nationalists, including the Army's African officers and soldiers, were allowed to freely speculate on the cause of the killings. Many white Rhodesians believed that guerrillas were picking off missions as "soft targets" because they could, perhaps in order to underline the failure of the government to control the situation militarily, and to mobilize international opinion and thus make a settlement more likely. African nationalists believed that the attackers were members of Ian Smith's dreaded Selous Scouts, a secretive fifth column unit, membership of which was 80 percent African. Joshua Nkomo, the independence leader in Matabeleland, claimed that the gunman who had killed a priest and a nun at a Roman Catholic mission the Friday before the Usher killings, had been attached to Smith's forces. In general, he blamed Rhodesian intelligence officers for being the killers of "priests and missionaries in order to put the blame on our nationalist

---

4. Murdoch interview with Sylvia Nevanji, R.N., at Gweru, Aug. 23, 1998.

The 1978 Deaths at Usher Institute 153

guerrillas." Their alleged intent was to bring African nationalists into disrepute with Western governments at a time when the United Nations, Britain, and United States were supporting majority African rule.[5] Nkomo did not specifically mention the Usher killings in his analysis. John Wesley Kurewa, an African Methodist minister who served in the new African-majority Zimbabwe Parliament in 1980–89, claimed that "Rhodesia security forces" had killed "many church leaders, both lay and ordained." He cited a Roman Catholic study as support for his contention.[6]

Although Andrew Young, the American Ambassador to the United Nations, argued that Ian Smith's forces had planned the Usher attack, he also provided an alternative explanation—that "uncontrolled rebel gangs" did the killing. He alleged that if such gangs had been even loosely attached to Nkomo's forces, they "would have been immediately crushed by the nationalists." But at the same time, Young found "no documentary or oral evidence to support the allegation that the Selous Scouts perpetrated the killings." In the end he concluded that other "partisans of Smith's interim government were responsible for the massacres of white missionaries" as "part of a planned operation against the missions."[7]

The Rhodesian police did not arrive at the scene until four hours after the killings occurred. When they arrived they failed to interview any African eyewitnesses yet they concluded that Joshua Nkomo's ZIPRA soldiers had done the killing. They gave this report to the censored white Rhodesian media, released it to the British and international press, and gave this conclusion to Salvation Army spokesman, Colonel David Ramsay from England, who was Chief Secretary (second-in-command of the Salvation Army in Rhodesia). The police gave as their evidence the presence of communist AK47 weapons, but Smith's Selous Scouts were also said to carry weapons manufactured in communist bloc countries in order to deflect blame onto the African guerrillas. It must be said that there are Africans, as well as whites, who accept the view that the attackers were from Nkomo's forces.[8] One also needs to remember that there were Africans in the Rhodesian regular forces as well as in the Selous Scouts.

5. Nkomo, *Nkomo: My Life Story*, 168–69.

6. Kurewa, *The Church in Mission*, 156, cites a Roman Catholic study to confirm his view: *A New People, A New Church*. Hertogenbosch, Holland: Dutch Missionary Council, 1980, 96.

7. Letter from N. Mukura to Murdoch, Dec. 4, 1996, in which Miss Mukura quotes from Zimbabwe National Archives Ref.: MS 308/59.

8. Two of my African interviewees in Bulawayo on August 20, 1998, cited personal and local opinion for believing that it was Nkomo's forces, whether disciplined or loosely attached, who did the killing.

But whoever did the actual killing, the Rhodesian police and media reports were based on shoddy police work and there was no investigative journalism to inform the media. Unless evidence can be secured by interviews with white policemen, or with the African attackers, or from unpublished files of Nkomo's ZIPRA forces or Smith's Security police, it is impossible to know for certain who killed Diane Thompson and Sharon Swindells.[9] At this late date it may be irrelevant to our investigation since the truth will not alter the fact that those who supported Smith and minority rule, and those who supported African nationalist rule, lined up on opposite sides in what was, in the absence of evidence, a propaganda war. In such situations it is more important to claim a political victory than it is to seek the truth.

David J. Maxwell's study of the ZANLA (Robert Mugabe's army) guerrilla attack on the Elim Pentecostal Emmanuel Mission School in the Eastern Highlands in late June 1978 may shed light on the nature of the Usher attack. The leaders at Elim were what Maxwell terms missionaries whose "intellectual response to the war [was] limited by their conservative evangelical theology" that focused on "individual transformation to the exclusion of social justice and structural change." Could that have been said of the Army's missions? In each case African Christians and missionaries, but not the denominational leaders in America, sought ecumenical support for their isolated mission. Both missions depended on African workers in the area for their protection and that, according to Maxwell, is where deficiencies lay.[10]

White commercial farms surrounded Usher's primary and secondary schools. Isolated from villages in the area, Usher did not provide a Salvation Army Corps (church) for Africans.[11] Without these vital connections with Africans in the area, Usher had little advanced warning of a guerrilla attack from friendly neighbors, although there was some evidence of intruders in the area. Since Usher closed immediately after the killings, there is no

---

9. Letter from Mark Ncube, National Military Museum at Bulawayo, to Murdoch, Jan. 20, 1997 says that "it will not be easy to find the fighters who operated in Usher, but it is not impossible as ZIPRA was a well-structured army and people are now willing to talk on the war freely." During my 1998 visit to Bulawayo and Usher I did not interview a fighter in Nkomo's forces, nor have I been able to contact any members of the Selous Scouts in South Africa.

10. The Catholic Church, however, consistently opposed the policies of the Rhodesian government in the name of social and political justice, but some of its personnel, including a bishop, were also killed.

11. According to Nyandoro's 1993 history, Dianne Thompson, who was Corps Officer for the school (chaplain) as well as a teacher, "showed special interest in the people living in the surrounding villages, and did all she could to be of assistance and encouragement to them." Nyandoro, *Flame of Sacred Love*, 123.

evidence that the dead missionaries achieved "martyrdom" in the village of Figtree any more than Cass had achieved it among Africans in the Mazoe area in 1896. At Elim the missionaries, eight adults and their four children, were saluted as "martyrs" and the school reopened with African leaders in charge. The overseas reaction was similar in both cases. In Britain a neofascist National Front distributed a leaflet with a picture of the Elim massacre victims in order to discredit the World Council of Churches, whereas the Zimbabwe press in 1988, after independence and majority rule, blamed the Selous Scouts for the killings.[12]

The Salvation Army conducted an impressive funeral for Diane Thompson and Sharon Swindells at St. John's Anglican Cathedral in Bulawayo on June 13. A crowd of 500 viewed a procession that was led by the flag of the Salvation Army's International Headquarters in London, flown in for the occasion, and the Rhodesian flag. Twelve African nationals and missionary officers carried the two caskets, and placed them next to the Usher Institute flag and a floral wreath from the Army's General, Arnold Brown, and his Chief of Staff. Mr. and Mrs. John R. Thompson and Brother and Sister William Swindells, the deceased women's parents, came from the United Kingdom to attend their children's funeral. The Matabeleland Anglican Bishop John Haynes, and the Roman Catholic Bishop Henry Karlen attended. The Salisbury Citadel band, joined by Bulawayo bandsmen, and 300 Salvationists marched to the cemetery playing "Promoted to Glory," a term the Army uses for death. Then the congregation sang, "Safe in the arms of Jesus" as the caskets were lowered into a double grave that the parents requested.[13] The Army's African Divisional Commander for Matabeleland, Major Jabel Ndhlovu, prayed, "O God, forgive our people for this wrong that has been done." William Swindells later responded: "Tell your people, we bear no grudge . . . we only pray that they may come to know the God we love and serve." Bulawayo Citadel's officer, Captain Shaw Clifton, gave the benediction.[14]

---

12. Maxwell, "Christianity and the War in Eastern Zimbabwe: The Case of Elim Mission," 63–64, 69, 74, 82, 86, 88. Maxwell cited "Comrade Marovha," a Salvationist who was a guerrilla and was well known for having a Christian background. Maxwell's point was that in areas around Elim where the "brokers of popular religion were Christians, guerrillas were forced to seek legitimacy from priests and Black pastors, rather than spirit mediums."

13. Jean Caldwell, the Usher Principal, had both of these songs sung at her funeral in 1993.

14. David W. Ramsay, Chief Secretary, "Report on Funeral of Lieutenant Diane Barbara Thompson and Sister Sharon Faith Swindells," 2 pages.

General Eva Burrows visits the grave of Sharon Swindells and Lieut. Diane Thompson in 1987. To the left of the General are Major Philemon Ndhlovu, Mrs. Major Georgina Ndhlovu, and Commissioner David Moyo. To the right, Mrs. Commissioner Selina Moyo, Mrs. Commissioner Brenda Coles and Commissioner Alan Coles.

Since January 6, 1978 the Salvation Army in Rhodesia had been under the Joint Command of Colonel Richard Atwell, an American who had been territorial commander since April 1973, and the first African to be promoted to this position in Zimbabwe, Lieutenant Colonel David Moyo.[15] The Army's General in London had appointed Moyo to this position six months before the killings at Usher in his native Ndebele area of southwest Rhodesia. The International Secretary for Africa at the time of the killings was George Nelting, another American, whom Atwell would replace in that position in March 1979. The Salvation Army *Yearbook* reported that 1978 had been "unusual and sensitive," a first class understatement. The events at Usher were not reported in the *Yearbook*.

---

15. On March 15, 1979 David Moyo, having held joint command with Richard Atwell, became the first African Salvation Army officer to hold the office of territorial commander in Zimbabwe, after Atwell's departure. Moyo served as territorial commander until 1987 when Alan Coles, a British officer who had previously worked in Zimbabwe, succeeded him. "Joint Territorial command" was an administrative device the Salvation Army hierarchy employed in a number of developing world countries for a few years in this period, where it belatedly felt under some pressure to advance indigenous officers to this senior role but was reluctant to trust them with full responsibility after having failed to prepare them adequately in previous years. Nyandoro notes that Moyo was unprepared for the role (*Flame of Sacred Love*, 192).

The Usher Institute would not reopen until the end of the war, in March 1980, with 240 students. When it closed in June 1978, it had 267 secondary boarding pupils, and 260 primary pupils of whom 60 were boarders.[16] The Salvation Army reported that there was "continuing dissident activity in the area" in early 1980, but it did not define what it meant by "dissident."[17]

16. "Rhodesia," *The Salvation Army Year Book, 1979*, 176–77. The information is current up to September 30, 1978, and thus should have covered the period of the Usher killings of June 7, 1978.

17. Silk, "Usher Institute: A Rehabilitation Success Story," *All the World*, Jan.–Mar. 1982, 169–70. In the early 1980s, tension between erstwhile supporters of Nkomo and Mugabe respectively culminated in the "Gukurahundi" (Shona: "the early rain which washes away the chaff before the spring rains"), a secretive Government military campaign after majority rule to eradicate a perceived separatist Ndebele threat in Matabeleland, in which some 20,000 are believed to have been killed by North Korean trained Zimbabwean troops. "Dissident activity" could have referred to the opening phase of this catastrophe.

Chapter 12

Salvation Army Reaction to the Usher Killings, 1978–83

> Despite unusual and sensitive situations, the year under review produces evidence of ever-increasing outreach to the people, particularly in rural areas. There has been a marked increase in soul-saving; almost 3,000 soldiers have been sworn-in and over 4,000 recruits are in training to become Salvationists. Eleven new corps have been opened and a number of societies have commenced.
>
> —Entry on "Rhodesia" in *The Salvation Army Year Book* for 1979[1]

On June 18, 1978, just after a band of African fighters killed two women Salvation Army missionaries from Britain, Colonel Richard Atwell, the Army's Joint Territorial Commander in Rhodesia with Lt. Colonel David Moyo, wrote to his friend "Paul." "Paul" was almost certainly the Army's National Commander in the United States, Commissioner Paul S. Kaiser (1977–79). Kaiser later mentioned that he had inside knowledge of the Rhodesia situation when he spoke to an ecumenical group in New York City, possibly pointing to information he had received from Atwell.[2] Atwell's letter charged that since the "terrorists" carried "communist made weapons" they "represented Nkomo." He came to this conclusion based on police reports since neither he nor any other Salvation Army leader interviewed the African eyewitnesses to

---

1. *The Salvation Army Year Book 1979*, 176. No reference was made in the Year Book to the events at Usher Secondary School.

2. Letter, Mrs. Paul S. Kaiser to Murdoch, July 21, 1995, informed me that "when we left Ohio [in] 1987 Paul's diaries were unfortunately destroyed . . . ."

the crime. Rhodesia's government-censored media had also based their articles on information released by the Security Force police.

Commissioner Paul Kaiser presenting classroom maps to Howard Secondary School, 1977, with Lieut. Linda Schearing and Headmaster Lemuel C. Tsikirayi. (Photo, The Howard Annual 1977.)

In his letter to "Paul," Atwell indicated where his sympathies lay by expressing pleasure that a "London paper refers to the attackers rightly as Terrorists," not "Freedom Fighters," which "would be out of character with their actions." Since the international media also drew their knowledge of the case from a superficial police report and censored Rhodesian newspapers, it is hardly surprising that they used the Smith term, "Terrorists," rather than the African nationalist designation of the pro-independence soldiers as "Freedom Fighters."

Linking the Usher killings to those of "19 other missionary friends" in Rhodesia, Richard Atwell, along with most whites in Rhodesia, aligned himself with those who blamed African "terrorists" for all missionary massacres. In fact, it is possible that many black Africans accepted this conclusion, unsupported by evidence, drawn by Smith's government and given to the white-controlled media. Atwell, like Smith and most white Rhodesians, blamed the British and American governments for supporting the Patriotic Front of Robert Mugabe and Joshua Nkomo, which Atwell claimed denied "human rights and [the] democratic concept." But in the West the term "democratic concept" was taken to mean one-man one-vote majority rule since the late nineteenth century, an idea Ian Smith had resisted since he assumed power as Prime Minister in 1964. Ian Smith's declaration of Rhodesia's "unilateral independence" in 1965 was a direct repudiation of democratic principles, and Western democracies were treating Smith's regime as illegal in 1978. Britain claimed that it would retain legal sovereignty over the country until Rhodesia agreed to a constitutional settlement and majority rule. This would not happen until 1980, after over a decade of armed struggle.

Colonel Atwell's letter to his friend "Paul" also raises important church-state questions for the Salvation Army, since the Army's official policy had long been one of non-involvement in political issues. What was the Army's relationship with Ian Smith's government in 1978, both as a London-based international organization and in terms of its Rhodesian leaders' political leanings? Atwell's letter raises an important question. Did Colonel Atwell in Rhodesia and General Brown in London lobby to alter Anglo-American foreign policy that favored majority rule in Rhodesia-Zimbabwe in 1978?

Group of retired Salvation Army officers at Mazowe with Commissioner Richard Atwell and Mrs. Doris Atwell. In the centre of the group is Major Leonard Kirby O.F. and top right, Major Ben Gwindi, both then aged over ninety.

Atwell's letter praised General Arnold Brown, the Army's international leader, for writing a letter to British Foreign Secretary David Owen, to seek a change in British foreign policy that supported what Atwell termed "the Communist-backed Patriotic Front." Atwell told "Paul" that he had written a similar request to President Jimmy Carter, "as a matter of Christian principle." Atwell alleged that Smith had agreed to support "Independence and African rule by 31 December." [1978][3]

It is true that under British and South African pressure in March 1978 Smith had begun to negotiate an Internal Settlement with Africans of his choosing that would lead to their participation in the Rhodesian government.[4] The Patriotic Front of Joshua Nkomo and Robert Mugabe, the principal forces who were fighting for majority rule, were not parties to these negotiations. In fact, in 1979 Smith would choose Abel Muzowera, a Methodist Bishop, to replace him as Prime Minister, without the benefit of a legitimate democratic election. Smith had only agreed to negotiate with Africans whom he felt he could manipulate. These negotiations produced neither a cease-fire with the Patriotic Front nor majority African rule. Rather it was a political ploy to continue Smith's fourteen-year program of white settler government in spite of the modest attempts by Britain, the United States, and many Rhodesian whites to change his mind.

Did Richard Atwell's and Arnold Brown's letters violate Salvation Army regulations against political activity and its claims to the World Council of Churches that, unlike the WCC, the Army was apolitical? General Brown did not respond to specific questions concerning the content of the letter Atwell said Brown had written to the British Foreign Secretary David Owen. While Atwell may be a credible witness in stating his understanding of Brown's involvement in this matter, there is no evidence to support his assertion. David Owen states that he does not have a copy of correspondence with Brown if such an exchange occurred.[5] My attempts to find his letter through correspondence with the Public Records Office were to no avail. The Army's Archives in London also have no record of the letter.

---

3. Letter, Richard Atwell to "Paul," 28 June 1978, in the author's possession.

4. An intermediate stage in 1978 was the formation of a government to be led month-about by Ian Smith (Rhodesia Front), Bishop Abel Muzorewa (African National Council), Senator Chief Jeremiah Chirau (Zimbabwe United Peoples' Organisation) and the Rev. Ndabaningi Sithole (founder of ZANU). Muzorewa defeated Sithole in the subsequent election, in which Mugabe and Nkomo were unable to participate.

5. Letter, General Arnold Brown to Norman H. Murdoch, 20 March 1995; Letter, Norman H. Murdoch to General Arnold Brown, 7 November 1994. Letter, David Owen to Norman H. Murdoch, 21 November 1994.

The Salvation Army officially asserts that it is apolitical. A recent official history of the Army that covers this general period states that the Army's "only official comment on the [Vietnam] war confirmed . . . its refusal to take a stand on issues that its leaders regarded as merely political or social."[6] The prohibition against political meddling by Salvationists goes back to the Army's Wesleyan past.[7] Although the Army has honored this dictum rather casually on several occasions, including William and Catherine and Bramwell Booths' participation in debates over public issues of Sabbath-keeping and the age of consent of young women in the late nineteenth century, it is a principle that the Army has continued to claim to uphold in the 1970s and 1980s.

Should it be regarded as "official comment" if the Army's commander in Rhodesia and its General in London (if Atwell is right about Brown) communicate political views to an American President and a British Foreign Minister? And did Atwell's reaction to the killings at Usher represent the views of African Salvationists, about 98 percent of its members in Rhodesia, and its African and missionary officers whom Atwell commanded? It is hard to say. Salvation Army officers in Rhodesia, native and expatriate, represented a wide range of political opinion. One Canadian missionary doctor, Major Jim Watt at Howard Hospital, spoke of wanting to join the guerrillas in Chiweshe at one point in the war. But other Salvationists, including Africans, were members of the government Army. Many Africans had a family tradition of serving in the military, long pre-dating the Smith government. White Salvationists were conscripted.

It is possible that many if not most Salvationists tried to stay within the boundaries of the Army's policy to avoid political involvement, even at the risk of being treated as traitors by fellow Africans. Unlike other churches the Army had no official internal debate over such policy issues as supplying chaplains to one side or the other. To a large degree the Salvation Army was a stealth mission about which little was written or known by historians or by other churches. When it suspended its membership in the World Council of Churches in 1978 as a direct result of the Usher killings it no doubt created a louder noise than it intended.

---

6. McKinley, *Marching to Glory*, 256, 179, 211, refers to the Army's policy on political involvement. He refers to support of the 18th amendment as its only political stand down to 1992.

7. For the Methodist transition from a policy of no political involvement to involvement in the mid-nineteenth-century election of Abraham Lincoln and support for the American Civil War, see Carwardine, "Methodists, Politics, and the Coming of the American Civil War," which covers a similar internal struggle and a similar division in a church such as the one I am discussing here.

Salvation Army Reaction to the Usher Killings, 1978-83

An international storm erupted in September 1978 when the World Council of Churches' Program to Combat Racism gave an $85,000 (US) grant to the Patriotic Front of Joshua Nkomo and Robert Mugabe just three months after the killing of two British women Salvationists at Usher Institute. In response General Arnold Brown suspended the Salvation Army's membership in the World Council soon after news of the grant hit the press. The WCC claimed that critics of the 1978 grant were "a relatively small number of member churches in the North Atlantic area." In fact, there were only three churches that suspended their WCC membership: the Salvation Army, the Irish Presbyterians, and the Evangelical Lutheran Church of West Germany. The WCC defended its grants to the Patriotic Front on ground that the decision was based on "theological and political principles undergirding the inception of the Fund . . . ."

The World Council of Churches accused the Salvation Army and others of engaging in "well organized attempts to discredit the work—in fact the very essence—of the WCC, through a distortion of the aims and nature of this program." It maintained that its Program to Combat Racism had: 1) "demonstrated ecumenical commitment to the struggle of the racially oppressed," 2) "helped reveal the depth and pervasiveness of racist attitudes and structures . . . often fostered by the mass media" and 3) "encouraged many Christians and churches in the poor countries to remain united with the victims of racial oppression." It asserted that "the doctrine and practice of apartheid is a perversion of the Christian gospel," and asked all churches "to examine in penitence their own involvement in racism."[8] There was little international objection a year later when the Program to Combat Racism aided the Patriotic Front delegations at the 1979 Lancaster House negotiations that ended the war and brought majority African rule of the new state of Zimbabwe.

From 1974 to 1981 Salvation Army Generals Clarence Wiseman (1974-77) and Arnold Brown (1977-81), both Canadians, tried to mollify both sides in the Army's internal struggle over World Council of Churches' membership. The Army's US leaders called for it to leave the WCC because of its "political" support for Marxist liberation movements, while Africans and international Salvationists (the Army was active in nearly ninety countries at the time) supported both majority rule and the Army's membership in the WCC and other conciliar-ecumenical movements. Wiseman and Brown hoped to ease the strain within Army ranks between the Americans and the rest of the world, and to present a united international front to its friends and potential foes, but by 1978, pressure from the North Americans led Brown to suspend the Army's WCC membership, which later led to a complete break.

8. "Unit II: Justice and Service," *World Council of Churches Central Committee, Nairobi to Vancouver*. Geneva: WCC, 1983, 150-56.

The Army's WCC representative was Commissioner Dr. Harry Williams, a British-born missionary surgeon, whose international service, including appointments in India, Australia, New Zealand, and Vietnam, made him sensitive to a world-view.[9] As the Rhodesian independence war continued in the 1970s, Rhodesian branches of the British Council of Churches, Christian Aid, Christian Care, Oxfam and other organizations, distributed humanitarian aid through churches, organized groups, and individuals. This was particularly true in Chiweshe in Rhodesia, an area in which the Salvation Army had worked in schools, hospital and corps for more than seventy years.[10] The WCC Program to Combat Racism was giving aid directly to the Patriotic Front to supply educational materials and food to Zimbabwe's war refugees in Mozambique and Zambia, including Salvationists.

To place balm on the wound, General Brown clouded the real cause of the Salvation Army's withdrawal from World Council of Churches membership in 1981. He did not want to appear insensitive to the Third World where well over half of all Salvationists lived. Thus he did not repeat the report that African "terrorists" had killed the two missionaries. Instead, he placed the blame on "political" actions taken by the WCC through its grants to the Patriotic Front. But his attempt at crisis management, by de-emphasizing the connection between the suspension and then withdrawal, and the killing of missionaries, was undercut by reports in Salvation Army magazines and later analysis in its official histories.

An official American Salvation Army history in 1980 recorded that the Army suspended its WCC membership after the World Council had "authorized a grant of funds to guerrilla organizations in Rhodesia-Zimbabwe, members of which were implicated in the murder of unoffending Salvation Army missionaries in that country."[11] Official Army public relations statements showed that Army leaders were out of touch with the reasons why Africans had decided, by whatever means, to overthrow white minority rule. They did not grasp, whether due to ignorance or due to their own con-

---

9 For the views of these three men see: Wiseman, *A Burning in My Bones*; Brown, *The Gate and the Light*; Harry Williams, *I Couldn't Call My Life My Own*. The latter two men have corresponded with me.

10. Chiweshe people were moved into fenced locations ("Protected Villages") under urgency by the Rhodesian Government in mid-winter in 1974 in an attempt to isolate guerrillas operating in the area. After protests from local Salvationists and missionaries alerted public opinion to peoples' hardship, Oxfam provided a lorry and building materials and the Salvation Army seconded an officer to arrange the building of homes for elderly people and others who could not do this for themselves in the new locations.

11. McKinley, *Marching to Glory*, 218–19; and 2nd edit., 284. Since Salvation Army authorities approve official histories, characterizations that they approve can fairly be regarded as the Army's official position.

servative political leanings, why the World Council had chosen to support African liberation movements in the 1970s.

In 1907, Commissioner George Scott Railton, a Salvationist who scouted southern Africa as an aide to General William Booth, asked: "Will the great God and Father of all much longer allow the white races, calling themselves Christians, to go on ignoring the rights and the highest interests of all other peoples?"[12] Railton, a committed evangelist and Booth's first general secretary, with little love for structural social reform, endorsed African independence. His hatred for injustice was shared by few contemporaries in Cecil Rhodes' South Africa and perhaps not, in southern Africa, by William Booth. Surprisingly, the views of Western Salvationists had changed little by 1978, in spite of independence movements in Asia and Africa that followed World War II.

What problems faced the Salvation Army in Zimbabwe when its African soldiers protested against General Brown's decision to terminate the Army's World Council of Churches membership in 1981? But first we will look at the internal tensions in the Army's international leadership prior to that decision.

General Arnold Brown. (By permission, The Salvation Army.)

12. Coutts, *The Salvationists*, 127, 129. Railton was a man of broad sympathies and learning. He argued for allowing Africans who practiced polygamy to become Salvationists.

First, tensions between international Salvation Army leaders and the World Council of Churches increased after General Brown suspended the Army's membership on August 21, 1978, in the wake of the Usher killings. Before he would officially terminate the Army's WCC membership Brown had promised international leaders that he would seek a vote. Unlike more democratic denominations that joined the Army in suspending their WCC memberships, the Lutheran Evangelical Church of West Germany, and the Presbyterian Church of Ireland whose vote was 561 to 393, the Salvation Army had no democratic polity to inhibit or incite its leaders to vote.[13] In fact, William Booth had abolished voting in 1878 when he formed his "army." The British Council of Churches, an ecumenical body to which the Army belonged, had suspended its contributions to the Program to Combat Racism under pressure from member churches, realizing that support of the PCR was voluntary.

In spite of his right as General to make decisions on his own authority, at the time of his 1977 election as General by the Salvation Army High Council, Arnold Brown had promised to "require the support of the majority of Commissioners" before he would withdraw the Army from the World Council.[14] There are references in Army records to a poll in 1978–81, but if Brown took such a poll he did not publish the results for Salvationists to see what was in the minds of their leaders. The basis on which Brown made his decision to withdraw in 1981 is therefore unclear. However it is abundantly clear that American commissioners were placing Brown under tremendous pressure to end the Army's fifty-three-year-long membership in the world's leading ecumenical body.

In January 1979 Commissioner Dr. Harry Williams, at a meeting of the World Council of Churches Central Committee in Jamaica, tried to amend a resolution that approved a grant to the Zimbabwe Patriotic Front. Williams said that he abhorred racism as "one of the evidences of human sinfulness," but he claimed that Christians differed on how best to combat this evil. "Some of us question the making of grants" with a primary intent of "showing solidarity with selected groups whose aim is political and whose methods include violence." He asked, "Should not the actual expression of concern be by the Churches at work in the country concerned, so that WCC funds are mediated through such Church Councils" and not

13. Smith, *Fraudulent Gospel*, 15–18, praised the Army for suspending its WCC membership, but he did not mention the June 7 Usher incident. He did note that the August 11 WCC grant came three weeks after "the slaughter of eight British Pentecostal missionaries and their four children" at the Elim mission.

14. Letter from General Arnold Brown to Commissioners, Sept. 8, 1978, in the author's possession.

through a "militant organization?" He argued that "in areas of conflict WCC aid should be impartially given to all."[15] His amendment lost by a 2 to 1 vote of Central Committee members.

In September 1979 General Arnold Brown called a meeting of the Army's international leadership at Toronto, Canada, where a vigorous debate ensued over the Army's WCC membership. Denis Hunter, a British colonel who had served in Rhodesia, listed documents that informed the discussion. They included: 1) Brown's September 8, 1978 statement when he suspended the Army's WCC membership; 2) a summary of December 1978 meetings of the Army and WCC representatives; 3) correspondence between Brown and WCC General Secretary Philip Potter, published in *The Officer*; and 4) Harry Williams' articles in *The Officer* and his statement to the WCC Central Committee in Jamaica. Hunter asked a pivotal question: "Is it the case that the soul of the World Council of Churches has so far died that it would be impossible to revive it?" Hunter argued that the fact that Williams' Jamaica amendment lost by a 2–1 margin indicated that there was "an important evangelical grouping within the Central Committee" that "would be weakened by our departure."

Not wanting to raise the ire of the anti-Program to Combat Racism group, Hunter asked that the leaders privately inform General Brown of their positions on WCC membership. Hunter may have expected the vote to go against withdrawal. That was the calculated expectation of the Americans. But until Brown made his decision, Hunter agreed to accept a proposal made by American National Commander Ernest Holz, that the Army would "remain in our present 'suspended' position" and that "eventual action be now passed to the General" without future need to consult commissioners. This action would release Brown from the promise he made to the 1977 High Council when he promised to consult with the commissioners before he would make any decision regarding WCC membership. Hunter asked the leaders to be sensitive to Salvationists of Rhodesia/Zimbabwe who had "felt the weight of the decision" to suspend WCC membership. The WFS, the "world fellowship of Salvationists" was his primary concern.[16]

When General Brown spoke he traced the Army's protest over the Program to Combat Racism grants, but he claimed that the World Council of Churches had given "no re-action." In December 1978 Army representatives had met with WCC leaders to challenge "aid given to non-acceptable groups." Apart from speeches by Philip Potter and Pauline Webb in defense

15. Harry Williams, Statement at the WCC Central Committee, Jan. 2, 1979 (3 pages).

16. Denis Hunter, "World Council of Churches," Toronto Meeting of Salvation Army Leaders, Sept. 1979 (7 pages).

of the WCC position, the meeting had been "a good day of Christian fellowship," nothing more, according to Brown. The Army had not withdrawn its membership in 1978, only suspended it. Brown claimed that there were Salvationists who found it hard to understand that the WCC "has entered into the political arena." But "the eyes of the world [are] on this Conference."

Harry Williams mentioned areas of concern, but in most cases they were apparently not issues of debate in the 1979 meeting of Army leaders. The seven areas of concern between the Salvation Army and the World Council of Churches that he cited were: "1) The Army's Militant Evangelism; 2) An Acute Social Conscience; 3) Emphasis on the Participation of Soldiery (i.e., the laity); 4) Female Ministry; 5) Internationalism; 6) Our Sacramental Positions; 7) Holiness Teaching." He commented on only two areas. First, the WCC had at some time in the past expressed "hope that eventually we would accept the sacraments," but it had not threatened to expel the Army if it refused. Second, only the Army and Moravians were international members of the WCC, and Williams found it difficult to represent an organization made up of Salvationists in eighty-four nations. He did not mention the Army's internal struggle between North Americans and Africans over WCC aid to Marxist liberation organizations. That the Army was an international body was not the WCC's fault, but it could be a reason for the Army to resign its membership. Membership gave it a voice and a vote that caused fissures in the Army. The Army could seek another affiliation with the World Council or join another international body that would not require an Army representative to speak for its international constituency. But would another group accept the Army's idiosyncrasies?[17]

Williams listed consequences if the Salvation Army chose to withdraw from the World Council of Churches. First, it would have to reapply if it wanted to rejoin. Second, it would relinquish its "distinct contribution" and forfeit this relationship to world Christianity. Third, it would lose WCC financial aid for its missionary projects. Fourth, it could no longer participate in the Council's debates. Fifth, it could join another world Christian fellowship. Sixth, it could accept "advisor status," like the Seventh Day Adventists, if the WCC offered it. And seventh, it would need to write a statement of grounds for withdrawal.

The Toronto Conference of Leaders' secretary recorded that twenty-six Army leaders chose to speak their minds on the issue of the Army's membership in the World Council, apart from Brown and Williams. Of those who spoke, twenty-three favored some form of WCC membership, at

---

17. This discussion is extracted from: Minutes, International Conference of Leaders, Toronto, Sept. 22, 1979.

least for the time being. Fifteen wanted to continue as a full member. Eight preferred to continue a suspended relationship or to seek observer status. Three favored total withdrawal and two Americans, Richard Holz and John Waldron, favored immediate withdrawal.

Eleven leaders from the Third World wanted to remain in the World Council; two preferred another type of membership. Richard Atwell, now in London, wanted to continue the suspension. Seven Europeans voted for full membership and four for observer status, but none wanted to leave the WCC. Two Australian leaders wanted observer status that would mean having a voice but no vote. Officers from the West who served overseas mainly favored WCC membership. Of the twelve leaders from the Third World only two were Africans; one was an Indian national. Of the nine Third World missionaries, seven wished to stay in the WCC, including two Americans. Of the four Americans serving overseas, none chose to leave the WCC.

Eva Burrows, an Australian who would be elected General of the Salvation Army in 1986 and would receive a note of congratulations from Zimbabwe's President Robert Mugabe, explained that her service as a teacher and school principal in Rhodesia had caused her to identify with the African people and their accusations of injustice. She complained that the Army had not protested against the Rhodesian political situation until the World Council of Churches had made its grants. For this reason Africans saw the Army's suspension of its WCC membership as a censuring of their Patriotic Front.

David Moyo, the Army's first African commander in Rhodesia-Zimbabwe, seconded Burrows' position. He argued that "many people in Zimbabwe/Rhodesia . . . think that The Salvation Army has aligned itself with the other political parties," by which he apparently meant Ian Smith and Abel Muzorewa. Since the Army suspended its WCC membership "many Salvationists have been killed." Caughey Gauntlett, a British officer who had served in Rhodesia, noted that the Americans' longstanding objection to WCC membership was not wholly linked to grants to the Patriotic Front. Lawrence Smith, an American serving in New Zealand, pleaded against a vote that would further alienate Africans who had legitimate aspirations for independence.

Thus almost every leader who had served overseas, including Americans, wanted to retain some form of WCC membership. That Americans with little foreign exposure would ask to leave the Council exposed their parochialism. The General had begun to send Americans to appointments abroad to modify their nationalism. Several leaders, mainly Americans, claimed to speak for Salvationists in their country in spite of the fact that they had certainly not taken polls or votes from American officers or soldiers.

Harry Williams pointed out that WCC rules did not provide for "suspension" of membership, and that "observer" status was for non-members. Arnold Brown expressed chagrin that "some opinions expressed did not tally with correspondence [he had] received previous to this conference." He must have expected more than three members to ask to leave the World Council, and a more vocal response from Americans. Among the Americans, the group that had most strongly opposed the WCC, three spoke in favor of staying in, two would get out, and four would maintain suspended status in spite of the fact that there was no such status. In spite of the Holz-Hunter proposal to let the General decide, Brown stated that he would not "take The Salvation Army out of the WCC without a two-thirds majority decision of the Commissioners," as he had promised the 1977 High Council. If this was the sentiment in September 1979, how and when did Brown and the leaders reverse their decision not to leave the WCC just two years later?[18]

In August 1980 Harry Williams, at the end of his five-year term as the Salvation Army representative on World Council of Churches' Central Committee, challenged WCC General Secretary Philip Potter's theology of sin. According to Williams, Potter saw sin as something nations did, particularly "the 'West' or 'Capitalism' or 'Colonialism,' . . . for which nations must repent." To the Army, Williams argued, "sin is personal, to be repented and forgiven personally."[19]

But corporate sin was an Old Testament theme. Israel, God's chosen nation, as well as "heathen" nations that surrounded were often cited by prophets as sinful and in need of repentance. God had his own liberation apologetic that favored humanitarian concern for his chosen, the poor and dispossessed.[20] Had not Potter claimed that the WCC grants placed the church on the side of the oppressed? How would Williams explain evangelicals in America who were, by 1980, embracing Ronald Reagan's corporate judgment of the Soviet Union as an "evil empire?" Why did American evangelicals embrace Reaganism if he believed in national sin? Were not the Patriotic Front "terrorists" being judged collectively by white Anglo-American Salvationists?

The Salvation Army was not unique in its concern for the Program to Combat Racism (PCR) grants and philosophy. The World Council of

---

18. "Salvation Army Quits World Council of Churches," *The Herald*, Harare, Aug. 25, 1981, 1.

19. Williams, *I Couldn't Call My Life My Own*, 130, was reflecting on an August 1980 meeting of the WCC Central Committee.

20. Banana, "The Politics of the Methodist Church," 124–27.

Churches grants to liberation movements opened divisions in nearly all churches on issues of corporate vs. individual sin, the nature of a "just war" and the use of violence to achieve honorable ends like "liberation" and "majority rule." WCC grants exposed traditional language that had separated the 1890 African and Asian colonizers' "Christian world" from the "heathen world" of people whose land they took and whose people they forced to labor on their farms and in their mines to pay illegal taxes. When Western churches followed Cecil Rhodes into Mashonaland and Matabeleland few leaders protested against the injustice and cruelty of the British South Africa Company.

A new day dawned after World War II. Africans saw the European theft of their land and the killing of their people as sinful, possibly a concept that missionaries had taught them. Was Africa heathen and sinful and Western civilization Christian? These were colonial terms that served as excuses for ruling other people and demeaning other cultures. By 1979 these ideas were dying, partly due to the success of missionary teachers like the two women killed at Usher, who believed in equality and kindness.

Canaan Banana, a Methodist minister who became Zimbabwe's first State President 1980, recalled the 1890s when "the Church was caught up in the middle of a war of aggression by the British settlers." Only the British Methodist missionary John White, a friend of Salvationist pioneers John Pascoe and Edward Cass, publicly opposed the violence. One of White's Methodist colleagues had penned the typical white settler sentiment: "the Matabele have of course brought this war upon themselves [and] now the only way to put down the uprising is by sword or our own lives would be in great danger." White disagreed. He charged that the British South Africa Company "ought to be held responsible for actions of their servants. Some of these fellows think less of shooting a Mashona than they do of shooting a dog. Burning huts, stealing meat, raping their women are common occurrences." The Methodist Mission House in London praised White for his "firm stand" on the side of natives "against a vicious white man."[21] Here was corporate sin being denounced along with individual responsibility.

Could it be that William Booth, on his visits to Southern Africa, did not see that his friend Cecil Rhodes was committing corporate sin in Africa, but that he could see the corporate sin of English brewers in East London? Why was the perspective of missionaries on the scene so different from their compatriots at home? Did they grasp the corporate injustice of a business or a government because they saw it up close? Professor Roger Green, a Salvationist theologian, says that in 1889 William Booth's theology changed.

---

21. Sjollema, *Isolating Apartheid*, 131.

Previously he had used "individual categories, such as personal conversion and personal sanctification." After 1889 he used "both individual and institutional categories such as corporate sanctification and the establishment of a physical kingdom of God on earth, with the most dramatic change being in his understanding of redemption."[22] This was an enormous change for a revivalist like Booth. One wonders, did Booth's theological progeny miss the point? Did they not realize that the Salvation Army's Founder acknowledged sin as individual *and* corporate? As it happens there is evidence that Zimbabwe's African and missionary Salvationists opposed what they saw as corporate as well as individual sin in both the 1890s and in the 1970s.

The Army eventually settled on maintaining its association by adopting non-voting "fraternal" status in 1981. This relationship derived from the Army's character as a "Christian World Communion," which it shared with such bodies as the Roman Catholic Church, the Conference of Seventh Day Adventists, the World Methodist Council, the Lutheran World Federation and the Baptist World Alliance. This reflects the Army's international polity as distinct from membership of the Council by separate national churches of each denomination. This association is now referred to as "advisor" status, a category shared by all participants in the Conference of Secretaries of World Communions. This means they are invited to participate in Central Committee meetings and General Assemblies of the World Council of Churches but do not have a vote.

---

22. Green, *War on Two Fronts*, 12.

Chapter 13

African Salvationists React to the Salvation Army's Withdrawal from the World Council of Churches, 1981

Zimbabwe Salvationists criticize resignation from World Council

The August decision by the international Salvation Army to resign as a member of the WCC prompted protests from Salvationists in Zimbabwe. Colonel David Moyo, Salvation Army territorial commander for Zimbabwe, said, "we see no conflict" between liberation movements which "fight for human rights" and "the gospel of love, charity and the liberation of the total man." *Target*, a newspaper related to the National Christian Council of Kenya, reported similar unhappiness with the Army decision in that country.

In London, the Army issued a one-sentence statement. It said Moyo "has been in communication with the Salvation Army international headquarters pledging that the Salvation Army in Zimbabwe will maintain its 90-year tradition of serving the spiritually and physically needy."

An Army spokesperson in London emphasized the importance the Army attaches to the "fraternal status" with the WCC which it requested and was granted in connection with the termination of its membership.

—EPS[1]

---

1. *The Ecumenical Review* 34.1, January 1982, 83–84.

On August 25, 1981, the *Harare Herald* headline read: "Salvation Army Quits World Council of Churches—Protest against the ecumenical movement's aid to armed liberation movements, the World Council of Churches said yesterday." World Council leaders rejected Salvation Army General Arnold Brown's charge that the WCC "was motivated more by politics than by the gospel." In fact, the WCC leaders claimed that while Brown "had written to ask for 'membership to be discontinued,'" he had also asked that the Army and World Council maintain "harmonious relations." His charge, as they saw it, did not support his aim.

In Zimbabwe, the *Herald*, now the newspaper of the new Patriotic Front government, reported that the Salvation Army's withdrawal was a "protest against a [1978] grant [of $120,000 US or £75,000] from the organization's anti-racism fund to Zimbabwean nationalist guerrillas."[2] But the *Herald* did not report that in January 1980, the World Council of Churches' Commission on Inter-Church Aid, Refugee and World Service had given the Army a £100,000 grant for rehabilitating returning African war refugees from Zambia, Zaire, and Mozambique. These were the people the WCC had assisted with its 1978 Program to Combat Racism humanitarian grant for health and education programs that led the Salvation Army to suspend its membership. The refugees who had been displaced by war were now moving home, and they were still in need of humanitarian aid. The Mugabe government turned to what was now an African-led Salvation Army to do the job of rehabilitation thanks to its trust in the Army's indigenous leaders.

Baldwin Sjollema, the head of the WCC Program to Combat Racism, claims that the total amount of WCC humanitarian assistance to all of Africa between 1970 and 1979 was $2,055,000 US. Of that amount the WCC had sent about a sixth, $348,500 US, to Zimbabwe.[3] Thus, the Salvation Army's complaint about WCC aid to "communist guerrillas" did not keep the Army from accepting grants from the same organization for its own humanitarian assistance to refugees at the time it was suspending its membership in the WCC. Was the Salvation Army claim that it was more apolitical in its motivation for taking WCC grants than was the Patriotic Front in accepting grants for the same purpose from the same source? And was the Army apolitical when it engaged in an effort to rehabilitate the refugees back into the new Zimbabwe's culture with WCC funds? African Salvationists who supported the liberation war did not think so. They were extremely grateful

---

2. "Salvation Army Quits World Council of Churches," *The Herald*, Harare, Aug. 25, 1981, 1.

3. Sjollema, *Isolating Apartheid*, 131.

for WCC support during and after the war. They were more skeptical of the Salvation Army's attitudes towards their freedom and democracy.

On August 31, 1981, Zimbabwe Salvationists gave General Arnold Brown, the Salvation Army's international leader, a surprise response to his decision to terminate the Army's membership in the World Council of Churches. The *Herald*'s headline read: "Salvationists Protest World Council of Churches Split." Between seventy-five and 200 Zimbabwe Salvationists marched to the Army's headquarters through Harare's main streets under police protection.[4] Corps Sergeant Major (lay leader) Jonah Blessing Matsvetu led the march to petition the "British-based head of the church, General Arnold Brown, to restore the Army to full membership of the World Council of Churches."[5] Salvation Army soldiers engaging in a public petitioning of the Army's leaders is sufficiently rare to make this march historically novel and significant.

Sergeant Major Matsvetu met with the Army's Territorial Commander for Zimbabwe, Commissioner David Moyo, and other leaders in the Army's headquarters boardroom. He told them: "We believe the word of God came to all mankind to save all men . . . and we members of the Salvation Army feel we should live within the World Council of Churches." Moyo told reporters afterwards that he admired the World Council's "fight for human rights and we see no conflict between such ideals and the gospel of love, charity and the liberation of the total man." Moyo closed his remarks to the press with his own petition to his superior, General Brown: "restore the Army to full status in the World Council of Churches. The Salvation Army in Zimbabwe maintains its 90 years' tradition as part of the universal church of Christ with a strong social conscience, serving the spiritually and physically needy without political bias and regardless of color, creed or culture."[6]

David Moyo's courageous public challenge to Arnold Brown broke with the Army's 116-year history of tough internal military control. Moyo must have been aware that his petition violated his "Memorandum of Appointment," which obliged him to discharge the General's decisions as is the duty of any military underling. In fact, Moyo confessed that he knew he was under orders to accept Brown's decision to withdraw from the World Council, but he claimed that "he had advised very strongly against" the decision when Brown had made it. It is reasonable to assume that a European member of Moyo's

---

4. A Deputy Chief of Police was a Salvationist.

5. "Salvationists Protest World Council of Churches Split," *The Herald*, Sept. 1, 1981, 1.

6. Matsvetu, "Salvationists in Zimbabwe Protest against Some Decisions Made by the Leaders During the Liberation War of Zimbabwe," 1993 (9 page ms. written at my request for this research).

staff advised him on his statement before he made it to the press, but it is also clear that it was Moyo's decision to challenge his commander.

Jonah Matsvetu observed that Zimbabwe's "Salvationists [had] protested against some decisions made by the Leaders during the Liberation War in Zimbabwe." He did not elaborate on what decisions the protests had challenged, nor who the leaders were that made them. But the statement must have been clear to those who realized that during the war the Army's leadership in Zimbabwe was American or British.

Matsvetu then offered, for the first time in print, an African perspective on what had occurred at Usher Institute on the evening of June 7, 1978. In his opinion "Selous Scouts," a wing of Ian Smith's forces, had killed the two British women missionaries. And he complained that African Salvationists had also died to end "the evil system and government of Rhodesia, which sought to perpetuate the succession of white rulers." But those deaths had gone largely unnoticed by the Army's leaders; they had certainly not been celebrated as "martyrdoms."

Matsvetu felt strongly that the end of the Salvation Army's World Council of Churches membership had "isolated" Zimbabwe Salvationists "from the rest of the Christian community," an international community that had created "one human Christian family." He reminded readers of the *Herald* that the WCC had helped needy people in "emerging countries during their times of hardship" with "food, shelter, clothing and spiritual comfort to the bereaved and maimed." It had not deserted "us during our liberation war to perish under the Rhodesian government who were bent to . . . maintain the evil system of government at all costs."[7] The Sergeant Major did not name those who had deserted African Salvationists, but he could have done so.

The matter of the World Council of Churches was not the only issue about which Matsvetu was unhappy. He was especially upset concerning farms Cecil Rhodes had given to the Salvation Army in the 1890s, particularly Pearson Farm in the Mazoe Valley on which Captain Cass had lived before he was killed in the First Chimurenga in 1896. Matsvetu argued that those farms now belonged to the African people from whom Rhodes had taken them. It was therefore up to Africans to decide whether or not the Army should sell the farms and whether or not it could evict the elderly African farm-workers from its land. After all, he reasoned, Rhodes had given the farms to the Salvation Army to "raise revenue for the church and sustain its Christian programs and welfare of the people." Africans could use the farms for "service to the people" and also as guarantees for bank "loans or

---

7. Ibid., 1–2.

overdrafts."[8] To Matsvetu the farms were a patrimony Rhodes ultimately deeded to the Africans of Rhodesia and now Zimbabwe through the Salvation Army.

In my oral history interview with J. B. Matsvetu in 1998, he pointed to an interesting personal attachment to the land on which the Army's Pearson farm in the Mazoe Valley stood. Behind this BSAC gift to the Army was an important African tale of Mazoe as the homeland of the Hwata people. The BSAC had removed the Hwata, a part of the Shona group of tribes, from their land in 1897 at the end of the First Chimurenga. The Hwata and their spirit medium, Nehanda, fought in the war in which the Salvation Army's Captain Cass had been killed. That Matsvetu was a Hwata was almost certainly unknown to Salvation Army leaders in Zimbabwe or even to many African Salvationists. Although Matsvetu is an urban-dweller and a professional social worker, he still identified with his family's tribal lands and his ancestors who lived there in the nineteenth century. Land is extremely important to Africans. Even when they move to the city they continue to visit their families and ancestors' graves, and they often build a home in the family's village.

Pearson Farm had been a financial problem for the Salvation Army during several stages of its long history. Captain Cass had moved to the land to create a farm in 1894. The British South Africa Company had given the land to the Army's original pioneers led by Major Pascoe in 1893, and the pioneers ceded the land to the Salvation Army in 1894. Of the original 2,500 acres (500 acres for each pioneer) about 600 were under cultivation by 1930 when Pearson farm showed an income deficit of £800. In fact, from 1925 to 1930 Pearson had an average annual deficit of £474 for a total of £2,843. Salvation Army General Edward J. Higgins stopped at Pearson on September 4, 1930, after the Financial Secretary issued a report on the deficits. The Territorial Commander in Salisbury, Colonel Soul, was urging that Pearson be sold. In his opinion it was impossible to make the farm pay. Higgins met Minister of Agriculture Robert A. Fletcher at the suggestion of Prime Minister H. U. Moffat and asked him to arrange for an agricultural expert to visit the farm and advise the Army on whether it could be made a financial success.

Fletcher observed that "for years past everything has been taken out of the land and nothing put in." In his opinion the Army's "only hope for successful farming was up-to-date scientific methods." Fletcher told Higgins that he would check the files for the conditions on which the British South Africa Company had given the farm to the Army. Prime Minister Moffat suggested that if the Agriculture Department reported that Pearson could

---

8. Ibid., 2–3.

not be made financially viable, then the Army could sell it without difficulty as far as the Government was concerned. The BSAC's 1894 conditions for giving the land to the Army said nothing about resale. It read: "Roads and thoroughfares over the land shall remain free and uninterrupted; all precious stones shall remain the property of the [BSAC] Company; the Company shall have power to construct roads, railways, telegraph lines, etc., over the land; [and] beacons should be constructed, etc." Moffat promised Higgins that if the Army decided to sell the farm, he would do his best to see that the Army would not have to pay the government a refund.[9]

When he returned to London General Higgins wrote to Colonel Soul on September 10, 1930, concerning the Army's work in Rhodesia, but he did not mention Pearson Farm. "I think that all whom I came in contact with are anxious to do what they can and really believe the Army can accomplish more than others."

On October 6, 1930, Ministry of Agriculture's expert J. H. Hampton gave a gloomy "Report on Pearson Farm," but he had a positive recommendation for how to treat the problem. "Pearson is one of the fertile farms in the maize belt," but its "lands have been almost continuously cropped to maize [the principal food in Zimbabwe] since about 1910. Very little, if anything, was put back into the soil, with the result that land, where yields of 10 to 15 bags of maize were recorded previously, now gives 3 to 5 bags." The land was hilly so erosion had occurred. "The main idea in the past has been revenue and there has been no thought of the future."

The Farm Superintendents from 1909 to 1930, Major and Mrs. John Thomson, attested to the fact that the Salvation Army had operated the farm after 1909 solely for the purpose of raising funds to support missionary work. Since 1923 mission work was taking place at Howard Institute after Captain Leonard Kirby had moved the corps and school work to Chiweshe, while at Pearson the Army's purpose was now exclusively social work. The Thomsons took charge of the Farm just after they were commissioned as Lieutenants, perhaps without education in agricultural methods. To purchase farm implements Thomson made lime from the limestone deposits at Pearson, a product that he said was used in many of Rhodesia's early buildings. In 1930 the Thomsons moved to Cato Manor, a social farm at Durban, South Africa, and Leonard Kirby returned to Pearson Farm, apparently to transform it into a productive agricultural enterprise.

Hampton's frank 1930 inspection notes concluded that the 200 head of mixed cattle were "only a little improvement on native stock and there is not an inch of fencing on the place." The farm had been "denuded of timber"

---

9. From "Pearson Farm" documents at the Salvation Army Archives, London.

and nothing had been done to replace it. With careful management the farm "ought to prove an ideal mixed farming proposition," but it would take capital outlay and time. Leonard Kirby, a Canadian, took over the Mission side at Pearson, which was also a Native Settlement. He and his wife had trained African cadets there after 1920, but in 1930 they became the Farm's managers. A "great number" of African families farmed the 1,000 acres of land in 5 to 10 acre plots that they rented. Although fairly inexperienced in agriculture, Kirby was a builder with practical skills. He lacked "good implements" and began work with what he thought must have been "one of the original ploughs bought in 1910."

If the Army intended to use Pearson as a "training center for youths from Great Britain," an adaptation of William Booth's "back to the land" scheme of 1890, Hampton's report advised that the Army would need to adopt "more diversified lines" than it was presently using. He recommended dairy farming, pig breeding, and forestry that would require additional buildings, dairy cows, and a competent stockman. General Higgins asked Colonel Lotz to survey the site and advise on the cost of revitalizing the farm.[10] A memoir by Leonard Kirby says nothing about the state of Pearson in 1934, the year he and his family moved to the Army's Social Farm at Rondebosch, in Cape Town, and then to Usher Institute near Bulawayo where they developed a large first class Boarding School.[11]

In 1947, when John Lewis, a trained farmer, arrived at Pearson he found the results of what J. H. Hampton had proposed in 1930, and what Leonard Kirby and his successors had achieved. He described the Farm as consisting of 2,000 acres, where there were "up-to-date tractors and implements," with 500 acres under plough with irrigation for crops grown during the six-month dry season. Africans who worked the land had their own village with three-room semi-detached houses. A new school educated the children to Standard III, half from the Army's workers and half from nearby farms. They also provided for European delinquents who needed "care and protection," and built a cottage for women addicted to drink or drugs. There was also a small African corps. Brigadier Lewis gave no indication that Pearson was failing to make a profit in the 1940s.[12]

By 1981 Pearson was again suffering hard times, possibly for the same reasons it had declined in the 1920s when the Salvation Army's focus was

---

10. From "Pearson Farm" documents at the Salvation Army Archives, London.

11. Kirby, "Memories of Long Ago," 3–4, 13–15, at the Salvation Army Archives, London.

12. Lewis, "500 Acres Under the Plough," *All the World*, Oct.–Dec. 1966, 137.

on revenue for headquarters to allocate elsewhere and not for the long-term effects of good farming.

Sergeant Major J. B. Matsvetu made his general charges explicit in 1981: the Army's leaders in Zimbabwe had not been "concerned with the many African Salvationists who had died during the Liberation War," nor for their desire to attain "freedom and liberty like any other free country the Army operates in." Because of that, the new Zimbabwe government "identified the Salvationists and their church as people who only wanted freedom of worship, which is insecure without the freedom of the total human being in a free country." While Matsvetu's board room interview with the Army's new African commander, David Moyo, went well, Matsvetu was disappointed that Salvation Army leaders in London did not respond to the Soldiers' protest over the sale of Pearson Farm to white commercial farmers. He was also upset at the leaders' failure to involve African Salvationists in the decision-making process, especially as it concerned Pearson.[13]

Prior to planning the Salvationists' march on the Salvation Army's Harare headquarters, J. B. Matswetu and his Soldiers' Committee decided to visit Pearson Farm to assess the situation, since sale of farms "did not go down well" with African Salvationists and the native people of Zimbabwe. The Soldiers' Committee decided to make an appointment to inspect Pearson after they met for prayer at Harare Citadel in the African township of Highlands. The committee consisted of J. B. Matswetu, Chairman; S. Muchenje, Secretary; M. G. Mtukwa; and L. Nhari, Vice Secretary. In their inspection report they noted all the buildings, including the church, machinery, servants' quarters, and the number of people who would lose their jobs if the Army sold the Farm. Some of the farm workers were elderly with no homes or income with which to start life elsewhere. At the end of their visit they prayed again and drove back to Harare "to devise a plan of action."

Methodist Bishop Crispen C. G. Mazobere, with no reference to Pearson Farm, observed that neither Cecil Rhodes nor church leaders in the 1890s had consulted African landowners about the distribution of their stolen land. "The Missionary and colonial settlers became hand in glove" in this regard. Besides this lack of consultation, Rhodes and other Europeans were convinced that "the British Empire was God-appointed to civilize and Christianize the world," a demeaning view of Africans as "heathen" that whites held throughout Africa.[14] African Salvationists chastised the Salvation Army's leaders for making colonialism a guiding principle in the late

---

13. Matsvetu, "Salvationists in Zimbabwe Protest against Some Decisions Made by the Leaders During the Liberation War of Zimbabwe," 4–5.

14. Mazobere, "Christian Theology of Mission," 162–63.

twentieth century when they discovered that the leaders had a plan to sell Pearson Farm to a white commercial farmer.

Matsvetu's Soldiers' Committee planned the March of 200 uniformed Salvation Army soldiers from the Harare Central Police Station through the city's streets to the Army's Territorial Headquarters with a police escort. They would arrive at 11:30 carrying placards. Their goal was to cement the Army's relationship with the new Mugabe government and "register our protest and defuse the action taken by the Salvation Army leadership." Matsvetu claimed that "Salvationists, Christians of all denominations and the general public of Zimbabwe" would be assured "that we are for the maintenance of good relations [with] them and the new government of Zimbabwe." The march would convince Zimbabweans that "we support [World Council of Churches] principles" and "universal peace for mankind." The Zimbabwe Council of Churches welcomed statements from Matsvetu's Soldiers' Committee and so did politicians, white and African, who had been unhappy with the former Ian Smith regime. Former Rhodesian Prime Minister Garfield Todd told Matsvetu that he supported his Committee's actions.

Matsvetu was correct in his interpretation of the history of Rhodes' BSAC land grants. The BSAC had donated land to church missions to make it possible for them to raise revenue for Christian programs and to provide for the welfare of the African people, something that concerned Queen Victoria's government in London. African Salvationists hoped that the Army would continue to use the farms for this intended purpose.

Assured of the Salvation Army's loyalty to his government, Prime Minister Robert Mugabe asked the Army's Harare Citadel, where Matsvetu was Corps Sergeant Major, to serve as a reception center for freedom fighters and other refugees who were coming home to rejoin their families. For this program the World Council of Churches had given the Salvation Army a grant of £100,000 grant in 1980 in spite of the fact that the Army's international leaders had suspended the Army's membership in the World Council.

Matsvetu added to a letter he wrote to me another concern he had about the Salvation Army. He charged that if it wanted "credibility and fuller participation" by its soldiers and officers the Army would have to change its internal polity to become more democratic, something it had not been since 1878 when it adopted its military style to replace the Methodist democratic conference system it had used since 1865. Matsvetu argued that the Army needed to develop an "electoral base [with] adequate channels of communication." And only if it restored its full membership in the World Council of Churches could it provide "a valid presence and contribution" to that body. The Soldiers' March of 1981 demonstrated "how strongly we all believed in these actions and [the] concern we have for our Army in Zimbabwe." Again

Matsvetu reassured Salvation Army leaders of his loyalty.[15] They were rightly concerned that his protest might lead to a schism in a land where it had become a successful mission and a growing church.

Matsvetu found that the Salvation Army's handling of complaints from his Soldiers' Committee and the Protest Marchers lacked a sincere engagement. General Brown sent the International Secretary for Africa, Richard Atwell, and a financial expert to Zimbabwe to "find out more information." According to Matsvetu these officers asked him to meet them at the Headquarters in Harare where "we restated our case and how we felt about these two important issues," the sale of farms and the Army's resignation from the World Council of Churches. It was Matsvetu's feeling that "they did not like our action and ideas because they did not come back to us with the results of their findings which [they] reported back to the General."[16]

---

15. Matsvetu, "Salvationists in Zimbabwe Protest against Some Decisions Made by the Leaders During the Liberation War of Zimbabwe," 6–7.

16. Ibid., 5.

Chapter 14

Conclusions

> Almost every one of the men who led the countries of black Africa to Independence after the Second World War was educated by missionaries. . . . What these men preached in their maturity meant the end of a great deal that the missionaries had always cherished. It meant the end of European supremacy on the once Dark Continent. It meant the rejection of many European values, like the one about the inherent superiority of the white man over the black man. It also meant the beginning of the freedom to control one's own life, to stand up in the congress of the nations with the right to speak as an equal on the affairs of the whole world. The missionaries were agents of that freedom. This was not a small gift.
>
> —Geoffrey Moorhouse[1]

Each Christian mission that arrived in Mashonaland and Matabeleland in the 1890s immediately asked Cecil John Rhodes' British South Africa Company (BSAC) for land. To each the BSAC granted urban stands and/or rural farms. The farms the BSAC gave to missions were often Native Settlements as well as centers for religious worship, education, and health care. They operated mainly under the supervision of European and North American missionaries who preached a Christian gospel that was so intertwined with Western culture that few missionaries distinguished their Western culture from that of Christianity's Jewish Middle-Eastern founder, even less from African cultural practices. Missions taught English language and culture

---

1. Moorhouse, *The Missionaries*, 334–35.

to African children and adults whom they held to be "heathen" for their deviations from Anglo-American norms. None of this is surprising given the nature of human ethnocentrism, but it did dawn on some missionaries that their Western obsessions were offensive to Africans and injurious to their mission.

When Zimbabwe's Africans won independence from minority rule at the Lancaster House Conference in 1979 and established their own nation state with elections in 1980, ownership of Zimbabwe's land became a central issue in their transition to democratic rule by their own African political parties and churches. Until the land returned to its original owners it would continue to be the most important issue of Zimbabwe politics into the twenty-first century. Therefore, it is no surprise that land was an issue of control when Africans took a leading role in what had been white-led churches like the Salvation Army. The Army in Zimbabwe was in a particularly problematic position since Africans composed 98 percent of its members and over 90 percent of its officer-clergy. The quality of the transition would be determined by the quality of relationships established by whites and Africans in the church's polity. The rigid authoritarian relationships established by the Army's military system inhibited an open exchange of views during the years of the independence struggle and transition to African voices in its polity.

Issues of land redistribution and democratization were thus central to efforts to remove the residue of colonial-mindedness in the Rhodesian state and in Zimbabwe's churches. That meant that the Salvation Army and other churches led by missionaries would have to develop new church-state-conciliar relations locally and internationally. Good relations meant open discussions of hard issues that had for a century divided races as well as local and international denominations of Christians. Poor communications also divided the churches and the state.

Unfortunately the Salvation Army, in its internal governance, had been slow to develop African leadership in the post-World War era of the 1950s to 1970s. And many of its last-minute decisions to involve Africans created bitter opposition from within white and black communities. Like other churches, from its beginnings in 1891 the Army had chosen to tie itself to the white settler community. It had identified the Edward Cass killing of 1896 as "martyrdom" for the faith, rather than blame it on the Army's ties to white settlers who had taken African land. In 1965 Army leaders identified with Ian Smith's white government, apparently in a hope that white supremacists would gradually accept African majority rule, although the Army had not accepted African leaders in its church structure. In 1978 the Army accepted, without question, unsupported charges of the white

Rhodesian state and media when they identified killers of Diane Thompson and Sharon Swindells as "terrorists" under the Patriotic Front control, without evidence that the police or journalists or Salvation Army leaders had interviewed eyewitnesses. And in 1979 the Salvation Army identified with Smith's Internal Settlement, a mistake it shared with several other missions.

As we have seen the Salvation Army's constituency was not like that of other missions. Its membership was nearly all African and many of its corps, schools, and its hospitals were in dangerous war zones in the 1970s, where Mugabe's and Nkomo's Patriotic Front was in ascendancy. In the most dangerous situations missionary officers in the field supported the independence movement. The isolation of a largely Anglo-American staff in Harare, as opposed to missionary and African officers, teachers and physicians at its schools and hospitals in war zones, led the Army's leaders to misread the complicated political situation. Thus when the Usher attack occurred in 1978, and the Soldiers' March took place in Harare in 1981, Army leaders, locally and internationally, went into a defensive mode and cut themselves off from African Salvationist spokespersons.

Because they misread the situation on the ground, Salvation Army Anglo-American leaders placed their interest in defeating communism and disputing World Council of Churches' grants ahead of the interests of African officers and soldiers. African Salvationists depended on the support of national and international sympathizers. Salvation Army leaders in the U.S. embraced American political interests in a period defined as a "Cold War." American Salvationists drew from community support large funds in the name of social services. This was not the case for African Salvationists who had good reason to appreciate a Christian fellowship that supported their quest for political freedom and supplied their spiritual and physical needs.

In many ways the Salvation Army in the U.S., with tremendous wealth gathered from the public that made it one of America's leading charities, had become rather like a state-supported church that lived off the financial support of outside contributors rather than its own members. But the Americans' poor African comrades were largely subsistence farmers. The Rhodesian state under Ian Smith had cut off their access to public funds by taking away the Army's village primary schools. Thus Rhodesia's Salvationists had become dependent on good church-state relations. The World Council of Churches and the Rhodesian Council of Churches buttressed their faith in a community of faith that would stand against a government that they saw as oppressive. There is no doubt that a lack of international Salvation Army support for the Zimbabwe liberation struggle that most African Salvationists favored, was compounded by American Salvationists' rejection of World Council of Churches support for the liberation effort.

The root cause of American Salvation Army leaders' refusal to embrace the Zimbabwe Patriotic Front and the reason they sought international Salvation Army opposition to the liberation war was Cold War anxieties in the aftermath of the 1972 defeat and withdrawal of American forces from Vietnam. American political sensibilities also caused them to oppose any change in the status quo, a new look at Africa or the Third World. Their effort to connect an African nationalist war for independence with a global ideological struggle was compounded by the American leaders' lack of international experience and a blindness to Third World problems. Holding on to African colonies had become a dead issue in Europe at least a decade before the struggle for majority rule began in Rhodesia in 1963.

British and American governments fostered the 1979 Lancaster House settlement that indicated they were aware that a new day had dawned in Africa, even in Rhodesia. As early as the mid-1960s the World Council of Churches and Rhodesian Christian Council were aware that white minority rule could not be sustained, but in the struggle against apartheid and colonial regimes in Southern Africa the Salvation Army lagged behind. Its international and Rhodesian leaders had neglected to develop African leaders in the 1950s and had failed to distinguish between the West's fight with communism as a political-economic-cultural system, and the straightforward African fight for independence in the 1960s and 1970s.

In 1965 British Methodists appointed Andrew Ndhlela as their first African District Chairman and General Superintendent in Rhodesia, and Africans succeeded him in that post. In 1968 the American Methodist church appointed their first African Bishop, Abel T. Muzorewa, and Africans also succeeded him.[2] Muzorewa became Ian Smith's choice to serve in his place as Prime Minister when African majority rule appeared to be inevitable in 1979. The Salvation Army did not appoint its first African Territorial Commander in Rhodesia, David Moyo, until 1979, and the Army acknowledged that Moyo was regrettably unprepared for the assignment. Moyo's successors from 1987 to 2000 were a Britisher, an African, and an American; and subsequently African officers. Usually the Chief Secretary, second in command, was white when the Commander was African. Often white commanders had finance and property as primary concerns.[3]

2. Banana, *A Century of Methodism in Zimbabwe, 1891–1991*, 221; Kurewa, *The Church in Mission*, 179.

3. For many years now it has been international Salvation Army policy to have the two leading positions in a territory, Territorial Commander and Chief Secretary, to be filled by one national officer and one from another territory. Moyo's successor, Alan Coles, had earlier been Financial Secretary for the Army in Zimbabwe, and his appointment back to Harare was probably related to the need to repair the damage inflicted by

Conclusions

In many ways the Salvation Army in Zimbabwe was more fortunate than it deserved. Insights and protests of African soldiers after 1963, many of whom were eligible to be called "saint" and "martyr" alongside whites who received accolades for shedding blood for the faith, saved the Army from schism or demise in 1981. African Salvationists tried to save the Army from ridicule when it suspended its World Council of Churches membership in 1978 and then resigned from the WCC in 1981. Africans attempted to get Army leaders to communicate with its soldiers. It remains to be seen if they will be more successful in this endeavor in the future than they were in the past. Fortunately for the Salvation Army African Salvationists are forgiving people. As they claimed during their protests against actions taken in London, they love the international Salvation Army. This affection was grounded in appreciation for the sacrifice of talented missionary teachers, doctors and corps officers who served in Zimbabwe over many years. Many expatriates spoke for the human rights and political independence of their African brothers and sisters.

A NOTE ON HISTORIOGRAPHY: RESEARCH IN THE 1990S

I began in 1991 and 1998 with interviews with Salvation Army leaders in Britain and North America, with World Council of Churches leaders in Geneva and with African Salvationists and expatriate missionaries in Zimbabwe and by email and snail mail. I read documentary evidence in the history of missions in Rhodesia and Zimbabwe at various archives for the period of 1890–1983. I began to probe what those involved in the independence war had to say about Zimbabwe's history. My questions were based on research I had done, but they were open-ended in the hope that those questioned would feel free to speak their minds. I wanted to hear the voice of those who had taken part in the events and had fresh memories of what happened and why.

Because the 1978 Usher killings, the Salvation Army struggles with the World Council of Churches' grants, and its problem comprehending an African fight for independence had all happened in the previous twenty-five years, the participants were still alive. I was able to engage many of them through letters or face-to-face and taped interviews. This work was new to me as an historian. I had never before done research that brought history up to the recent past where most of the participants were still alive—although

---

a massive fraud perpetrated by a non-Salvationist employee at headquarters in Moyo's term.

many had become octogenarians and could fairly claim that they had a loss of memory concerning events in the 1950s to 1980s. In general, responses to letters and requests for personal interviews paid off, albeit with a measure of dogged persistence in some cases. Naturally not all participants were anxious to discuss old wounds or unpleasant memories.

Letters to Canadian General Arnold Brown brought three gracious letters, but little fresh information. Brown did not recall Sergeant Major Matsvetu's 1981 charges concerning the Army's sale of land at two of its farms, Usher and Pearson, or the African soldiers' protest, although Brown did recall the march, possibly from seeing it on TV in London. He did not recall sending representatives from London to meet Matsvetu and his colleagues in Harare. Salvation Army histories, including Brown's memoir, *The Gate and the Light* (1984), make no mention of the 1981 protest or the Army's split with the Rhodesian Christian Council in the early 1970s.

Brown's autobiography did cover the Army's rift with the World Council of Churches at length, even appending correspondence with WCC General Secretary Philip Potter. Overall Brown fills no gap in what historians term "bottom-up" history, history of the Army from a soldier's perspective. This sort of history is also missing from official Army histories, as it is in the public face put forward by nearly all public institutions. Brown almost never refers to Third World participation in Army decision-making that is almost always exclusively the prerogative of its ruling councils of leaders.

Brown responded only vaguely to evidence I found that he and Richard Atwell, the American Salvation Army commander in Rhodesia/Zimbabwe in this period, had acted politically in spite of the Army's regulation against such activity. But if the claim that Atwell made was correct, that he and Brown had written to President Jimmy Carter and Foreign Secretary David Owen to protest against actions by the U.K. and U.S. in support of majority African rule in Rhodesia, then they may have engaged in political activity. Brown, who did not confirm that he had written such a letter, responded to my request for confirmation by writing that "S.A. action is always motivated by humanitarianism—which may or may not have a 'political' effect."[4]

In a 1992 letter Arnold Brown claimed that negative reactions to the Salvation Army's separation from the World Council of Churches, including the reaction of David Moyo, the Army's leader in Zimbabwe in 1981, "seemed to fade." Brown held that this was "perhaps due to increasing anti-WCC attitudes expressed through the media of the world." As for David Moyo's 1979 statement at the Toronto Conference of Army Leaders, Brown read Moyo's words at the time as an indication that he understood

---

4. Arnold Brown to Murdoch, 19 November 1991.

the official Army position and would explain it to his African constituents. That, Brown held, "was the last we heard of the matter."[5] But it was not the last word or the last protest. The Toronto conference preceded the Army's 1981 withdrawal from WCC membership by two years. Moyo's remarks following the 1981 march called on Brown and the Army to maintain WCC membership the Army had established in 1947.

As for the sale of farms at Pearson (Mazoe) and Usher (Figtree), Brown called these sales "unrelated matter[s]." They were part of a series of "financial challenges [that] were ongoing." As such they were under the control of the Army's Chancellor of the Exchequer and International Secretary for Africa.[6] Either Brown was not personally engaged in exchanges with the Soldiers' Committee over the sales and Matsvetu's call for democracy in the Army in such decisions, or his memory failed to recall the matter.

After four letters to request Commissioner Richard Atwell's aid, the former Salvation Army commander in Rhodesia/Zimbabwe responded in a detailed four-page letter. He said that my letter caused him to engage in "a deep painful emotional experience for me to reflect on the war that resulted in the death of hundreds of dedicated Salvationists and others, including the two beautiful Salvation Army Missionaries." The wounded Usher missionaries, David Cotton and Gunvor Paulsson, did not respond to my letters, possibly because of the pain of memory. Atwell set out to clear up issues of his role in the Usher killings and their aftermath. He was worried that "you have been misinformed or perhaps uninformed."

The first issue Atwell addressed was whether or not the Africans who had killed the missionary women at Usher were attached to Joshua Nkomo's ZAPU or to Ian Smith's Selous Scouts. Atwell was certain that it was ZAPU and not the Scouts that had done the killing. He based his opinion on a "report given to me directly," apparently by Smith's Military Police, that he cites throughout his letter. Atwell went to Bulawayo Hospital to identify the bodies of the two women who were brought there at 3:00 a.m. by Military Police, along with two wounded colleagues. Atwell was advised, apparently by the Police, that ZAPU had done the killing and wounding since they had spoken in "both the local dialect [Ndebele] and in English prior to the shooting." The principal, Jean Caldwell, and two other staff members also mentioned ZAPU. The police told Atwell that "they had a report of the presence of a group of Freedom Fighters in the general area before the Usher incident and it was being checked out, they were believed to be Zapu." This information I confirmed with African teachers at Usher. In his account

5. Arnold Brown to Murdoch, 17 March 1992.
6. Arnold Brown to Murdoch, 20 March 1995.

Atwell did not mention any attempt to interview African teachers who saw the shootings and who understood the gunmen when they spoke Ndebele. Instead he relied on the partisan Rhodesian police who were fighting an insurrection.

On the issue of the World Council of Churches' grant of £143,000 to the Patriotic Front, Atwell quoted an Anglican bishop, likely Paul Burrough of Mashonaland, an Ian Smith supporter, who said: "the World Council by their decision have created the possibility of Religious Schisms." Burrough held that "it is not the function of a Christian World Body to advocate Force and Terrorism." Atwell did not see "the Rhodesian incident" as the only reason the Army withdrew "but it did reflect . . . that the Salvation Army and some churches could not ascribe to [the grant]." Burrough spoke for white Anglicans who voted for the Smith regime's new constitution and Land Act aimed at continued white rule. Bishop Skelton, Burrough's fellow Anglican bishop in Bulawayo, opposed those acts. Atwell sided with Rhodesian conservatives represented by Burrough, but most Rhodesia Christian Council members supported their president, Bishop Skelton. The WCC would not accept the Burrough charge that it advocated "Force and Terrorism." Rather the WCC claimed that it provided humanitarian support for the Patriotic Front's quest for majority rule and the right to self-government.

The third issue Atwell addressed was the March 1981 Soldiers' March to the Salvation Army headquarters in Harare. He recalled a different occasion for the march, stating that it occurred during Zimbabwe's Independence Day Celebrations that featured the Army's Harare Citadel Band. President Mugabe had invited the Army "to play a vital role." At the time "Mr. Matsvetu and some of his friends and others marched near the Salvation Army Headquarters building and someone carried a placard alluding to the World Council withdrawal." General Brown saw the news on TV and read an article with a photo. Atwell, by now in London as the Army's International Secretary for Africa, "contacted Commissioner David Moyo for an explanation." Moyo assured him that "there was no crisis or problem, mentioning this was a one-time spontaneous incident at the time the Country was celebrating Independence and the General should not worry. Salvationists would remain loyal to the Army's Principles, Doctrines and policies." Atwell wrote that he had visited Zimbabwe, but he did not mention a discussion with Matsvetu or his Soldiers' Committee, nor was he "aware of details in connection with the actual disposition of the farm."

On the letter Atwell claimed to have written to President Jimmy Carter and a letter he wrote to his friend "Paul," Atwell said that he had no copies of the letters, nor did he recall "writing to President Carter or any other official regarding political issues." I sent Atwell a copy of his letter to "Paul" which I have in my possession. I also asked him if the widow of his friend Paul Kaiser, the Army's American National Commander at the time, might have his letter. In correspondence with Mrs. Kaiser I discovered that her husband's correspondence had been accidentally destroyed. I heard nothing more from Atwell who has since passed away.

In Rhodesia/Zimbabwe Atwell claimed "our Missionary Officers in particular strongly believed in Independence." He qualified "independence" to mean "freedom to vote, for free speech and free expression and equal rights." He did not mention majority rule, but chose to connect independence to the Army's educational, medical, and social programs, and to African leadership in the Army. The missionary role had moved after he arrived in Rhodesia in January 1950, from "leadership" to "fellowship" to "followership" as supporters of African leadership. He argued that local and world pressure for majority rule had built up "before the war escalated." Since "majority rule was inevitable," all Salvationists hoped that "it would come about without bloodshed."[7] This last note indicated that he felt that Salvationists should not support conflict to resolve Rhodesia's problem of white minority rule.

Rhodesia/Zimbabwe had a special appeal to the missionary in the field, sometimes described as "the bush," quite a different perspective from mission leaders who resided in Salisbury's white enclaves where whites dominated the life of the city in the colonial period. To some extent whites dominated the architecture and business of the city after independence, but rural villages belonged to Africans and missionaries who became comfortable with living in their midst. In history the voices of these missionaries in "the bush" are overwhelmed by press releases from mission headquarters. I wrote to or met with Salvation Army missionaries in the field, U.K and U.S. conservatives, and more liberal missionaries from Scandinavia, Switzerland, New Zealand, Australia, and Canada.

Eva Burrows, an Australian missionary teacher in Rhodesia/Zimbabwe, served as Principal of Usher Institute from January 1967 to December 1969, after she had taught and administered at Howard Institute for fourteen years. She responded to my questions about the war, the World Council of Churches, and missionaries and Africans. She demonstrates how views of missionaries in the field differed from those at mission headquarters in Salisbury. Burrows recalled that "though not a policy of Nkomo or Mugabe, to the minds of many of the freedom fighters (a term preferred to terrorists) the missionaries were identified with the white minority and therefore [were] justifiably an object for their hatred." She recommended that on my

---

7. Richard D. Atwell to Murdoch, June 12, 1995.

1998 research trip to Zimbabwe I should speak with "thoughtful salvationists such as Jonah Matsvetu," leader of the 1981 protest. By contrast with Burrows, I met a Salvation Army officer in London in 1998 who had served as pastor of the white Harare City Corps located on the headquarters building. He called Burrows' friend Matsvetu the "Mafia."

To Burrows, who delved deeply into African culture and was fluent in the Shona tongue, the liberation struggle was not "a conflict between Christianity and Communism," the focus of concern by U.S. Army leaders who had no knowledge of Africa. For her, "Communistic support was the only tool the Africans could find for help, and when it had served its purpose they could devise their own future in an African way."[8]

Salvationists who corresponded with me during my research provided a clear, albeit varied view of what concerned them during the last stages of minority rule and the first stage of Zimbabwe independence. While their sympathies differed on the African struggle against white settler rule, they united in their fear that my historical investigation might do damage to the story of the affection that missionaries had for their mission. Eva Burrows wrote, "I cannot see any serious reason to make the study in which you are involved, Professor. Today is a new day for Zimbabwe, and Salvationists rejoice in the vibrancy and growth of The Salvation Army as a strong evangelical and social service agency in the land." Lt. Colonel Ruth Chinchen, who taught at Usher from 1958 to 1963, answered my questions about the Usher killings and then responded to a question I asked about Salvationists siding with Smith or the Patriotic Front. Her experience had told her that "the army does not take sides . . . it tries to serve the needy people whoever they are and seeks to help them develop their highest potential."[9] Fair enough.

My lengthiest correspondence was with Colonel Lyndon Taylor, a missionary from Britain who responded to my broad generalizations with candor. His seventeen years of teaching and administering in Rhodesia began in 1955 at Howard Institute in Chiweshe. He and his wife Ethel also spent four years in Zambia as Officers Commanding. They ended their African mission as Territorial Leaders in Ghana from where they retired to Bromley, Kent. Historians dream of sources that are knowledgeable, open and frank,

---

8. Burrows to Murdoch, 10 January 1996, from South Yarra, Victoria, Australia. Burrows became the Salvation Army's second woman General in 1986. A former Harare City Corps Officer, with whom I spoke in London, asked for anonymity when I asked him to confirm his description of Matsvetu as "Mafia." He insisted that our conversation was "off the record." He did not withdraw his allegation concerning Matsvetu or deny that he said it.

9. Chinchen to Murdoch, 7 January 1996, from London.

and connoisseurs of historical endeavor. Such was Lyndon Taylor who in Salvation Army terms was "promoted to glory" in 1997.

On my observation that missionaries tended to be immersed in the white Rhodesian community rather than mix with Africans, Taylor countered that some in 1955 had become immersed in African culture and languages. But he "had lived through a period when African folk were seen as relatively primitive (from a Western standpoint)" and needed guidance. Missionaries "had links with the white population which, while often paternalistic, had even more difficulty in appreciating the speed of African advance." Missionaries became convinced that Africans "were not ready for self-government" when newly independent countries in other parts of Africa faltered.[10] In 1956 Taylor formed the Salvation Army Students' Fellowship (SASF) in Rhodesia and held the Army's first non-racial conference where whites and blacks openly discussed issues. While these were not political discussions, since the Army prohibited party politics, they often nibbled at the edges of political debate. The races ate together and later many lived together in Howard's school dormitories. Joint officers' meetings of blacks and whites came later, possibly due to the success of the SASF.

Taylor gave three reasons why the Salvation Army found it difficult to support the liberation movement. First, Salvationists were appalled at violence as a means to overthrow the government. Second, the Army had "cooperated with the government for a long time" and had accepted its support for African education and medical programs. Third, "a good deal of terrorist/freedom fighting was inspired by socialist/communistic/Marxist attitudes and tended to be anti-church." Eva Burrows, Taylor's colleague at Howard, did not share this view. I asked Taylor if missionaries from some countries adapted better to African culture than others. He responded that "Australian officers seemed more at home in the southern hemisphere—also New Zealanders. They were not used to a class structure as it has obtained in the UK. On the whole they were more extravert and open to change." Taylor commented on the work of three such colleagues: Eva Burrows, Ruth Wilkins, and Philip Rive, who had mastered African languages and mixed with Africans with more ease than some British and American officers.

Taylor agreed that Methodists were more "politically outspoken." Taylor, in Zambia by this time, was "disturbed" about the Army's withdrawal from the World Council of Churches. He feared that it would affect the Army's membership in Christian Councils in Africa, where the Army had

10. The collapse of the Belgian Congo into civil war upon the Belgian government's hasty withdrawal in 1960, without having prepared Africans for responsibility in any way, led to refugees streaming across the borders into Central Africa. This disaster probably contributed to the electoral success of the Rhodesia Front party in 1962.

gained status and influence. He also "suspected that this was a reaction following the Usher murders." At the 1979 Leaders' Conference in Toronto he opposed the move to leave the World Council. He was aware that "American leaders in particular favored membership of an evangelical body rather than of the WCC." He was aware of the Army's problem of representing an international constituency that did not always think alike.

As for the Army's political stance, Taylor acknowledged that "the SA has nearly always been suspicious of revolutionary political movements." This may have been due to "early hostility" before the Army gained status in the community. And "leftish movements were sometimes anti-religion. Salvationists have served the poor without being sentimental about them." As for African leaders, "The Army system required efficient management (so much paperwork and finance involved) which was not readily forthcoming from Africans." The Army "had not attracted . . . enough well educated and able officers." Pay was low. General Frederick Coutts was "uncomfortable in the Rhodesian situation" and "was pushing African leadership."[11] Taylor wrote to me fifteen months before he died: "Don't be too hard on the Army. It is trying to do all the good it can in the world. . . . We still try to be at the battle's front." He mentioned the Army's work at the time in the former Soviet Union, Rwanda, and Bosnia.[12]

Two Salvation Army medical missionaries, Dr. Paul du Plessis of South Africa and Dr. Jim Watt of Canada, lived in areas of conflict during the independence war. Both, like the three teachers, deserve full-blown biographies, but only a sample of their thinking fits this historiographical summary. I met Dr. du Plessis while I was doing research on my book on Salvation Army origins at the Army's London headquarters in 1981, soon after he had served as Chief Medical Officer at Chikankata Hospital in Zambia (1968-80). In 1979 he was in the zone where Zimbabwean refugees fled from the war and where Nkomo's forces prepared to stage raids into Rhodesia. In 1991 I corresponded with him in India, and in 1998 I talked with du Plessis in South Africa where he was territorial commander. Dr. Jim Watt, whom I met at Howard Hospital in 1998, spent most of the war in Chiweshe, an area north of Salisbury where there was fighting between Mugabe's ZANU guerrillas and Rhodesian government forces. In addition to our long discussions at Howard, Watt has permitted me to read his memoirs and corresponded with me.

---

11. Taylor to Murdoch (sometime after my first letter to him of 19 September 1995). He asked that I not quote his evaluation of the characteristics of colleagues.

12. Taylor to Murdoch, 12 February 1996.

Conclusions

195

Paul du Plessis was superintendent of Chikankata Hospital in Zambia from 1968 to 1980. Zambia had already gained independence and was a place of refuge for Zimbabwean émigrés. Inevitably southern Zambia was a hot spot. Toward the end of the Zimbabwe liberation war, in 1979, Du Plessis managed to run into Rhodesian, Zambian, and ZAPU Patriotic Front forces. When his Chikankata community health team got caught in a Rhodesian offensive aimed at Joshua Nkomo's ZAPU forces, du Plessis and colleagues went to their rescue. One of their vehicles detonated a mine that destroyed it. He was also apprehended by a ZAPU guerrilla who allowed him to continue his leprosy reviews, and Zambian authorities arrested him following a house search and detained him briefly, "apparently on suspicion that I was a spy." From this context du Plessis wrote to General Brown to sympathize with his dilemma on how to deal with the World Council of Churches after the 1978 killings of the missionaries at Usher, but he urged him to "act circumspectly."

Besides his mission work in Zambia, Paul du Plessis was a Salvation Army delegate to the World Council of Churches meeting in Vancouver in 1984, the first meeting after the Army's withdrawal from membership and its adoption of "fraternal membership" status. He had told the Chief of the Staff (second to the General) that he felt that "our withdrawal from the WCC had been untimely and felt that the world would not understand the background discontent we had had over the sacraments and the awkwardness of representation of an international movement. They would interpret our action as retaliatory, pique and racism." He would defend the Army's position "only by arguing that our emphasis is on personal conversion as the only way to lasting change, justice and peace. The use of force to create a new social order is therefore out of keeping with our denominational style and theological position."[13] When du Plessis and his wife Margaret returned to South Africa as the Army's commanders in the mid-1990s, he led his Salvationist countrymen in writing a submission to the Truth and Reconciliation Commission to apologize for the Salvation Army's racial discrimination during the years of apartheid. In retirement, Commissioner du Plessis worked as a physician in a hospice.

Dr. Jim Watt's memoirs contain a record of a physician in the African bush who "went native" in his sympathies. When I met him in 1998 he had contracted several diseases and anticipated his return to Canada in a year to recover his health. Unlike any other missionary I met he was unabashedly

13. Du Plessis to Murdoch, 20 November 1991, from Madras, India. Dr. du Plessis has described his experiences in an unpublished paper, "The Zimbabwe Liberation Struggle and Chikankata," 1996, and his "The South African Freedom Struggle and The Salvation Army, 1977–1994: Some Observations," 1996.

partisan to the cause of the African Patriotic Front and said he had even considered joining them in their struggle against the Rhodesia Front government. He blamed Smith's regime for mistreatment of the African populace in confining them in gated camps during the war and he also blamed the regime for mistreating missionaries and African Salvation Army officers. He certainly questioned the Army's national and international leadership in withdrawing from the Rhodesian Christian Council and the World Council of Churches. He was as far to the left as any of his compatriots in the Salvation War were to the right. This is remarkable in an organization in which, so far as I can tell, most officers in nearly all nations are on the political right. I base this conclusion on interviews with officers in North America, the U.K., India, Chile, and Southern Africa. A British officer who referred to J. B. Matsvetu as "Mafia" was one such contact. Is it because Watt is a doctor that he is so independently-minded, or is it simply due to the fact that he lived his life, as others who nudged the left did, close to the people he served in the "bush"?

Of course I am most grateful to Corps Sergeant Major Jonah Blessing Matsvetu to whom, with his fellow African Salvationists, I dedicate this book. I also appreciate the time and thought given to responses from General Arnold Brown and Commissioner Richard Atwell, for their candid statements of what occurred as they saw it and their role in this history. One does not expect unalloyed candor from institutional leaders. Readers must understand that on the whole a historian gives more credence to the testimony of on-the-scene eyewitnesses than to those who receive information at second or third hand.

Therefore J. B. Matsvetu's account of what happened in the Soldiers' March must be given more credence than Richard Atwell's second hand account, although Atwell adds interesting detail. Credence must also be given to the on-the-scene African teachers, especially John Ncube, who told me of the killing and wounding of his white teacher colleagues that he witnessed at Usher Institute. The African teachers heard the killers' conversation in their own Ndebele language and recall the commander's chilling command to fire. These are more credible witnesses than either of the warring parties, ZANU PF or Rhodesian Military Police, and they carry more weight than biased media or police reports, neither of which were at the scene or interviewed eyewitnesses. As Atwell revealed, the Salvation Army and media received reports only from the police and not from interviews with the staff. That evidence, tainted by partisanship and a lack of thorough investigation, contains details of the identification of the victims at Bulawayo Hospital, but historical conclusions must rest on a more solid base. Nevertheless, information from letters of Salvation Army leaders also help to enlighten us on the relations between the Salvation Army, the World Council of Churches and the Rhodesian Christian Council, and Rhodesian and Zimbabwean states in 1978 to 1981, in which they were primary actors.

Such is the work of historical investigation and the process of drawing conclusions from evidence. The work includes adventure in gathering documentation, but it cannot claim to have a God's-eye-view in making deductions from diverse sources of conflicting evidence. The basic chore is to remain objective by keeping an arms-length detachment form the various parties and debates under investigation. This is done to a major extent by drawing on the advice of fellow historians who read and critique the work. Thus every historian is in the debt of colleagues who agree to do this arduous task.

Epilogue

Internationally, the Salvation Army in 1999, the year after my second visit to Zimbabwe, was in 107 countries. In 2014, according to its 2013 Year Book, the Army operated in 126 Countries and Territories. As three countries (Kenya, India, and the USA) comprised more than one Territory, the comparable figure is now 117. The 1999 statistics given below are followed by the 2014 figures in square brackets

The Salvation Army's statistics listed 17,362 [17,105] active officers (clergy), 947,603 [1,150,666] senior soldiers (members aged 14 and over), 400,078 [368,749] junior soldiers (ages 8–14) and 82,893 [108,786] salaried employees, nearly five times [now 6.3 times] more employees than officers. In 1999 the Army in Zimbabwe had 404 [508] active officers, 86,921 [123,346] senior soldiers, and 1,382 [1,303] employees. The Army in the U.S. had 3,627 [3,394] active officers, 87,502 [83,941] senior soldiers, and 39,883 [58,529] employees. In the U.K. and Irish Republic the Army had 1,583 [1,091] active officers, 41,240 [27,183] senior soldiers, and 3,948 [4,800] employees.

From these relatively reliable statistics it is apparent that the Salvation Army in Zimbabwe had far more soldiers per active officer at 215 to 1 [now just under 243:1], than did either the United States with 24 to 1 [almost 25:1], or the United Kingdom and Ireland with 26 to 1 [25:1].[1] Philip Halcrow's analysis in *The Salvationist*, a British Salvation Army journal, indicated that the Army's 1998 statistics showed that "the United Kingdom Territory is part of the only zone in the international Army which is in numerical decline." But while the Army in Europe was losing soldiers, "numbers are booming in the African and South Asia Zones which, combined, now account for almost 66 [74.8] per cent of the Army's soldiers worldwide." He found that the U.K., in spite of its "continually falling soldiers' rolls" had

---

1. Margaret Sutherland, ed., *The Salvation Army Year Book: 2000*, 37, 227-28, 235, 266. Jayne Roberts, ed. *The Salvation Army Year Book: 2014*, 234, 240, 273.

"more soldiers than any one of the four prospering USA territories" [still, just, the case]. In Europe, only in Russia/CIS was the Army's membership growing. [Rolls continue to fall in Europe.]

Africans made up 38.1 [41.69] percent of Salvationists worldwide in 1999; South Asia (the Indian sub-continent) had 27.7 [33.1] percent.[2] When Latin America and East Asia were added to the 66 percent in Africa and South Asia, over 70 [84.75] percent of Salvationists live in the two-thirds world.

Former Salvation Army colonies in Africa and Asia have issued a warning against the continuing over-lordship of what an Indian officer termed reliance on "Our father who art in London." They warn that the Army must become more democratic. But the Army's London headquarters has in turn prodded colonial Salvationists they once saw as "children," toward self-management and self-support. Each Third World command has developed its own leaders after decades of knee-jerk subservience. The Army's leaders, and the leaders of all Christian sects, have asked former colonials and their new, sometimes minimally educated clergy, to address issues of how the Christian gospel and social services could appeal to their people in a way that would fit their own liberated cultural milieu. Both the West and the Third World, often within the structures of the World Council of Churches and other conciliar groups, are seeking to develop a Christian community that would break the cord of financial and cultural dependence on the West. But, in spite of this goal, all Third World "territories" of the Salvation Army still report to leaders at the London headquarters and obtain their external funds from North America, Europe, and Australia-New Zealand.

Thus the Africans, Asians, and Latin Americans are still, to a large degree, colonies striving to loosen the colonial cord at the beginning of the twenty-first century. In this book I have tried to move beyond institutional history to ask why Salvation Army leaders, missionaries, and Africans often did not communicate their anxieties and aspirations to each other at times of crisis. Was it because democracy was lacking in the Army's Western countries that Anglo-American officials in Africa acted as they would have acted at home where they expected deference from the Army's soldiers and from the poor to whom they rendered social services? At many Army corps in the West the educational level of soldiers (laymen) and officers (clergy) has not been much better than that of many Third World soldiers and officers, particularly in cities where the elite of the Third World live. In neither the developed nor the developing world did the Salvation Army's soldiers

---

2. Halcrow, "The Army is Growing around the World."

discuss or vote or control church polity and finance, nor did they elect their leaders, apart from the High Council that elects the General.

Voting was anathema to William Booth after he left behind the democratic Christian Mission conference system and exchanged it for a military-type autocracy. By the beginning of the twenty-first century such authoritarian rule was becoming antiquated. The rough and tumble of open debate, such as was the rule in other denominational councils was time consuming, but it encouraged members to claim ownership of the body that Salvation Army soldiers seldom could claim. Possibly Africans will teach the West a lesson in democracy.

It may be surprising that the Salvation Army's authoritarianism seems most in vogue in the United States where the command system and dependence on external funding leaves its American soldiers with no policy-making power. As America's favorite charity the Army ranks above the Red Cross in private donations although it seldom heralds this fact. Most of its $68.9 million in private donations in 1994 came from the United Way and its own Christmas appeals. Unpublished member contributions undoubtedly provided much less.[3]

Could a Third World challenge to the Army's authoritarian system encourage democratic changes in the West in the twenty-first century? Might it loosen control over what Western leaders fear might be an unacceptable expression of Christianity in the Third World? Lately charismatic Christianity's appeal in the Third World has unveiled a desire for both a more democratic polity and a more spiritually robust expression of faith. This exuberance is no longer present in many Salvation Army meetings in the West where the Army has screened over-exuberance from its style of worship. Army polity and dogma will face new challenges from Third World Salvationists as they call for majority rule in their church. In turn Third World Salvationists may face the discomfort of severing their ties to Western financial support and cultural heritage.

Yet some Salvation Army leaders have begun to see that shared decision making and more spirited worship can help the Army experience membership growth, something Western Salvationists now regard as desperately needed. This would almost certainly mean a more limited role for international leaders in the affairs of local congregations. In the United States weak support from soldiers has given the Army the aura of a state church, dependent on external funding, whereas in Zimbabwe, for survival sake, soldiers have assumed an increasing financial role by the late 1960s

---

3. Roha, "Charities You Can Believe In," placed the Salvation Army ahead of the American Red Cross which had $535.8 million in private donations in 1994.

and with it sought an increased voice in governance. For this reason is it possible that democratic impulses in Africa might resonate in America, Europe and Australasia?

Matsvetu's vision of democratic reform is attractive but the Army's military, hierarchical structure may militate against such an outcome. While Africa does have traditions of consultative and participative leadership, it also shares traditions of authoritarian control and the latter are more readily fostered within the Salvation Army system of governance. Sadly, indigenous African Salvation Army leadership can be sometimes as controlling as its colonialist predecessors. It remains to be seen which tradition emerges as normative.

Bibliography

Adlam, Frederick J. "What is Best for the African People Today?" *The Salvation Army Yearbook, 1965.* London: Salvationist, 1965.
Anon. "Under One Flag." *The War Cry,* 24 Oct. 1896, 12.
———. "Where the Shamrock Grows." *All the World,* March 1905, 139.
Banana, Canaan S., ed. *A Century of Methodism in Zimbabwe, 1891–1991.* Harare: Methodist Church-Zimbabwe, 1991.
———. *Politics of Repression and Resistance: Face to Face with Combat Theology.* Gweru: Mambo, 1996.
———, gen. ed. *Turmoil and Tenacity: Zimbabwe 1890–1990.* Harare: College Press, 1989.
Baxter, T. W., and E. E. Burke. *Guide to the Historical Manuscripts in the National Archives of Rhodesia.* Salisbury, Rhodesia: National Archives of Rhodesia, 1970.
Beach, D. N. "The Initial Impact of Christianity on the Shona: The Protestants and the Southern Shona." In *Christianity South of the Zambezi,* edited by A. J. Dachs, 25–40. Gwelo, Zimbabwe: Mambo, 1973.
———. *The Shona and Zimbabwe, 900–1850: An Outline of Shona History.* Masvingo, Zimbabwe: Mambo, 1980.
———. *War and Politics in Zimbabwe, 1840–1900.* Gweru, Zimbabwe: Mambo, 1986.
———. *A Zimbabwean Past: Shona Dynastic Histories and Oral Traditions.* Gweru, Zimbabwe: Mambo, 1994.
Begbie, Harold. *The Life of General William Booth.* 2 vols. New York: Macmillan, 1920.
Boggie, Jeannie M. *Experiences of Rhodesia's Pioneer Women.* Salisbury, Rhodesia: Philpott and Collins, 1954.
Booth, Catherine. *Female Teaching.* 2nd ed. London: Stevenson, 1861.
Booth, Catherine Bramwell. *Catherine Booth: The Story of Her Loves.* London: Hodder and Stoughton, 1970.
Booth, William, *Heathen England and What to Do for It.* London: Partridge & Co., 1877.
———. *In Darkest England and the Way Out.* London: The Salvation Army, 1890.
Booth, William, and Alfred J. Cunningham. *The Bible: Its Divine Revelation, Inspiration and Authority.* London: The Salvation Army, 1961.
Booth, W. Bramwell. *Echoes and Memories.* London: Hodder & Stoughton, 1925.
Booth-Tucker, F. de L. *The Life of Catherine Booth: The Mother of The Salvation Army.* 3rd ed. London: Salvationist, 1924.

Bourdillon, Michael F. C. *Religion and Society: A Text for Africa.* Gweru, Zimbabwe: Mambo, 1990.

———. *The Shona Peoples: An Ethnography of the Contemporary Shona, with Special Reference to Their Religion.* 3rd ed. Gweru, Zimbabwe: Mambo, 1987.

Brown, Arnold. *The Gate and the Light.* Toronto: Bookwright, 1984.

Brash, Alan. "World Council and the Gospel." *Outlook,* Sept. 1974, 13.

Burrows, William. "Outlook: Evangelism and Dialogue." *War Cry,* US, Aug. 31, 1974, 2 and Nov. 29, 1975, 2.

Carpenter, Joel A., and Wilbert R. Shenk, eds. *Earthen Vessels: American Evangelicals and Foreign Missions, 1880–1980.* Grand Rapids: Eerdmans, 1990.

Carwardine, Richard. "Methodists, Politics, and the Coming of the American Civil War." *Church History* ? (September 2000) 578–609.

Charmley, John. *Churchill's Grand Alliance: The Anglo-American Special Relationship, 1940–57.* New York: Harcourt Brace & Co., 1995.

Chennells, Anthony J. "White Rhodesian Nationalism—The Mistaken Years." In *Turmoil and Tenacity,* edited by C. S. Banana, 123–39. Harare: College Press, 1989.

Coutts, Frederick. *Bread for My Neighbour: The Social Influence of William Booth.* London: Hodder and Stoughton, 1978.

Coutts, John J. "Half a Century in Nigeria." *Salvation Army Yearbook, 1970.* London: The Salvation Army, 1969.

———. *The Salvationists.* London: Mowbrays, 1977.

Cox, Ronald. "Village Schools in Rhodesia." *All the World* (January–March 1966) 4–6, 8.

Craig, E. T. *Cooperative Society Illustrated.* London: Reeves, 1880.

———. *History of Ralahine and Cooperative Farming.* London: Trubner, 1882.

———. *An Irish Commune: The History of Ralahine.* Dublin: Lester, 1919.

Dachs, A. J., ed. *Christianity South of the Zambezi.* Gwelo, Zimbabwe: Mambo, 1973.

Darley, Gillian. *Villages of Vision.* London: Architectural Press, 1975.

du Plessis, Paul A. "The South African Freedom Struggle and The Salvation Army, 1977–1994: Some Observations." Unpublished paper, 1996.

———. "The Zimbabwe Liberation Struggle and Chikankata." Unpublished paper, 1996.

Eason, Andrew Mark. "The Salvation Army and the Sacraments in Victorian Britain: Retracing the Steps to Non-observance." *Fides et Historia* 41.2 (Summer/Fall 2009) 51–71.

Ervine, St. John. *God's Soldier: General William Booth.* New York: Macmillan, 1935.

Gale, W. D. *One Man's Vision; James Johnston, M.D., Reality Versus Romance in South Central Africa.* New York: Revell, 1935.

Gariepy, Henry. *Christianity in Action: The International History of the Salvation Army.* Grand Rapids: Eerdmans, 2009.

———. *Mobilized for God: The History of The Salvation Army, Vol. 8, 1977–1894.* Atlanta: The Salvation Army, 2000.

Garnett, R. G. "Robert Owen and the Community Experiment." In *Robert Owen,* edited by Sidney Pollard and John Salt, 39–64. Lewiston, NY: Bucknell University Press, 1971.

Gauntlett, S. Carvosso. "The Salvation Army as a League of Nations." *The Salvation Army Yearbook, 1933.* London: Salvationist, 1933.

George, Henry. *Progress and Poverty.* New York: Robert Schalkenbach Foundation, 1981.

Glass, Stafford. *The Matabele War.* London: Longmans, Green, & Co., 1968.

Bibliography

Green, Roger. "Settled Views: Catherine Booth and Female Ministry." *Methodist History* 31.3 (April 1993) 131–47.

———. *War on Two Fronts: The Redemptive Theology of William Booth*. Atlanta: The Salvation Army, 1989.

Haggard, H. Rider, *The Poor and the Land: Being a Report on The Salvation Army's Farm Colonies in the United States and at Hadleigh, England*. London: Longmans, Green, 1905.

Halcrow, Philip. "The Army is Growing Around the World." *Salvationist* 631, 23 May 1998, 12–13.

Hallencreutz, Carl F. "A Council in Crossfire: ZCC 1964–1980." In *Church and State in Zimbabwe*, edited by Carl Hallencreutz and Ambrose Moyo, 51–113. Gweru, Zimbabwe: Mambo, 1988.

Hargreaves, J. D. *Decolonization in Africa*. London: Longman, 1988.

Hill, Harold, "Howard: The Years That Have Gone." *All the World* 7.20, July-September 1973, 219–22.

Hobsbaum, Eric. *The Age of Empire, 1875–1914*. New York: Vintage, 1987.

Hochshild, Adam. *King Leopold's Ghost: A Story of Greed, Terror and Heroism in Colonial Africa*. Boston: Houghton Mifflin, 1999.

Holbrook, Olive. "Salvationist Survey, XIV—Rhodesia." *The Officer*, Jan. 1953, 34–41.

Hope, Noel. *Lucy in Lion Land*. London: Salvation Army, 1928.

Horridge, Glenn K. *The Salvation Army: Origins and Early Days, 1865–1900*. Godalming, UK: Ammonite, 1993.

Isichei, Elizabeth. *A History of Christianity in Africa: From Antiquity to the Present*. Grand Rapids: Eerdmans, 1995.

Kendrick, Kathleen. "Missionary Education." *All the World*, July-September 1960, 78–81.

Kessler, J. B. A. *A Study of the Evangelical Alliance in Great Britain*. Goes, Netherlands: Oosterbaan & Le Cointre, 1968.

Kirby, Leonard. "Early Days in Rhodesia" (1965). Unpublished manuscript at the Salvation Army Archives, London.

———. "Memories of Long Ago." Unpublished paper at the Salvation Army Archives, London.

Kurewa, John Wesley. *The Church in Mission: A Short History of the United Methodist Church in Zimbabwe, 1897–1997*. Nashville: Abingdon, 1997.

Lapping, Brian. *End of Empire*. New York: St. Martins, 1985.

Larsson, John. *1929: A Crisis That Shaped The Salvation Army's Future*. London: Salvation Books, 2009.

Lewis, Donald M. *Lighten Their Darkness: The Evangelical Mission to Working-Class London, 1828–1860*. New York: Greenwood, 1986.

Lewis, John. "500 Acres under the Plough." *All the World*, October-December 1966, 137.

Mahlah. "Away to Mashonaland." *All the World*, June 1891, 468–70.

Manson, John. *The Salvation Army and the Public*. London: Routledge, 1906.

Marsden, George M. *Fundamentalism and Culture: The Shaping of 20th Century Evangelicalism, 1870–1925*. Oxford: Oxford University Press, 1980.

Matsvetu, Jonah Blessing. "Salvationists in Zimbabwe Protest against Some Decisions Made by the Leaders during the Liberation War of Zimbabwe." Unpublished paper, 1993.

Maxwell, David J. "Christianity and the War in Eastern Zimbabwe: The Case of Elim Mission." In *Society in Zimbabwe's Liberation War*, edited by Terence Ranger and Ngwabi Bhebe, 65–78. Oxford: Curry, 1996.

Mazobere, Crispen C. G. "Christian Theology of Mission." In *A Century of Methodism in Zimbabwe, 1891–1991*, edited by C. S. Banana, 149–74. Harare: Methodist Church-Zimbabwe, 1991.

McKinley, Edward H. *Marching to Glory: The History of The Salvation Army in the United States, 1880–1992*. 2nd ed. Grand Rapids: Eerdmans, 1995.

McLynn, Frank. *Hearts of Darkness: The European Exploration of Africa*. New York: Caroll & Graf, 1992.

McMillan, Christine. "The Salvation Army and the United Nations." *The Salvation Army Yearbook, 1966*. London: Salvationist, 1966.

Meath (Earl of), (Lord Brabazon). *Brabazon Potpourri*. London: Hutchinson, 1928.

———. *Prosperity or Pauperism?* London: Longmans, Green, 1888.

———. *Social Arrows*. London: Longmans, Green, 1886.

Merritt, John G., ed. *Historical Dictionary of The Salvation Army*. Metuchen NJ: Scarecrow, 2006.

Millin, S. Gertrude. *Rhodes*. London: Chatto & Windus, 1933.

Moorhouse, Geoffrey. *The Missionaries*. London: Eyre Methuen, 1973.

Moyles, R. Gordon. *The Salvation Army and the Public*. Edmonton, Alberta: AGM, 2000.

Moyo, Sam, *The Land Question in Zimbabwe*. Harare: Sapes, 1995.

Murdoch, Norman H. "Anglo-American Salvation Army Farm Colonies, 1890–1910." *Communal Societies* 3 (1983) 111–21.

———. "Female Ministry in the Thought and Work of Catherine Booth." *Church History* 53.3 (1984) 363–78.

———. "Frank Smith, M.P." In *Historical Dictionary of The Salvation Army*, edited by John Merritt, 516–18. Metuchen NJ: Scarecrow, 2006.

———. *Frank Smith: Salvationist Socialist (1854–1940)*. Alexandria, VA: The Salvation Army, 2003.

———. "Rose Culture and Social Reform: Edward Bellamy's *Looking Backward* (1888) and William Booth's *Darkest England and the Way Out* (1890)." *Utopian Studies* 3.2 (1992) 91–101.

———. "The Salvation Army and the Church of England, 1882–1883." *Historical Magazine of the Protestant Episcopal Church* 55, March 1986, 31–55.

———. *Soldiers of the Cross: Susie Swift & David Lamb, Pioneers of Social Change*. Alexandria, VA: Crest, 2006.

———. "William Booth's Darkest England and the Way Out: A Reappraisal." *Wesleyan Theological Journal* 25.1 (1990) 106–16.

Needham, Philip. "Arkansas Traveler with a World View." *The Southern Spirit* 5.18, July 11, 1988, 4–5.

Nicol, A. M. *General Booth and The Salvation Army*. London: Herbert and Daniel, 1911.

Nkomo, Joshua. *Nkomo: My Life Story*. London: Methuen, 1984.

Nyandoro, Misheck. *A Flame of Sacred Love: The Salvation Army in Zimbabwe 1890–1991*. Harare: The Salvation Army, 1993.

Orsborn, Albert. *The House of My Pilgrimage*. London: The Salvation Army, 1958.
Pakenham, Thomas. *The Scramble for Africa: White Man's Conquest of the Dark Continent from 1876 to 1912*. New York: Avon, 1991.
Parkin, Christine. "Pioneer in Female Ministry." *Christian History* 9.2 (1990) 10–13.
Paton, Andrew. *'Mzilikazi': A Biography of Lieut. Colonel John Tudor Usher*. Johannesburg: The Salvation Army, 1987.
Porter, Bernard. *The Lion's Share: A Short History of British Imperialism, 1850–1970*. London: Longman, 1975.
Railton, George S. *General Booth*. London: Salvationist, 1912.
Ranger, Terence O. *Revolt in Southern Rhodesia, 1896–97: A Study in African Resistance*. Evanston, IL: Northwestern University Press, 1967.
———. "Taking Hold of the Land: Holy Places and Pilgrimages in Twentieth-Century Zimbabwe." *Past and Present* 117 (1987) 158–94.
Ranger, Terence O., and Ngwabi Bhebe, eds. *Society in Zimbabwe's Liberation War*. Oxford: Curry, 1996.
Roha, Ronaleen R. "Charities You Can Believe In." *Kiplinger Personal Finance Magazine*, November 1995, 75–80.
Rossiter, C. The Bureaucratic Struggle for Control of U.S. Foreign Aid: Diplomacy versus Development in Southern Africa. New York: Westview Republican Edition, 1988.
Said, Edward W., *Culture and Imperialism*. New York: Vintage, 1993.
Samkange, Stanlake. *Origins of Rhodesia*. London, Heinemann, 1968.
Sandall, Robert. *The History of The Salvation Army*, vols. 1–3. London: Thomas Nelson, 1947–55.
———. "Native Work in Africa." *All the World*, Oct. 1905, 541–45.
Schmidt, Elizabeth, *Peasants, Traders and Wives: Shona Women in the History of Zimbabwe, 1870–1939*. Harare: Baobab, 1992.
Silk, Heather. "Usher Institute: A Rehabilitation Success Story." *All the World*, Jan.–Mar. 1983, 169, 175.
Sjollema, Baldwin. *Isolating Apartheid: Western Collaboration with South Africa: Policy Decisions by the World Council of Churches and Church Responses*. Geneva: Program to Combat Racism, World Council of Churches, 1982.
Skelton, Kenneth. *Bishop in Smith's Rhodesia*. Gweru, Zimbabwe: Mambo, 1985.
Smith, Bernard. *Fraudulent Gospel: Politics and the World Council of Churches*. London: Covenant, 1991.
Smith, Ian. *The Great Betrayal*. London: Blake, 1997.
Smith, J. Allister. *Zulu Crusade*. London: Salvationist, 1945.
Spence, Clark C. *The Salvation Army Farm Colonies*. Tucson, AZ: University of Arizona Press, 1985.
Swift, Susie Forrest. "Editor's Diary," *All the World*, March 1892, 210.
Thomlinson, Ronald. *A Very Private General: A Biography of General Frederick Coutts, C.B.E., D.D.* London: The Salvation Army, 1990.
Thompson, Victor J. *Delayed Harvest: A Brief Record of the First Five Years of The Salvation Army in Mashonaland, Central Africa*. Salisbury, Rhodesia: for Private Circulation, 1957.
Todd, Judith. "White Policy and Politics 1890–1980." In *Turmoil and Tenacity: Zimbabwe 1890–1990*, edited by C. S. Banana. Harare: College Press, 1989, 116–22.

Tuck, Brian. *Salvation Safari: A Brief History of the Origins of The Salvation Army in Southern Africa, 1883–1993*. 2nd ed. Johannesburg: The Salvation Army Southern Africa Territory, 1993.

Waldron, John, ed. *The Salvation Army and the Churches*. New York: The Salvation Army, 1986.

Walker, Pamela J. "Proclaiming Women's Right to Preach." *Harvard Divinity Bulletin* 23.3/4 (1994) 20–23, 35.

Webb, Pauline, ed. *A Long Struggle: The Involvement of the World Council of Churches in South Africa*. Geneva: WCC, 1994.

Weiss, Ruth, with Jane L. Parpart. *Sir Garfield Todd and the Making of Zimbabwe*. London: British Academic Press, 1999.

Whitlow, J. R. "Environmental Constraints and Population Pressures in the Tribal Areas of Zimbabwe." *Journal of Zimbabwe Agriculture* 81.2 (1980) 41–48.

Wiggins, Arch R. *The History of The Salvation Army*, vol. V. London: Nelson, 1968.

Williams, Harry. *I Couldn't Call My Life My Own*. Worthing, UK: Churchman, 1990.

Williams, Richard, "At Work in a Changing World." *The Officers' Review*, Jan. 1948, 28–33.

———. "Rhodesian Dawn." *The Salvation Army Yearbook, 1950*. London: The Salvation Army, 1950.

Wiseman, Clarence D. *A Burning in My Bones*. Toronto: McGraw-Hill, 1979.

Woods, Reginald. "The Army and the World Council of Churches—Some Questions Answered." *The Officer* 12, Sept.–Oct. 1961, 291–94, 323–24.

———. "New Delhi Speaks: A Glance at Some of the Questions Raised." *The Officer*, Mar.–Apr. 1963, 125–28 and 161–67.

Zvobgo, C. J. M. *The Wesleyan Methodist Missions in Zimbabwe, 1891–1945*. Harare: University of Zimbabwe Publications, 1991.

Index

Adlam, F.J., 100n14, 127, 142
Alice Mine, 23–25
African National Congress (Rhodesia), 112
African National Council (ANC, South Africa), 122
African Voice Association, 112
Anderson, A.M., 96
Anglican Church, Church of England, 7, 11, 16–18, 27, 34, 42, 46, 49, 94–96, 104, 109, 113, 116, 134–35, 144, 190
Ashton, Lord Thomas, 64
Asquith, Herbert Henry, 60, 62
Atwell, Richard, 112, 144, 150, 156, 158–62 (*illus* 160), 169, 182, 188–91, 196

Bailey, Abraham, 60- 62 (*illus* 61), 65–67, 70- 72, 74, 76–67, 79- 82, 84, 88
Baird, Catherine, 125
Banana, Canaan, 16, 128, 143, 171
Baptist Church, 172
Barker, James, 95, 97
Battersby, Agatha, 100
Beach, D.N., xvi, xx, xxi, 18–19, 20n24, 21n2, 30
Beatrice Mine, 24
Begbie, Harold, 43
Bellamy, Edward, 40
Bhebe, N. M., xiii, xiv, xx
Bickersteth, Edward, 132
Blackwell, Benjamin, 125
Blake, Eugene Carson, 141–42

Blakistone, J.L., 24–25
Blowers, A.R., 95n9, 101
Boer War, 44
Bond, Linda, 129n19
Booth, Bramwell, xxiv, 18, 43, 45, 49, 53–88 (*illus* 54), 120, 125, 126, 129n19, 135, 162
Booth, Catherine, xxix, xxx, 10, 58, 126–27, 131–33, 162
Booth, Emma, 59
Booth, Evangeline, 54, 63, 129n19
Booth, Florence, 55, 77
Booth, Lucy, 55, 59
Booth, William, xxviii, xxi, 9, 10, 12–14, 18, 36–88 (*illus* 54), 91, 93–94, 120, 125–27, 129n19, 131, 133–35, 162, 165, 171, 179, 201
Booth-Helborg, Emanuel, 59
Booth-Tucker, Frederick, 59, 75, 81
Bourdillon, Michael, xviin2, 31
Brabazon, Reginald (Earl of Meath), 41–43
Bradley, Frank, 37
Bradley Secondary School, 110
Brash, Alan, 148
Brethren in Christ Church, 12, 95–96
British Council of Churches, 166
British South Africa Company (BSAC, "Chartered Company"), xvi, 2–3, 6–7, 9–16, 18–19, 22, 27, 29- 30, 32, 34–35, 46–49, 52, 55–57, 60- 62, 64–66, 78–81, 83–86, 89–92, 95–97, 112, 119, 121, 171, 177–78, 181, 183

Index

Brown, Arnold, xvii, xix, xxvii, xxviii, 5, 121–22, 129n19, 138, 155, 160–68 (*illus* 165), 170, 174–75, 177, 182, 188–90, 196
Bumhudzo Rest Home, 110
Burns, John, 79–80, 87
Burrough, Paul, 190
Burrows, Eva, xix, 129n19, *illus* 156, 169, 191–93
Burrows, William, 148

Caldwell, Jean, 151n3, 152, 155n13, 189
Campbell-Bannerman, Henry, 47, 62
Carpenter, George L., 129n19
Carter, Herbert, 16
Carter, Jimmy, 161, 188, 190
Cass, Ada, 23, *illus* 26–27, 30
Cass, Edward T., xvi, 3, 9, 17, *illus* 22–33, 155, 171, 176–77, 184
Charity Organization Society, 49
Charmey, John, 110
Chase, Samuel, 132
Chennells, Anthony J., 5, 6n10, 33, 46n28
China Inland Mission (CIM), 13
Chinake, J., 105
Chinchin, Ruth, xix, 192
Chirau, Jeremiah, 161n4
Chiweshe, 28–29, 90, 97, 104, 164, 173, 194
Christian Council of Rhodesia (CCR) 2, 4, 109, 114–16, 119, 129, 143, 190, 196
Christian Council of Southern Rhodesia, 105, 114
Church Army, 42
Church of Christ, 144
Churchill, Winston, 46, 60, 62, 110
Clack, Charles, 91
Clifton, Shaw, 129n19, 155
Coles, Alan and Benda, xx, *illus* 156
Cotton, Angela, 150–51
Cotton, David, 151–52, 189
Coutts, Frederick L., xxix, 120–21, 124–25, 127, 129, 131, 135, 194
Coutts, John, xxvii–xxxi, 89, 125, 126, 138

Coutts, John and Heather, xix, xxi,
Cox, Andre, xx, 130n19
Cox, Ronald, 99, 107–8
Craig, E.T., 40, 43
Crewe, Charles Preston, 71, 73–74
Crewe, Lord (Earl of), 71
Cripps, Arthur Shearly, 16
Crook, David, 9, 17
Cunningham, Alfred G., 125–26, 135–36
Cunningham, John, 70, 73, 84–86

'Darkest England' social reform program, 38–42
De Beers Company, 60, 71, 74, 79, 81–82, 88
Dickinson, James, 24–25
Dodge, Ralph, 16
Dunne, Finlay Peter, 36
Du Plessis, Paul, xix, 55n2, 194
Dutch Reformed Church, 11, 19, 63, 95, 104, 109, 128, 144

East London Special Services Committee, 133
Elim Pentecostal Emmanuel Mission, 154–55, 166n13
Epps, Dwayne, xx
Ervine, St. John, 47
Estill, Thomas, 9, 20
Etherington, Norman, xxi
Evangelical Alliance, 131, 133, 136–37

Fabian Society, 49
Faull, William, 24–25
Federation of Rhodesia and Nyasaland, 112–13
Fewster, Ernest, 115
Finney, Charles G., 10, 126
Fletcher, Robert A., 177
Foster, April, xx

Gale, W.D., 22
Gariepy, Henry, xviin3, 3, 4n8
Gauntlett, Carvosso, 125, 135
Gauntlett, Caughey, 169
George, Henry, 38–39, 43
Gilmour, A., 58
Gladstone, Herbert, 46

Gould-Adams, Hamilton, 63
Gowans, John, 127, 129n19
Green, Roger, 171
Grey, Lord Albert, 34
Grey, Sir Edward, 48
Griffin, Ada (Mrs Cass), 20
Groves, C.P., 12
Gwindi, Ben, 160

Hadleigh Farm, 58
Halcrow, Philip, 199
Hampton, J.H., 178
Hardie, Keir, 64
Hartman, Janine C., xx, xxi
Hawksley, Bourchier, 65, 71
Haynes, John, 155
Heads of Denominations Forum, 115, 117
Heim, C.D., 14
Henderson, Arthur, 64
Higgins, Edward J., 76, 129n19, 177–79
High Council, 122, 166–67, 170
Hill, Harold and Pat, xix, xxi
Hill, Harold, 102n18
Hobsbaum, Eric, 36, 46
Hochshild, Adam, 8n3
Hole, Marshall, 33, 51, 85, 88
Holz, Ernest W., 167, 170
Holz, Richard E., 145–46, 169
Hope, Noel, 32
Howard, T. Henry, 28, 76, 87, 97
Howard Institute, 94, 97–98 (*illus* 98), 100–102, 104–5, 110, 178
Howard Hospital, 100, 102, 105, 110
Hunter, Denis, xix, 167, 170
Hutson, Don, xxi
Hwata people, 29, 90, 177

In Darkest England, and the Way Out, 9, 13, 43
Isichei, Elizabeth, 73n26

Jameson, Leander Star, 11, 14, 17, 24, 47, 51, 56–58, 60- 62 (*illus* 61), 70–71, 76, 79–80, 85–88
Jeffries, Charles, 135
Jenkins, Edward, 43
Jesuit Order, 11, 18, 34, 90

Johansen, Judith, xx
Johnson, Frank, 15
Judd, Charles, 13
Judson, Dan, 24
Jumbe, Clement, xx

Kaguvi, 24
Kaiser, Paul S., 145–46, 158–59 (*illus* 159), 191
Karlen, Henry, 155
Kaunda, Kenneth, 141
Kellner, Paul and Jajuan, xx
Kendrick, Kathleen, 99n12, 104
Kirby, Leonard , xix, 94, 97, *illus* 160, 178–79
Kitching, Theodore, 53, 56, 60–62, 66–67, 71, 74, 76–77, 80, 82–84
Kitching, Wilfred, 105, 127, 129n19
Kurewa, John, 153

Lamb, David C., xxxi, 57–58, 87
Lambon-Jacobs family, xx
Lamont, Donal, 16
Lancaster House Agreement, xvii, 163, 184, 186
Lapping, Brian, 15n13
Larsson, John, xxixn4, 45n25, 129n19
Lause, Mark, xx, xxi
Leopold, King, 8
Lewis, John, 179
Lewis, Thomas, 102, 104
Lloyd-George, David, 86
Lobengula, King, 11, 14–15, 18, 20–21, 34, 90
Loch, Charles, 44
Loch, Henry, 18
London Missionary Society (LMS), 11–12, 14, 18–19, 95
Loosley, J.S., 65
Lovedale Mission, 72–73

McCarthy, Joseph, 137
McDonald, Ramsay, 64
MacGregor, Alan, 37
MacKenzie, F.A., 64, 79, 86
McKinley, E.H., 14n12, 45n25, 162n6, 164n11
MacLaughlan, Janice, 16

McLynn, Frank, xviin2
McMillan, Christine, 135
Mabhiza, Sydney and Gladys, xx
Maguire, Rochfort, 14
Mahon, Edgar, 9
Makone, Bernard Mangizi, 106
Manson, John, 64, 87
Marsden, George M., 125
Mashayamombe, Chief, 21
Matsvetu, Jonah Blessing, *frontispiece*, xix, 29n18, 175–77, 180–82, 188–91, 196, 202
Matunjwa, Mbambo, 37
Maxwell, David J., 154
Mazobere, Crispen, 8n2, 180,
Mazoe, Mazowe, 3, 14, 17, 21, 24–27, 30, 34, 37, 49, 90, 97, 104, 110, 160, 176–77
Merriman, John Xavier, 59
Merton, Thomas, 140
Methodist Church, 7–8, 11–13, 16–18, 94–96, 104, 109, 112, 114, 128, 131, 143–45, 150, 162n7, 171–72, 186, 193
Mhlange, Moffat M., 151
Milton, Sir William, 51, 83, 85, 87
Millin, S. Gertrude, 8n4
Moffatt, Archibald, 101n15
Moffat, H.U., 177, 178
Moffatt, Robert, 11
Mondlane, Eduardo, 141
Moore, Margaret, 149
Moorhouse, Geoffrey, 1, 183
Morgan, Richard Cope, 132–33
Morley, John, 46
Mortimer, Kingsley, 102
Moyles, Gordon, xxi, 45n25
Moyo, David, 156, 158, 169, 175, 180, 186, 188–90
Moyo, David and Selina, *illus* 156, 173
Moyo, Gideon and Lister, xx
Moyo, Sam, 90
Mtukwa, M.G., 180
Muchenje, S., 180
Mufanechiya, Godfrey, xv
Mugabe, Robert Gabriel, xvi, xvii, 3, 4, 6, 122–23 (*illus* 123), 128, 150, 160–61, 163, 169, 174, 181, 185, 190–91

Muhambi, Ben, 37
Mukonyora, Isabel, xxi
Mungate, Stuart, xxi
Murdoch, Grace, xv, xxi
Murdoch, Norman, *xiff* (tributes), 38n5n7, 39n10, 40n12, 41n14, 42n17, 45n25, 132n4, 133n5, 135n8
Murray, Mary, 44
Muzorewa, Abel, 6, 150, 161, 169, 186
Mzilikazi, King, 11
Mzongwana, Philemon, 143

National Council of Churches (USA), 128, 137
Ncube, John, xix, 150–51, 196
Ndhlela, A.M., 114, 143, 186
Ndhlovu, Jabel, 155
Ndhlovu, Philemon and Georgina, *illus* 156
Needham, Philip, 149n1
Ngwenya, Aloisy, 151
Nehanda Nyakasikana, 24, *illus* 29, 177
Nesbitt, Randolph, 25
Nevanji, Sylvia, 152
Newberry, John, 63–64
Nhari, Joseph, 105–7
Nhari, L., 180
Nicol, A.M., 76
Nkomo, Joshua Mqabuko, xvi, xvii, 3, 4, 6, 112, *illus* 124, 128, 150, 152–53, 160–61, 163, 185, 189, 191
Nyachuru, 28, 97
Nyandoro, Misheck, 3, 4n7, 31, 94, 100n13, 105–6, 110n3, 117n16, 154n11
Nyathi, Pathisa, 151

Orpen, James, 70
Orsborn, Albert, 118, 129n19, 135–36, 138
Orthodox Church, 147
Owen, David, 160–61, 188
Owen, Robert, 40, 43
Oxfam, 164n10

Pakenham, Thomas, 15n14, 43n20, 48
Pallant, Stephen, xix

Index

Pascoe, John, 9, 13–14, 16–17, 20, 23–26 (*illus* 26), 171, 177
Paton, J.B., 42
Patrick, Mother, 11
Patriotic Front (PF), xvi, xvii, 3, 4, 5, 29, 112, 122, 129, 143, 147, 150, 161, 163–64, 166, 174, 186, 190, 195–96
Paulsson, Gunvor, 151, 189
Pearson Farm, 5, 27, 29, 97, 104, 176–80, 189
Perry, Geoffrey T., xix
Pfende, Joseph, 151
Pollard, H.H., 30
Porter, Bernard, 44
Potter, Philip, 142, 145–46 (*illus* 146), 167, 170, 188
Presbyterian Church, 12, 35, 96, 128, 144
Prestage, Peter, 11
Program to Combat Racism, 4, 122, 128, 138, 141–44, 146–48, 163, 166–67, 170

Quakers, 136–37

Radcliffe, Reginald, 133
Rader, Paul, 129n19
Railton, George Scott, xxix, 165
Raiser, Konrad, xx, 140
Ramsay, David, 153
Ranger, Terence O., xx, 6, 7n11, 21n2, 27–28, 30, 32–34, 112n7
Rauch, Joseph, 58
Rea, Fred, 143
Reid, Mary, 59
Rhodes, Cecil John, xvi, xxxi, 2, 5–9, 10, 12–15, 18–19, 22, 32, 36–38 (*illus* 37), 41–45, 51, 171, 176–77, 181, 183
Rhodesia Front (RF), 5, 150, 193n10, 196
Richards, W.J., 58, 62, 64, 66, 73, 77, 83–84, 86
Ridout, Audrey, xx
Ridsdel, William, 25
Rive, Philip, 102, 193
Roberts, John H., 143

Robinson, Earl, xix
Rogers, Jessie Stuart., 51
Roman Catholic Church, 2, 4, 6–7, 11, 16–17, 34, 94–96, 104, 109, 113, 116, 120, 125, 137, 152–54, 172
Rosebey, Lord, 46, 71
Rossiter, C., 90
Routledge, T.G., 24–25
Rudd, Charles Donnell, 14
Rumford, Count (Benjamin Thompson) 39–40, 43
Rushwaya, 151

Sagar, William, 80–81
Said, Edward, 21
Salisbury, Eileen, 100n14
Salthouse, J.W., 24
Salvation Army Student Fellowship (SASF), 110, 193
Samkange, S., 15n15
Sandall, Robert, 91, 92, 134n6
Schmidt, Elizabeth, xviin2, 22
Schearing, Linda, *illus* 159
Scott, (Rev) Bob, xx
Scott, Robert H., 9, 17n18
Searle, Theodore, 9
Sebotsiso, Moses, 95
Selborne, Lord (2nd Earl of) 60, 62–63, 75, 87
Selous Scouts, xvi, 152–53, 176, 189
Seventh Day Adventist Church, 12, 34, 95, 168, 172
Shackleton, David, 64
Shamuyarira, Nathan, 128
Shava, Kunzvi, 97
Shipe, Tadeous, xx
Simpson, Gordon, 136
Sithole, Ndabaningi, 161
Sjollema, Baldwin, xx, 122n10, 141n4, 148, 174
Skelton, Kenneth, 16, 114, 116, 121, 190
Sloman, Isabel, 105
Smith, E.W., 95n8
Smith, Frank, xxx, 38–40, 43, 49, 64–65
Smith, Ian Douglas, xvi, xxvii, 3–6, 91, 100, 109, 112–14 (*illus* 113), 116,

119, 121, 142n6, 149–50, 153, 160–61, 166n13, 169, 176, 181, 184–86, 189
Smith, J. Allister, 70, 73n26
Smith, Joseph, 102
Smith, Lawrence, 169
Soko, Cyrus, 32
Soul, Charles R., 177–78
Southern Rhodesia Bantu Christian Conference, 4
Stanley, H.M., 13, 38,
Stead, W.T. 38, 43, 53, 73
"Sweating" charges, 76, 79, 86
Swedish Church Mission, 95, 96
Swift, Susie Forrest, xxxi, 12, 13n9, 39, 43
Swindells, Sharon, xvi, 3, 151–52, 154–55, 185
Swinfen, John, xxi

Tambo, Oliver, 141
Taylor, Josiah, 20
Taylor, Lyndon, xix, 192–94
Tazitsona, Mrs, 151
Thomas, Anthony, 45n24
Thomlinson, Ronald, 120, 124, 125
Thompson, Diane, xvi, 3, 151–52, 154–55, 185
Thomson, John, 178
Thompson, Victor, 17n17, 20n25, 25n10, 25n13, 26, 32
Tilden Smith, Richard, 64, 80
Tillsley, Bramwell, 129n19
Todd, Garfield, 50n40, 104, 128, 181
Todd, Judith, 11n6, 15n15
Tongogara, Josiah, *illus* 123
Tredgold, Clarkson, 51
Tsikirayi, Lemuel, *illus* 159
Tuck, Brian, 73n26

Uchimura, Kanzo, 109
Unilateral Declaration of Independence (UDI), 3, 110, 112, 114–15, 160
Unsworth, Isaac, 76
Usher, James, 51

Usher Secondary School, Farm, 3, 4, 29, 110, 139, 149–59, 162, 166, 176, 189
Ushewokunzwe, Herbert, 143

Victoria, Queen, 2, 6, 10, 45
Villalon, Andrew, xx, xxi, xxiii–xxvi
Vintcent, Joseph, 23–24
Vorster, John, 142, 144

Wahlstrom, Jarl, 129n19
Waldron, John, 136n12, 169
Watson, Bernard, xxix, 125
Watt, James, xix, 127n17, 162, 194
Watt, James and Bette, xx
Weiss, Ruth, 50n40
White, John, 8, 16, 20, 171
Whitney, Sir John, 64–65, 87
Wickberg, Eric, 121, 127, 129n19, 138
Wilkins, Ruth, 193
Williams, Harry, xix, 146, 147, 164, 166–68, 170
Williams, Richard, 103–4
Wise, C.D., 83- 85, 87,
Wiseman, Clarence, 121, 122, 129n19, 144, 163,
Woods, Reginald, 125, 136n12, 138,
World Council of Churches (WCC), xv, xvii, xviii, xx, xxvii, 2, 4, 5, 112, 114, 119, 122, 125, 127–29, 135–38, 140–48, 150, 155, 163–76, 181–82, 185–90, 193–94, 196, 200

Young, Andrew, 153

Zimbabwe African National Liberation Army (ZANLA), 5, 154
Zimbabwe African National Union (ZANU), 3, 122, 128, 143
ZANU-PF (Combined ZANU and ZAPU), 122
Zimbabwe African People's Union (ZAPU), 3, 122, 128, 143, 189, 194
Zimbabwe Council of Churches, Zimbabwe Christian Council (ZCC), 4, 150

Zimbabwe Peoples' Revolutionary Army (ZIPRA), 5, 153–54,

Zvobgo, C.J.M., xx, 12, 13n10, 18, 21n2, 95n8, 100n13

NORMAN H. MURDOCH
Ph.D., M.Th., M.Ed., M.Div.
Professor Emeritus of History, University of Cincinnati

Norman Murdoch was born into a Salvation Army officer family. Throughout most of their careers his parents were corps officers, and Norman was immersed in all of the corps activities. He went to Asbury College and Seminary, intending to go into The Salvation Army as a full time officer.

After graduation, Norman and his wife, Grace, went to Cincinnati, Ohio to work for The Salvation Army. Norman was the director of the new youth center there and responsible for developing programs for inner city youth. This experience changed the course of his life and career. It was a painful year of soul searching and confusion. It became apparent to him that The Salvation Army was not a good match for his temperament, his intellect, and his education. At that time The Salvation Army did not work well with educated individuals who had been trained to think critically, ask questions, and explore options.

Norman went back to school and got his degrees in history. He accepted a position at the University of Cincinnati as a professor of American history, and he found his niche. He loved teaching and the university lifestyle. He got active in faculty politics, and was president of the AAUP (faculty organization), and then he was chief negotiator for the faculty union contract. He was an advocate for many faculty issues and for many young faculty members as they went through the tenure process. He was known as someone who would fight for what was right and fair.

But Norman never lost his love for The Salvation Army. His area of historical study was American intellectual history, which is the study of the evolution of ideas and how they influence historical events. His period was the late nineteenth century, and he chose The Salvation Army as the focus of his inquiry. His study of the history of The Salvation Army allowed him to blend both his intellectual pursuits and his attachment to the Army. He is the author of three books and several articles on Army history. His research has taken him to many parts of the world where The Salvation Army has work. He developed many friends around the world who were also interested in Salvation Army history and enjoyed discussions of related issues.

This is Norman's fourth book. For the last five years he has had Alzheimer's. While the narrative of the book was finished, it was not ready for publication. Because of his appreciation for Norman's work, Dr. Harold Hill organized a variety of people to assist him in putting the finishing touches on the work. The book is not only Norman's final work, but also a tribute to him for his valued contributions. This book is indeed a special conclusion to a life dedicated to the uncovering of truth and justice.

Grace Murdoch, Ed.D.

www.ingramcontent.com/pod-product-compliance
Lightning Source LLC
Chambersburg PA
CBHW051053230426
43667CB00013B/2272